WOMEN IN INDIAN POLITICS

WOMEN IN INDIAN POLITICS

(Empowerment of Women through Political Participation)

Editor

NIROJ SINHA

GYAN PUBLISHING HOUSE
NEW DELHI-110002

WOMEN IN INDIAN POLITICS
(*Women, Politics*)

ISBN : 81-212-0686-3

Published in 2006 in India by
Gyan Publishing House
5, Ansari Road, Darya Ganj,
New Delhi - 110002

Laser Typeset at: A S Printers, Delhi-94

Printed at: Raidhani Printers,:

CONTENTS

List of Tables

List of Contributors

1. Anuradha Dutta is Professor of Political Science, Guwahati University. Has been regularly attending the World Congress of Political Science since 1985.
2. Chandrakala Padia is Professor of Political Science in Benaras Hindu University. Has been attending the World Congress of Political Science since 1990. She has many published papers to her credit.
3. Niroj Sinha is Professor and Head of Political Science, M.M. College, Patna University. She has been attending the World Congress of Political Science since 1979. Participated in two international research projects as Co-author of India Chapter. She has several publications-papers and books to her credit.
4. Rashmi Srivastava is Professor of Political Science, Vikram University. Has been attending the World Congress of Political Science since 1985. Has several publications.
5. Rachna Suchinmayee is Lecturer in Political Science, Arvind Mahila College, Magadh University, Although very young, she is commited to research in Political Science and Women's Studies.
6. Sarojini Sharan is retired Reader of Political Science, Patna University. Has attended World Congress of Political Science and National Congress for the last three decades. She has five books to her credit. She is an avid reader and researcher.
7. Sharda Jain is Professor of Political Science, Kalindi College, Delhi University. She has published several papers.

List of Contributors

INTRODUCTION

It is a global experience that in any political system, right from the developed to the developing countries, women's presence in the political process is marginal and low except a few countries (the Nordic countries). Women's movements for their rights started in the later half of the 19th century and continued till the first half of the 20th century, ultimately crystallising to a demand for the 'right to vote'. Women in many countries had to wage long and grim battle to get this right. In most countries, they got this from the second decade of the present century. Despite their struggle for a long period, women have not yet been able to attain a rightful position in the arena of politics.

Radical feminists have gone beyond just the right to vote, maintaining that the demand for right to vote came from women of the elite class to find some room for themselves in the established power structure. There is now an emphasis on the right to participate in the political decision-making. And it is here that the crunch lies. The percentage of women as voters has increased considerably in most of the countries, but they have not been able to create a niche for themselves in the policy-formulating and decision-making bodies. Their political status remains secondary.

Barbare Nelson and Najma Choudhury, the editors of the book: *Women and Politics Worldwide*, maintain that a study has been carried out in 43 countries on women's political engagement, which reveals the fact that women everywhere have a secondary political status. They maintain that there have been women of substance in politics, holding on their own, but such women are exceptions and it's not the rule. They also imply that it does not mean that all women experience their subordinate political status in a similar way, or all groups of women are subordinate to all groups of men in a similar way. In most cultures there is a complex matrix of political power, composed of may social hierarchies, of which gender is only one component. Nevertheless, men of any group are more able to be active in politics than women of their group. They emphasise that the ubiquity of women's secondary political status demonstrates how politics is intertuned with other aspects of life. They see politics, economics, culture, religion and law as mutually constitutive, each creating itself and the other at the same time. The secondary position of women in each realm is reinforced by the total pattern of male privileges. But each sphere of society also creates unique elements of gender inequality and its own opportunities for resistance, innovations and transformation.

Women's political participation has to be discussed in the context of gender and patriarchy. Gender is defined as the social construction of relations between women and men and among various groups of women and men. Feminist scholarship places gender as the "sociocultural manifestation of being a man or women" at the focus of inquiry in research and study and arrived at a 'gendered' understanding of society. It has been a long battle to show that a woman is not a mere composite of female anatomy and physiology, sex and gender are not identical. Sex connotes a biological difference between the male and female. The difference between sex and gender is at once a liberator as well as an explorator, for if we are convicted that discrimination, oppression and exploitation that are ascribed to natural difference is false deduction, and that body differences do not warrant these differentiation, and they are socially produced, then we have a basis for action. Gender is the most potent, significant and enormously useful analytical concept that feminists have thrown up. It is a matter of social ascription, a sociocultural construction and provided a deeper analysis of inequalities existing between male and female. The feminist scholars through the application of the concept of gender have challenged the structures—socioeconomic, political and cultural processes. Simon de Beamvoir maintains, "one is not born but rather made a women". To quote her, "she is defined and differentiated with reference to men and not with reference to her; she is incidental and unessential as opposed to the essential. He is the subject, he is the absolute— she is the other". Nancy Chodorow maintains that since women have always been assigned the responsibility of primary parenting and nurturing, they develop a psychology of being most suited to the task of nurturing and caring, and thus, themselves choose the role of the care-give and 'confinement to the private'.[8] Rosaldo supports the theory that in most societies, so far gender has been a socially constructed category rather than biologically determined. Linda Nicholsan maintains that the gender structure in a particular time and space is less affected by other contemporary structures such as political, economic etc, more by the previous history of gender.[10]

The concept of gender, thus, explains the division of spheres of action into private and public. The private sphere belongs to women while the male is assigned the public spheres. Firestone argues against this separation of spheres of activity.

This public/private dichotomy has resulted in women being marginalised in all spheres of activity — social, economic and more specifically, political. Rationality, self-discipline, competition, universality to mention a few are the priced qualities of political parlance. These are inherent in male. On the contrary, irrationality, indiscipline, particularly, submissiveness, impulsiveness are some of the qualities associated with female nature.

Patriarchy looms large in feminist debate. Patriachy implies that power is imperative in gender relations. As a substantive, it usually refers to some form of systemic male dominance. Kata Millet in *Sexual Political* and Shulasmith in *The Dialectic of Sex* sees patriachy as a broad system of power of men over women. This patriarchal character of society pervades ideology and culture.[13]

Millet, Firestone, Mackennon and the whole movement behind them have drawn our attention to the pervasiveness of sexual domination and the role of force and male violence as a major social-historical reality.

The origins of the concept can be traced to the 19th century women's movement and in Marxism. Mark and Engels in their *German Ideology* had incorporated crucial insight about women. Engel's major contribution was to bequeath to the working class movement, a conceptualisation that women were not naturally the 'second sex'. They were in fact being exploited within an oppressive family structure. Though, he used the term 'father right', this was essentially a conceptualisation of patriarchy.

Contemporary feminist theories of patriarchy emerged primarily in reaction to and in confrontation with the mechanical materialistic form of Marxism that had developed. This was because in the Marxist tradition concepts 'patriarchy' was retained in, however, inadequate a form. It has avoided biologism and retrained the nation of a separate male-dominated family/reproduction system. Radical feminism has sought to replace economic class struggle with a nation of sexual class struggle.

Without going into the detailed analysis of the various theories of patriarchy and later its downfall, we can for our purpose of study infer that power is imperative in gender relations, in producing gender relations and in maintaining these in some way or other.

In actual practice, the rule of the patriarch over the household and family has been extended into the rule of the male over the female in wider society, economy and politics. Experiences in various political systems with very different hierarchy and cultural patterns proves the patriarchy mindset of the male over female in all spheres of life and its activities. The resistance of female participation in politics is also a direct result of this mindset. The resistance to female participation in politics is a direct result of this mindset, although other environmental factors cannot be ignored. Even the definition of politics for centuries has been the result of gender-patriarchy considerations.

The feminist academics have questioned the traditional definition and constituents of politics, and charged it with gender bias. Before going into the details of efforts at a redefinition of politics from feminist perspective, we turn to the conventional definition and constituents of politics.

What is Politics?

Politics has been defined in various ways, but there is a common thread running through all of them, that it is inevitable in any society. It is about representation, policy, position and power with government as its area. Miller maintains that it is the activity which aims at bringing government to bear in a particular direction, to secure particular results. Laswell maintained that political process is the shaping, sharing and exercise of power. Involvement in politics is directed towards influencing power channels and elites for protecting one's rights and self-interests and giving legitimacy to political elites and their decisions. Conventionally, politics deals with the formal political structures, but it has now been wined by political theorists to include movements, protests and struggle as legitimate expressions of political behaviour. Political sphere, thus, includes the "spheres in social relations, where power relations are generated, institutionalised and used to encourage, control or move people's attitudes, beliefs in a specified direction to control and regulate the distribution of resources.

Feminist scholars have been very concerned about what constitutes politics, that it is basically male activity. They have challenged the dominant hypothesis that politics is confined to public sphere. They maintain that traditional politics legitimises women's exclusion or absence from the power spheres and also devalues women's concerns.[15]

Feminists also argue for a redefinition of politics. An important feature of their efforts have been to proclaim the political nature of private life and the relation between sexes, which has brought traditional political science into question, and has forced the authorities to take account of problems hitherto regarded as belonging to private life.

Political participation has to be discussed and understood in this light.

Political Participation

Political participation has been defined in various ways, but in nutshell it refers to the participation of individuals in the political process, and that it ensures that individuals are able to take part in deciding the common goals of the society and the best ways of achieving it.[16]

Kazenstein Mary Fainshod conceptualises political participations as public membership of citizen 'sharing' justice and orienting their action towards a public or a common good.[17] Political participation also connotes activities for protecting one's rights and duties and advancing interest through competition.

The concept of participation as an instrumental action for having a close link with power is postulated by Laswell and Parsons Verba. Nie states political participation as "the activities by private citizens that are more or less directly aimed at influencing the selection of governmental personnel and/or the action they take.[18] Political participation as instrumental action is close to 'exchange theory'. Politics is depicted in the language of bargaining, exchange and efficiency. A rational citizen is considered to be a consumer of private benefits. Participation is thought of as cost incurred in the political market only when one's vital interests are at stake. The result is a cost-benefit account according to which rational citizens minimise costs and maximise benefits. Rayon terms such action as rational. It may be assumed that participation is rational in the sense that it consists of the examination of alternative actions and the selection of that alternative, which yield the greatest expected utility.[19] Self-interest, thus, is the main base for choice of ones action.

These two concepts are two different ways of representing rationality of political participation.

Milbrath maintains, "every person participates atleast passively in the political system in which he lives.... There is no such thing as not behaving."[20] Thus, apathy or passivity is a form of political participation for some.

In liberal democratic political systems, it is regarded as essential that more and more people participate in the system. However, various studies have revealed that only a very small percentage, even less than 10 per cent participate in the political process. Actually, participation and its extent is related to various factor — the psychological make up of the person, his total personality and external environment the social, economic, cultural, individual response to such stimuli, but his political attitude is outcome of his social personality and his political options reflect the characteristic modes of his adjustments to life.[20]

Milbrath holds that political participation differs in relation to four major factors: (i) the extent to which the individual receives political stimuti; (ii) the individual's personal characteristics; (iii) social characteristics; and (iv) the political environment in which the individual finds himself. Dahi is of the opinion that some people are indifferent to politics, others are more deeply involved. Even among those who are deeply involved, only some actually seek power and among the power seekers, some gain power than others.

Milbrath, basing on the intensity of participation divides input political activity mainly into three categories (i) active; (ii) passive or supportive; and (iii) apathetic. Active political activity is again categorised into conventional and unconventional. Participation, in protest process, is regarded by Milbrath as unconventional.

Women and Political Participation

Participation of women in the political process has been very low. Their presence in the legislative and decision-making bodies is scarcely above 10 per cent except some Nordic countries. It has been often stated that the personality traits of women (lack of self-esteem to be precise) and the socioeconomic cultural environment and, on the other hand, the political environment is to a great extent responsible for women's marginal participation in polities.

Preceding observations reveal that self-esteem, standing in the society, the culture which puts maximum premium on the male, and the political environment of instability, criminalisation and absence of political ideology are factors which influence the extent of political participation.

Women fall mainly into the group of those who are apathetic to politics because of the group of those who are apathetic to politics because of (i) their low status in society (ii) lesser exposure to education (iii) very low economic status; (iv) the restraining cultural norms; and, (v) the unhealthy political environment, the nature of political structure, such as party structure, process of political succession, which supports or opposes the recruitment of women to political offices.

In nutshell the sociopolitical environment determines the participation and involvement of women in politics. Culture is a very dominant factor. It deprives women of the self-esteem necessary for political leadership. Jean J Kirkpatrick observes "in a culture which values the male more highly than the female, women may never acquire the confidence and autonomy required to seek power and wield it effectively." Culture decides role choices, "The transition from the roles of housewife and mother to the role of political decision-maker is not easy, and has not been frequently attempted. The roles of housewife, mother, law-maker etc, do not have what Eulau and Spranger have called "professional convergence".[21] Kirkpatrick refutes the established relationship between power, politics, and maleness. According to her, the female psychology is no more a disqualification for politics. She maintained that in the ultimate analysis, "to many radical feminists culture, ideology and social structure are conspiracy. The enemies are male, and female are the most oppressed political caste in history."[22]

Levels and Areas of Political Participation

The most prevalent political action is voting in elections. Although the 'right to vote' was won after a grim battle in most of the Western liberal democracies, at present women constitute a reasonable percentage of total voters in almost all political systems with the exception of some Middle East Muslim states.

Although there has been a global awareness and realisation that political participation does not only mean the right to vote (right from the Mexico conference in 1975 through Copenhagen, Nairobi and Beijing), yet women's presence in legislative bodies is scarce despite the absence of legal constraints.

So, women have been accepted as voters but not as policy formulators and decision-makers. Women's movement has for the last two or three decades been demanding more space for women in the representative bodies, but things have scarcely changed. Demands for affirmative action/ reservation as an instrument for ensuring more space to women has been repeatedly turned down in many countries. The ERA never got passed in USA. In India, although 33 per cent reservation was provided for women at grassroot-level and local institutions through the constitutional amendment in 1993, the bill providing for 33 per cent reservation to women in the Lok Sabha and the state assemblies was not passed in 1996. It was not allowed even to be tabled in the Lok Sabha in 1998. This speaks a lot about the rigid patriarchal approach of the male political leaders. They will not let any effort for giving more space to women in politics go waste.

Even though democracy has made great gains in the 1990s, women average only 11.6 per cent of the world legislatures (inter-parliamentary union, 1997). Women essentially are appointed by men leaders in at least 37 undemocratic countries or are entirely missing from the national legislatures. In an additional 49 nations — the new democracies or the partially developed ones — men parliamentarians dominate the legislature with 93 per cent membership. Only in the 27 long-established but unfinished democracies do women have the greatest opportunity for equality in representation. Yet, women members of these parliaments average only 15 per cent.[23]

Government of the people, by the people and for the people — Abraham Lincohn's concept of democracy — is an ideal which remains unachieved in the world specially in the context of half the population of any country, the women.

Democracy falls short when women of whatever colour or ethnic groups cannot vote or caste votes, and cannot expect success in electing representation of their choice, or being elected to the legislative bodies, and have little hope for enactment of laws they believe are critically needed.[24]

The reasons — narrow gender roles, restrictive religious doctrines, unequal laws and education, discriminatory socioeconomic conditions, male biased leaders or other political elites and women-unfriendly election system. The barriers, while varying among countries typically, are interrelated and mutually reinforcing.

Anne Phillips in her The politics of presence maintains that the shift from direct to representation democracy has shifted the emphasis from who the politicians are to what they represent. She further maintains that men may consciously stand for women when what is at issue is the representation of agreed policies or programmes on ideals, but how can men legitimately stand in for women when what is at issue is the representation of women *par se*?

Phillips speaks about gender parity and accounts that a significant number of political parties have adopted the measures to raise the proportion of women elected. She recounts the experiences in South Africa and European countries like UK, Germany, the Nordic countries where, when one party adopted a gender quota and other parties also followed suit. The green party in Germany contributed to the quota — the Christian Democratic Party was adopted in 1986. There is consensus among major political parties in UK, atleast at the central level, in favour of selecting more women candidates.

She maintains that changing the gender composition of elected assemblies is a major and necessary challenge to the social arrangements, which have systematically placed women in a subordinate position and wether we conceive of politics as the representation of interests or need (or both) a closer approximation to gender parity is one minimal condition for transforming the political agenda. But she also mentions that this change cannot guarantee anything. The case for gender parity among our political representatives inevitably operates in a framework of probabilities rather than certanities.[25] She maintains that the politics of presence points towards rather different policy recommendation depending on the nature of the excluded group. In relation to women, a straight-forward quota seems entirely appropriate. In comparison to racial or ethnic quotas, the introduction of minimum quota for women and men is less inherently problematic because there are self-evidently two sexes.[26]

Phillips is, thus, in favour of politics of presence. It can ensure that there is a possibility of gender parity, as politics of presence can provide separate recommendation for the excluded group.[26]

Women in the Political Process in India

Women in India entered the political process in the early decades of the present century, through their massive participation in the national struggle for freedom under the leadership of Mahatma Gandhi. Gandhiji was able to reach out to women and draw them into the vertex of the freedom movement. Though Gandhi could not fully abandon gender bias and in some way perpetuated the traditional image of the Indian women, he did manage to appeal to women to join the movement. Women played a very important role in the Civil Disobedience Movement, the salt *satyagraha* and the Quit India Movement of 1942. Together, with their participation in movement against the colonial rule, the educated women were simultaneously struggling to get the right to vote and right to get elected. Generally, it is maintained that the women participating in the struggle, especially, those who were in key positions were from the elite class. Not much has been written about thousands of infamous women, who were poor and had rural background, but who in their own humble way had participated in the national freedom struggle.

Some women leaders were very articulate in their ideas and their awareness of the situation was prevalent. For example, in 1917, even before women in England got the right to vote, Sarojini Naidu had petitioned to the British Parliament the Indian women's demand for equal voting rights with men.

Gandhi had said as early as in 1929, "women must have the right to vote and equal legal status. But the problem does not end there. It only commences at the point where women begin to effect the political deliberation's of the nation."

Gandhiji brought an absolutely new dimension into the debate on women's problem. He began from the basic issue that subjugation of and exploitation of women was the product of "men's teaching and women's acceptance of them," and thereby broke away from the reform tradition by preaching the philosophy not only of absolute equality of rights between the sexes, but the pragmatic necessity of enrolling women's support to transform the nationalist struggle for the transfer of power from the British to India through social revolution.

There is little doubt that it was the willing and spontaneous participation of women in the Civil Disobedience Movement rather than the radical ideas of sexual equality that finally tilted the balance in favour of political equality between the sexes within the Congress party and later in the Constituent Assembly.

The Constitution of free India saluted the massive participation of women in the freedom struggle by equal rights to enter into politics irrespective of gender and other factors.

It is now nearly 49 years since the Constitution was adopted in 1950. Despite the opportunity of equal access to the political process guaranteed by law, the presence of Indian women in politics is still scarce. Their representation has never gone beyond 9 per cent in Parliament, 10 per cent in state assemblies and 15 per cent in the Council of Ministers. Even though India had a Prime Minister like Indira Gandhi — the longest surviving women Prime

Minister— women have not been able to find space in the representative and decision-making bodies.

Women's movements in India have been struggling for women's political empowerment for nearly five to six decades, yet women have only managed to get their demands for quota/reservation in Parliament and state legislatures included in election manifestoes of the political parties in 1991, 1996 and 1998 general elections.

The parties despite their promises have displayed their gender bias in giving tickets to women to fight elections. The Congress (I) has not been able even to put 15 per cent women candidates, although the party has the record of putting up comparatively the highest number of women candidates.

A major reason forwarded by all political parties is that the chances of women candidates winning are very thin compared to male candidates. However, the election reports display that the percentage of women winning in relation to their total candidates is much higher than male.

April 23, 1993 was a red letter day for Indian women, when the 73rd Constitutional Amendment gave statutory status to *panchayats* and provided 33 per cent reservation of seats to women at every tier of the grassroots political institutions. The elections have revealed that the number of women in *gram panchayats* is increasing steadily.

The granting of reservation to women at grassroot-level institution inspired women to make a similar demand with regard to Lok Sabha and state legislatures. Women activists and academics have been intensifying their demands in this regard, but it is being met with a constant protest by the males, as displayed in 1996 and 1998 by male members cutting across party lines.

Adequate representation in representative bodies is very important for women's empowerment in the political process, and reservation/affirmative action is being seen as the most potent strategy. The negative aspects are being heatedly debated not only by men, but also by some women activities. The debate still continuous.

An important shift is being noted in the last couple of years from representation to governance. The centre for women's development studies, New Delhi, organised a meeting on gender, democracy and governance in September 1997, in which Rajni Kothari opined in his paper that from focus on representation to focus on governance was an important transition. Why this emerging interest in governance? Because representation without participation in governance will only underscore the existing order. All feminists agree that gender represents a system of power relation. In Indian history, however, it can only be defined as an instrument to maintain a hierarchical social order designed to perpetuate in equality and diversity of a multi-ethnic, multi-lingual and multi-cultural population, said Vina Majumdar.

Caste is an important factor in Indian politics. Social scientists have been grappling with the phenomenon of caste for a long time, but only few have appreciated that the major instrument for maintaining the hierarchy even more than diversity is the subordination of women. Srinivasan's theory of Sanskritisation with increasing subordination/control on women believed to be applicable only to upwardly mobile. The studies by the Centre for women's Development Studies, New Delhi, find it equally manifest among all other groups, including the tribals, generally believed to be more generous in recognising women's right.[27]

Women by and large have demonstrated their stake in democracy, especially when they threw out Indira Gandhi's government which was the first major attack on democracy since Independence. With the resurgence of women's movement since the 1970s, it advocates that "transformational politics" have increasingly recognised the potential of the movement to deepen democracy in India. Most analysis, however, continues to harness the fear that women's largescale entry into power structures will only result in cooperation, instead of changing the undemocratic and corruptive elements in these structures.

Vina Majumdar suspects that these fears are based on

the continued undemocratic view of power and a narrow understanding of politics.[28]

Majumdar writes about 'social engineering' as democracy in India was a radical departure from the inherited social system. At present, social engineering has become politically incorrect and nation states are being asked to reduce their interventionist roles. In the kind of democracy India has this weakening and extremely negative impact on the quality of governance or the management of power.[29]

The chapters of this book have tried to examine the role of women in the political process in India within the conceptualism framework of gender and patriarchy. Women's role in the national freedom struggle has been analysed, and it has been found that gender equality was never the concern of our reformers in the late 19th century or our political leaders of the movement. They wanted a better place for women in the society, but for they never considered women's right as "individuals".

Similarly, the participation of women in formal political institutions and process has been severely restricted by gender considerations. The sociocultural norms still restrict the movements and behaviour of women. Despite all the changes, women's behaviour is still restricted by the private female and public/male dichotomy. A very recent example is from Haryana, where girls of 18 years are not allowed to cast their vote if they are unmarried. They can cast their votes only as married women if their husbands and family members permit and in the manner they want.

The opposition to women's reservation provided by the 81st Constitutional Amendment in 1996 by the male MPs and again in 1998 clearly mirrors the patriarchal attitude of our men in politics. It is very clear that they will not permit the loss of nearly 180 seats in Parliament to women, which will happen precisely if 33 per cent seats in Lok Sabha are reserved for women.

The gender and patriarchal norms have perpetuated the subordination of women in the family and extended their subordination in the wider society, economy and polity.

The environmental deterrents — social economic, cultural as well as political factors are in a close way related to these norms. India is characterised as a nation which is poor, has low level of education and awarness, is overridden by the feudal considerations. It is a multi-ethnic, multi-lingual and multi-religious society, and not all groups have equal access to the arena of politics. Yet, among all groups men have better enhances of access than women. The present Parliament in India consists of a majority of members from the backward castes and Dalits, but has the number of women of these groups or communities accordingly increased in number?

True, women need to be made conscious of their role in politics, the importance of their participation in parties and women's groups are continuously trying to train and mobilise them but centuries of subordination and passivity cannot be wished away in two decades. More than 50 years of Independence has not been able to ensure reasonable space for women in the representative bodies. It has not gone above 10 per cent. Therefore, there is a need for affirmative action in the form of quote/reservation for women. It is the prime need of the time.

Some of the papers in the book are revised version of papers presented in the seminar on "empowerment of women through political participation", organised by the department of political science, M M College, Patna University and held on February 7-8, 1997. The seminar was funded by the University Grants Commission and ICSSR.

While it cannot be claimed that all the papers in the book are very conclusive or all areas of the issue have been covered, yet it is an effort to conceptualise and discuss political participation of women in India to a reasonable extent.

I thank the contributors for their patience in revising and re-revising their chapters, and also thank Mr Amit Garg of Gyan Publishing House for his patient cooperation.

July 5, 1999

Niroj Sinha

References

1. Vina Majumdar, *In Symbols of Power* (Editor's note). Allied Publishers Pvt. Ltd., New Delhi, 1979.
2. Barbara Nelson and Choudhury Najma, *Women and Politics World-wide* Yale University Press, New Haven and London, 1994.
3. Barbara J., Nelson, *Women and Knowledge in Political Science: Texts, Histories and Epistemologies in Women in Politics*, 1989, p. 1-25.
4. Sapiro Virginia, *The Political Integration of Women's Roles Socialsation and Politics*, University of Illinos Press, 1984, p. 36.
5. Krishna Raj Maithreyi, *Feminist Concepts Part–III*, Research Centre for Womens Studies, SNDT. University, Bombay.
6. Simon de Beauvoir, *The Second-Sex* Harmondishwor Penguin, 1972.
7. *Ibid.*
8. Nancy Chodorow, *Family Structures and Faminist Personally* in M-2 in Resaldo & L Lamphere (ed) Women, Culture and Society Stanford University Press, 1997, pp. 43-46.
9. Michelle Z Rasaldo, *The uses and Abuses of Anthropology* 5/980 pp. 389-417.
10. Linda J, Nicholson *Gender and History*–Columbia University Press, New York, 1986, p. 83.
11. S, Firestone–*The Dialectic of Sex*, New York, Morrow, 1970, p. 225.
12. Coolies M. Diana, *Women in Political theory from ancient*, Misogony to contemporary Femanism (Introduction) wheat sheaf Sussex 1988.
13. Kate Millet, *Sexual Politics*, New York, Double Day, 1970.
14. Report of the UNESCO meeting of experts on the participation of women in political life and the means for increasing the participation. Lisbon, Dec. 13-16.
15. Sapiro Virginia, *What research on the political sociolisation tell us*, p. 163 Carol Pateman, Women and Political Issue in Politics Vol. 17, No. 1, p. 45.
16. T C Eakin, *Students and Politics – A Comparative Study*. Popular Prakashan, Bombay, 1972, p. 96.

17. Kazenstein, Mary Fainshod – *Women and Politics in India, in Women and Social Change*, 1980.

18. Nie Verba, and Kim – *Modes of Democratic Participation: Cross national comparision*, Beverly Hills, Sage, p. 9, 1971.

19. Alan Royan, *Two concept of Politics and Democracy*, in John Stuart *Mill Machiavelli and Nature of Political Thought* (ed.) M Fleister N Y Allenium p. 80, 1972.

20. L Milbrath, *Political Participation*, Rand, Macknell & Co. Chicago, 1965, p. 26.

21. Jean J Kirkpatrick – *Political Women*, Basic Books, INC Publishers, N.Y. 1974.

22. *Ibid*, pp. 1518-19, 12-13.

23. Elina Havio Manlla et. al.– *Unfinished Democracy*, Oxford, Pergamon, 1983.

24. *Refer to Democrateic Criteria in Arend Liphart Democracies*, New Haven, Yalu University Press, 1984, pp. 2-3.

25. Anne Phillips, *The Politics of presence*, Clarendon Press, Oxford, 1995.

26. *Ibid.*

27. Vina Majumdar, CWDS Seminar on gender, Democracy and governance 2nd March '98, New Delhi.

28. *Ibid.*

29. *Ibid.*

1

DEMYSTIFYING GENDER: A STEP TO SOCIAL EQUITY

Chandrakala Padia

The word 'gender' means much more than 'sex'. The gender of a man is masculine; that of a woman feminine. Neither a man nor a woman is sex alone or a biological species. So, the concept of gender may be said to be more inclusive than that of sex. But this distinction as such says nothing as to which of the two is inferior or superior. A bigger circle is only bigger than—not necessarily superior to—the smaller one, which it may include. In other words, the word gender' in my view is a value-free concept. Differences of value arise only when we take genders in relation to their functions in society and, what is more important, when our way of looking at the matter is merely external. The point may be brought out as follows:

When female child becomes a wife, she acquires the functions of a mother; similarly a male child becomes a father. Now the functions of a mother are mostly confined to activities which quietly take place within the house. The father, on the other hand, earns a living by working in the outer world. What takes place in the open is noticed easily. What happens at home does not strike the public eye. So by the average man, whose way of looking is confined to the externals – that is, whose *drishti* is *bahirmukhi*—the male is taken to be superior to the female. Those who are careful enough to take a comprehensive view of the human life, attach as much value to the mother's activities of producing and nursing children and keeping a family together as to the bread winners' outdoor activity of earning a living. It is really a defect in our ways of looking at things, and not the fact of gender as such, which is at the root of prevailing bias against women.

However, in the contemporary feminist literature, gender is not a value-free concept. It is a value-loaded term. It has acquired new dimensions and greater significance. It now refers to the 'social institutionalisation of sexual difference'. It aims at exposing the present masculinist hegemony in the name of natural sexual differences, and also at uncovering the male connotations of the existing vocabulary of reason, morality, autonomy, justice and history. It, therefore, aims at suggesting an alternative epistemology and methodology, which can uncover the present gender bias, and may reflect more accurately the experiences and needs of all human beings. Feminists assert that any discrimination based on the basis of sexual differences is unjust; the body differences do not warrant such discriminatory differentiation; and, that they are only socially produced. Catharine A Mackinnon says:

> "Our issue is not the gender difference, but the difference gender makes, the social meaning imposed upon our bodies – what it means to be a woman or man is a social process and, as such, a subject to change. Feminists do not seek sameness with men. We more criticise what men have made of themselves and the world that we, too, inhabit. We do not seek dominance over men. To us, it is a male notion that power means someone must dominate. We seek a transformation in the terms and conditions of power itself."[1]

Neglect of Gender in Political Theories of the Past

It would be relevant here to discuss how political theorists in the past have neglected gender.[2] John Locke defines political power as distinct from the power relations operating within the household.[3] Rousseau and Hegel have clearly contrasted the two spheres and have justified this contrast in legitimising male rule in the domestic sphere.[4] Locke has categorically mentioned that when "women hold the helm of government, the state is at once in jeopardy".[5] Rousseau believes that women pose a permanent threat to political order. The natural morality of women fits them only for the 'natural society' of domestic life. He argues in *Politics and the Arts*, "even if it could be denied that a special sentiment of chasteness was natural to women, would it be less true that in society...they ought to be raised in principles appropriate to it? If the timidity, chasteness and modesty, which are proper to them are social inventions, it is in society's interest that women acquire these qualities......[6]

Freud offers remarkably similar justification for women's confinement to domesticity. He writes, "for women the level of what is ethically normal is different from what it is in men. Their superego is never so inexorable, so impersonal, so independent of its emotional origins as we require it to be in men.... They show less sense of justice than men, they are more often influenced in their judgements by feeling of affection of hostility....."[7] Hence, Freud insists that the difference in moral capacity between the two sexes must be accepted.

Ironically, most contemporary political theorists continue the same neglect of gender by ignoring the family. Susan Moller Okin has rightly claimed, "the judgement that the family is 'non-political' is implicit in the very fact that it is *not* discussed in most works of political theory today".[8] A number of examples can be citied.[9]

However, there are a few exceptions. The works of Michael L Walzer, Philip Green, Allen Bloom and Michael J Sandel can be cited here.[10]

Contemporary Feminist Thought on Gender

Contemporary feminist scholars have used the word 'gender' after two decades of intensive thought and research.

To them gender is a social and political construct, related to and not determined by, biological sex difference.

In its most recent usage, gender seems to have first appeared among American feminists, who wanted to reject biological determinism implicited in the use of such terms as 'sex' or 'sexual difference'.[11] Two major theories of gender are prevalent today—the psychologically focused theory of gender; and, the historically and anthropologically focused explanation of gender.

The Psychologically Focused Theory of Gender

Simone de Beauvoir, in her work *The Second Sex*, a quintessential example of modern feminist inquiry and critique, claims that "one is not born but rather becomes a woman".[12] She claims that it is a whole process by which femininity is manufactured in society. To quote her, "she is defined and differentiated with reference to men and not he with reference to her; she is the incidental, the inessential as opposed to the essential. He is the subject, he is the Absolute – she is the Other".[13]

Beauvoir argues that it is the child-bearing role of women which excluded them from the productive process, and prevented them from seeing themselves as subjects in their own right. Thus, an artificial idea of womanhood was created by society. She exhorts: "No biological, psychological or economic fate determines the figure that the human female presents in society; it is civilisation as a whole that produces this creation, intermediate between male and eunuch, who is described female."[14]

Nancy Chodorow also subscribes to the above viewpoint and substantiates her argument from a psychoanalytical point of view. She argues that since women have always been assigned the responsibility of primary parenting and nurturing, they develop a psychology of being more suited to the task of nurturing and caring. Thus she chooses the role of a caregiver and confinement to the *private*. On the other hand, man from the very beginning is encouraged for more and more individuation and attaining status leading to personality traits, impelling him to associate himself with the *public*.[15]

Chodorow's use of the notion of gender identity presupposes three major premises: First, everyone has a deep sense of self, which is constituted in early childhood through one's interaction with his/her primary parent, and which remains relatively constant thereafter. The second premise is that, this deep self differs significantly for men and women, but is roughly similar among women and among men both across cultures and within cultures across lines of class, race and ethnicity. The third premise is that, this deep self colours everything one does.[16]

Historical and Anthropological Explanation of Gender

The second theory of gender proclaims that in most societies across cultures, so far, gender has been a socially constructed category rather than biologically determined. However, the proponents of this theory have also stressed that the nature of this social construction differs from one society to the other. So, there cannot be any unicausal, universalist and ahistorical explanation of it. Anthropologist Michelle A Rosaldo supports this theory on the basis of her cross-cultural research, which reveals that women are subjected to the authority due to the existing dichotomy between the public and the private.[17]

Historian Linda J Nicholson also rejects the unicausal explanation of inequality of the sexes. She emphasises that it has been affected by various causal factors in different social contexts. She stresses the need to fight against the powerful tendency present in political theory to reify the public-private distinction and to perceive it as rigid.[18] She believes that one can comprehend this distinctly only through the study of history, for the gender structure of a particular time and place is less affected by other contemporary structures, such as political, economic etc. more by the previous history of gender. Joan W Scott also stresses the centrality of history in analysing different aspects of the social construction of gender. She explains

(a) how cultural myths and symbols reify the suppression of women; (b) how these symbols create the 'binary opposition of masculine and feminine, male and female; (c) how social institutions like family, labour markets, educational institutions and polity reinforce this dichotomy; and, (d) how the subjective identity formation of individuals is psychologically determined.[19] She, therefore, emphasises the need to expose the social construction of gender by deconstructing it. This calls for:

> "a refusal of the fixed and permanent quality of binary opposition, a genuine historicization and deconstruction of the terms of sexual difference... (we must) revers(e) and displac(e) its hierarchical construction, rather than accepting it as real or self-evident or in the nature of things."[20]

In fact, all of them are unequivocal in proclaiming that the public sphere till today, has been constructed under the assumption of male superiority and dominance. It has avoided a number of compelling questions such as that of incorporating the responsibilities of child-bearing and child rearing into the fabric of job-structure.

The above analysis of gender has helped feminists in rejecting many of the existing dominant paradigms. First, they reject the claim that separation of the public and the private follows inevitably from the natural characteristics of the sexes. They argue that a proper understanding of social life is possible only when it is accepted that the two spheres, the private and the public, are inextricably interrelated. Unless the separation of the two worlds is not destroyed, the public life would always be conceptualised as the sphere of men. Carole Pateman has aptly remarked:

> "In popular (and academic) consciousness the duality of female and male often serves to encapsulate or represent the series (or circle) of liberal separations and oppositions: female, or–nature, personal, emotional love, private, intuition, morality, ascription, particular, subjection; male, or-culture, political, reason, justice, public, philosophy, power, achievement, universal, freedom."[21]

The most fundamental and general of these opinions associate women with nature and men with culture. Nature is always seen in a lower order than culture. The feminists like Ortner argue that the opposition between women/ nature and men/culture is itself a cultural construct and does not enist in nature.[22] S. Firestone, in her work *Dialectic of Sex*, argues against this separation of private and public. Women necessarily suffer from a fundamentally oppressive biological condition. It is their role as reproducers that has handicapped women over the centuries and made possible men's patriarchal power.[23]

The consequences of this public-private dichotomy are disastrous. Due to this, women have been deprived of political power and effective participation. Citizenship for women is always seen as 'an elaboration of their private domestic tasks'. Thinkers like Ruskin could argue that "man's duty as a member of the commonwealth, is to assist the maintenance, in the advance, in the defence of the state. The women's duty, as a member of the commonwealth, is to assist in the ordering, in the comforting, and in the beautiful adornment of the state."[24]

This has eventually led to the dichotomy between morality and power. Women, in the name of being more moral, have been excluded from the public realm. Even the suffragists argued in favour of women's franchise by claiming women's superior morality as it would usher the state in a reign of peace. This is why J B Elshtain alleges that suffragists instead of challenging the separation of the public and private, merely "perpetuated the very mystifications and unexamined presumptions, which served to rig the system against them."[25]

Against this background, one can understand the significance of the feminist slogan:

'The Personal is the Political'

The feminists argue that public realm of politics can be so rational, noble and universal only because like the messy content of the human body, meeting its needs for production, caretaking and attending to birth and death, as too in politics are taken care of elsewhere.

So, a modern reflective political theory should recognise that the glory of the public is dialectically entwined with exploitation and repression of the private and the people restricted to that sphere so that they can take care of the people's needs. In view of this, the feminist political theory concludes that the 20th century politics requires a basic rethinking of this distinction and its meaning for politics.

The feminists are trying to develop a theory of social practice on the following premises. First, there should be no sexual division of labour at work place and in political organisations of all ideological persuasions; second, there should be a differentiated social order within which various dimensions are distinct but not separate or opposed, and which rests on social conception of individuality, which includes both women and men as biologically differentiated but not unequal creatures.

Third, there is a need to base and expand the conception of politics on the understanding that power relations between men and women are not confined to the 'public' world of law, the state and economics, but pervade all areas of life. This means that contrary to the assumptions of traditional political theory, the family, reproduction and sexuality must be included in political analysis.

The question arises how far this public/private dichotomy and its deconstruction is relevant to the women of the Third World? Can this empowerment epistomology rooted in white women's experiences, subjectivity and identity fulfil the interest of the Third World women?

However, in the post colonial discourse, women of the North have understood the significance of the Third World women's realities, and they themselves have rejected the monolithic nature of the earlier feminist discourse on the grounds that it ignores difference, indigenous knowledge, and local expertise. For example, modernity is equated with westernisation, industrialisation and superiority, whereas non-modernity is equated with non-western countries, tradition and inferiority.[26] In the 1970s, Eshter Boserup's pioneering work *Women's Role in Economic Development*, asserted that modernisation had marginalised women and their contributions in the Third World. Chandra Mohanty also questions the western approach, when she asks:

> "Is it possible to refer to the sexual division of labour when the content of this division changes radically from one environment to the next, from one historical juncture to another? At its most abstract level...concepts such as the sexual division of labour can be useful only if they are generated through local, contextual analyses. If such concepts are assumed to be universally applicable, the resultant homogenisation of class, race, religion, and daily material practices of women in the Third World can create a false sense of the commonality of oppressions, interests, and struggles between and among women globally."[27]

G Sen and Crown too, are caution against adopting a concept of gender that ignores differences and diversities. They believe the this diversity is built on gender oppression and hierarchy. He exclaims:

> "Feminism cannot be monolithic in its issues, goals and strategies, since it constitutes the political expression of the concerns of women from different regions, classes, nationalities, and ethnic backgrounds. There is and must be a diversity of feminism, responsive to the different needs and concerns of different women, and defined by them for themselves."[28]

The most positive part of the whole discourse is that these concerns are reflected in practice also. Women involved in different social movements are fighting against injustice on their own cultural terms. Environmental activists like Vandana Shival are speaking of the need to decolonise northern assumptions such as the concept of sustainable development, and appeal to save environment through knowledge based on poor women's experience.

Thus, feminist scholarship has brought sweeping

changes to social and political theory. It has cautioned us against constituting gender as a superordinate category of analysis. It should neither be an automatic starting point of analysis of adjustment, nor should it be ignored as a potential starting point. We must avoid approaches that are gender-blinded or gender-blind. Then only we can have true meaning of democracy and participation.

References

1. Catharine A Mackinnon, *Feminism Unmodified*, Cambridge, Harvard University Press, Mass, 1987, p. 23.

2. A number of books have appeared in the past 30 years uncovering the sexism of political theory. See, for example, Susan Moller Okin, *Women in Western Political Thought*, Princetor, Princeton University Press, 1979; Lorenne Clark and Lynda Range, *The Sexism of Social and Political Thought* Toronto, Univ. of Toronto Press, 1979; Jean Bethke Elshtain, *Public Man, Private Woman: Women in Social and Political Thought* Princeton, Princeton Univ. Press, 1981; Carole Pateman and Elizabeth Gross (eds), *Feminist Challenges: Social and Political Theory*, Boston, Northeastern Univ. Press, 1987; Carole Pateman and Mary L Shanley, *Feminist Critiques of Political Theory*, Cambridge, Polity, 1990.

3. John Locke, *Two Treatises of Government*, (ed.) Peter Laslett, Cambridge, Cambridge University Press, 1960, p. 308.

4. Hegel states: "Womankind perverts the universal property of the state into a possession or ornament for the family" *The Phenomenology of Mind*, tr. JB Balie; London, Allen and Unwin 1949, p. 496.

5. *Ibid.*

6. A Bloom *Politics and the Arts: A Letter to D'Alembert on the Theatre*. tr. Ithaca, Cornell University Press, 1968. p. 87.

7. Freud, 'Some Psychical Consequences of the Anatomical Distinction between the Sexes' in *The Standard Edition of the Complete Psychological Works*. tr. J Strachey, London, Hogarth Press, 1961, Vol. 7, p. 342.

8. Susan Moller Okin, 'Gender, The Public and the Private', in David Held (ed.) *Political Theory Today*, Cambridge, Polity Press, 1991, p. 71.

9. See, for example, Bruce A Ackerman, *Social Justice in the*

Liberal State, New Haven, Yale University Press, 1980; William A. Galston, *Justice and the Human Good*, Chicago, University of Chicago Press, 1980; Ronald Dworkin, *Taking Rights Seriously*, Cambridge, Mass, Harvard University Press, 1977; Robert Nozick, *Anarchy, State and Utopia* New York, Basic Books, 1974.

10. Michael L Walzer, *Spheres of Justice*, New York, Basic Books, 1983; Philip Green, *Retrieving Democracy: In Search of Civic Equality*, Totowa, NZ, Rowman & Allanheld, 1985; Allan Bloom, *The Closing of the American Mind*, New York, Simon & Schuster, 1987; Michael J Sandel, *Liberalism and the Limits of Justice*, Cambridge Univ. Press, 1982.
11. See, Joan W Scott, 'Gender: A Useful Category of Historical Analysis', *American Historical Review*, 91, 1986, p. 1054.
12. Simone de Beauvoir, *The Second Sex*, trans, HM Parshley, New York, Vintage Books, 1974, p. 301.
13. Semone de Beauvoir, *The Second Sex*, Harmondsworth, Penguin, 1972, p. 16.
14. *Ibid.*, p. 295.
15. Nancy Chodorow, 'Family Structure and Feminine Personality' in MZ Rosaldo and L Lamphere (eds.). *Women, Culture, and Society*, Stanford, Stanford University Press, 1974, pp. 43-66.
16. See, Nancy Fraserand Linda J. Nicholson, 'Social Criticism without Philosophy: An Encounter between Feminism and Postmodemism' *in* Linda J Nicholson, (ed.) *Feminism/ Postmodernism*, New York and London, Routledge, 1990 pp. 19-38.
17. See, Michelle Z Rosaldo, 'The Use and Abuse of Anthropology', *Signs*, 5, 1980 pp. 389-417.
18. See, Linda J Nicholson, *Gender and History*, New york, Columbia University Press, 1986, p. 83.
19. Joan W Scott, 'Gender: A Useful Category of Historical Analysis', *American Historical Review*, 91, 1986, 5. pp. 1067-69.
20. *Ibid.* pp. 1065-66.
21. Carole Pateman, *The Disorder of Women*, California, Stanford University Press, 1989, pp. 123-24.
22. See, SB Ortner, 'Is Female to Male as Nature is to Culture? in *Women, Culture and Society*, (ed.) MZ Rosaldo and

L-Lamphere, Stanford, Stanford University Press, 1974, pp. 72-87.

23. S Firestone, *The Dialectic of Sex New York,* W Morrow, 1970, p. 255.
24. J Ruskin, 'Of Queens' Gardens', in *Free and Enobled,* (ed) C Bauer and I Pitt, Oxford, Pergamon Press. 1979, p. 17.
25. JB Elshtain, 'Moral Woman and Immoral Man: A Consideration of the Public-Private Split and its Political Ramifications', in *Politics and Society,* 4, 1974, pp. 453-61.
26. See, Hagen 1962; Huntington 1971; Lener 1964; Sutton 1963.
27. Chandra Mohanty, 'Cartographies of Struggle; Third World Women and the Politics of Feminism,' in Mohanty *et.al. Third World Women and the Politics of Feminism,* Bloomingyton, *IN.L Indiana University Press, 1991,* pp. 67-68.
28. G Sen C Grown, *Development, Crises* and Alternative *visions*: Third World Women's Perspectives. New York, Monthly Review Press, 1987, pp. 18-19.

2

PATRIARCHY, POLITICS AND WOMEN

Niroj Sinha

Patriarchy looms large in feminist debate. It implies that 'power' is imperative in gender relation, in producing and maintaining gender relations.

The basic value of the term patriarchy and importance of its use by women is that it denotes a structural system of male domination. In doing so, it contrasts with the ways of looking at women both in the academic social science and in the traditional left movement.

The term 'patriarchy' has double meaning: 'rule of men' and 'rule of the father', the later been its literal meaning. Its original use was to describe a specific type of male-dominated family - the large household of a patriarch, which included women, junior men, children, slaves and domestic servants, all under the rule of this dominant male.[1] The term patriarchy has not been as universally accepted by the academic feminists as it has been by the women's movement Rubin Gayle wants to reserve its use for the traditionally extended patriarchal family because she feels that it implies male domination as inevitable. She argues for using the term 'sex-gender' system on the grounds that these can bring equilibrium or perhaps even show aspects of female dominance.[2] Barrett Michels also objects that the term implies a system of male dominance that is completely historical and external to economic systems such as capitalism.[3]

Difference in terminology does not solve the problem of giving an adequate analysis of Patriarchy.

Focusing on the concept as used by the feminist theorists would be the first step. In analysing the development of the concept of patriarchy, it is useful to keep in mind the fallacies discussed in Barrett's recent book *Women's Oppression Today*.

(a) Dualism – which seen patriarchy and capitalism as separate parallel systems without comprehending their relation and interaction.

(b) Biologism – biological differences are highlighted between men and women to explain social differences.

(c) Functionalism (or reductionism, economism), which explains particular structures of female oppression in terms of their use for capitalism or any other general structure of oppression.[4]

It is to avoid this characteristic fault of Marxist analysis that feminists originally developed such concepts as patriarchy.

"The difficulty in avoiding these fallacies is that they all have seen in one way – more than a grain of truth. Patriarchy is not fully identical with the capitalist mode of production; gender differences or patriarchal structures do have atleast some biological base, and they do serve functions for economic structures. The problem is to develop an analysis, which can integrate all these facts without going to the extreme."[5]

The origins of the concept can be traced back to the women's movement of the 19th century and Marxism. Eisenstien maintains that women like Mary Wollenstonecraft, Elisabeth Lady Canton or Harriet Mill, "understood in their own fragmented way that men have power as men in a society organised into sexual spheres". But while they spoke of power in caste terms, they were only beginning to understand the structure of power enforced upon them through sexual division of labour in society. These feminists tended to accept the different 'sexual spheres' of men and women even while they argued for equal rights. They argued that motherhood was a basic reason why women needed more power and independence.

These feminists in their own way challenged the patriarchal structure, but could not develop a theory of patriarchy.

Marxist View of Women

In *The German Ideology*, Marx and Engles had incorporated crucial insights about women. Engel's major contribution was to bequeath to the working class movement a conceptualisation that women were not *naturally second sex;* that they were in fact exploited within an oppressive family structure; and, that this exploitative system was historically created and would historically disappear. Though he used the term father–right, this was essentially a conceptualisation of Patriarchy.

Contemporary feminist theories of Patriarchy emerged primarily in reaction to and in confrontation with the mechanical materialist form of Marxism which developed. This was because it was within the Marxist tradition that concepts such as Patriarchy were retained in however inadequate a form. It has had a theory of patriarchy, though it is inadequate. It has avoided biologism and retained the notion of a separate, male dominated family/reproduction systems.[7]

Radical feminism has sought to replace economic class struggle with a notion of sexual class struggle without re-examining Marxism or really attempting to develop a total social theory.

Patriarchy as the Rule of Men

Radical feminists see patriarchy as the 'rule of men.' It is represented in Kate Millets' *Sexual Politics* and Shulasmith Firestones' *The Dialectic of sex*, published in 1970. Both books see patriarchy as a broad system of the power of men over women, particularly over their sexual functions, and see it as historically preceeding and more fundamental than class division. As Kate Millet maintains.

"Our society is a patriarchy. The fact is evident at once if we recall that the military, the industry, technology universities, science, political offices, finance, in short every avenue of power within the society including coercive power, is in male hands."[8]

Mackinnon Catherine argues that gender in society is determined by sexuality and not vice versa.

Sexuality is to feminism what work is to Marxism—that which is one's own, yet most taken away. The moulding, direction and expression of sexuality organises society into two sexes – women and men, – which underlines the totality of social relations.[9]

Millet Firestone, Catherine and the whole movement behind them have drawn our attention to the pursuance of sexual domination, and the role of force and male violence as a major social historical reality.

Marxist feminism, through domestic labour debate, brought out a new conceptualisation of patriarchy. Discussion on domestic labour made it clear that traditional Marxism could be called inadequate not only because it made social and cultural (or sexual) oppressions simply a reflection of the economic oppression, but because it had too narrow a conception of the 'economic' itself.

Socialist Feminists' View

Those who took up the theory of patriarchy from this point of view are all consciously socialist feminists because they began from a partial acceptance of Marxism, an awareness of class oppression and a concern for revolutionary change. At the same time as they took up the feminist awareness of Marxism's inadequacies and the new issues brought forward in women's, movement on the one hand, they criticise traditional Marxists focus on economic class struggle. On the other hand, insights of the radical feminists and the domestic labour debate, which included both sexual psychological–cultural issues and a new version of 'economic', tended at first to take a dualistic approach, looking at male and female roles as conditioned by a set of dichotomies, wage labour/domestic labour public/private productive/reproductive, etc. Zillah Eisenstien's work best typified this dualism.

Socialist feminists historical materialism is not defined in terms of relations of production without understanding its connection to the relations that arise from women's sexuality — the relations of reproduction. And the ideological formulation of these relations is the Key.[11] The stress on ideology was new, both in comparison to the radical feminists, who had emphasised sex and force, as well as the Marxists domestic labour debates, who had talked only of a particular kind of labour. It apparently comes out of Marxist tradition, but not simply out of a Marxism that relegated women to the superstructure, but out of a Marxism that was itself in the process of developing towards a new stress on cultural-ideological factor. However, these two elements were not really integrated in Eisenstein's theory. It gave a name to structures and relations of male domination and asserted their importance along with class relations in understanding society.[12]

Patriarchy as Labour

Many theorists have moved in the direction of defining women's labour as a special kind of labour, and patriarchy in terms of male control of that labour.

We can usefully define patriarchy as a set of social relations among men, which has a material base and which, though hierarchical, establish or creates interest to dominate women. The material base on which patriarchy rests lies most fundamentally in men's control over women's labour power.[13] Characteristic of this approach is that it not only adds reproduction to the concept of production, but also very often makes it basic.

It is significant that nearly all versions of 'women's labour' or 'production of life' approaches to patriarchy involve a two-tier structure of exploitation with male hierarchy at the top, structured by the exploitation of women.[14]

Patriarchy as Ideology

The 'ideological theory' of patriarchy locates its essential features in the ideological-psychological cultural sphere. Juliet Mitchell's *Psychoanalysis and Feminism* and Gayle Rubin's *Traffic in Women*, were both published in 1975 They base their theory by interpreting the work of well-known anthropologist Levi-Strauss and founder of psychoanalysis Sigmund Fraud.

This approach comes to recognise the importance and of early socialisation and of sexual relation between human beings in the construction of personality and at the same time in showing their social base and not taking them as something simply biological and natural. The advantage of this perspective is that it gives a notion of a 'deep structure' at a psychological-ideological level, which can then interact with the economic system of production to produce the concrete forms of "male control of women's sexuality, fertility and labour."[15]

By the early 1980s, patriarchy was no longer a central concept in feminist theoretical discourse. Doubts about its usage and usefulness had emerged. There were four major problems with Patriarchy:

First, it lacked precise definition and the bases of patriarchal control. Mary Wollenstonecraft and Weber located patriarchy in the control of "fathers over household organisation and production", thereby controlling the labour of the household members. Gayle had tried to limit the concept to a certain historical form of control by fathers. Patriarchy should be reserved for a specific sex-gender system: the form of male dominance described in the nomad societies of old testament.[16] Later, feminists have, however, retained the concept for many forms of male domination. Michelle lodges it in 'kinship system'. As to the basic, some seek it in biology, some base it in the cultural and ideological sphere.[17] A third position embraces some form of economic materialism.

The second group of objections raised against patriarchy relates to its persistent universalism, Rowbothom and Barrett maintain that it is not useful to extend the concept because of its extreme. Variance in expression of role dominance.[17]

Third objection relates to charge of essentialism. Patriarchy assumes pre-given sexual characteristics of men and women. Often this means reverting to biological essence, which contradicts the ideas of second wave feminism. This maintains that gender is separable from biological sex and is constructed by social relations at large. Eisenstein maintains that assuming internal essence of gender can also lead to some politically very reactionary positions.[18]

A fourth objection has been the matter of dualism. Black and ethnic feminists talk about racism being another system of oppression.

A final question is, patriarchy is a system, a set of structured social relations or is it about individual men oppressing individual women?

R Coward has pointed out, in the past historical variety in forms of gender relations colluded in keeping forms of power and domination hidden, and this prevented certain questions. The problems remained regarding explanation of hierarchy between the sexes, and also how to deliver a historically/specific account at the same time.[19]

Several theorists, while rejecting container concepts like 'patriarchy' and oppression, have retained the basic ideas of both concepts that 'power' is involved in the production and maintenance of "gender asymmetry". American political scientist Nancy Harstock, who was the first to re-examine power from a feminist perspective, pointed out that feminists, aware of women having always been the object of domination, tended to avoid power. In this way they tacitly reproduced the idea that power is masculine. Examining the power theories, she affirms that power is a gender concept.[29]

Politics has been refined by feminist literature in the

context of gender and patriarchy. The elements of patriarchy are very visible in the perception of the political role and status of women.

Politics Redefined

Politics has been defined variously, but there is a common thread running through all of them, that is inevitable in any society. It is about representation, policy, position and power with government as its arena. Miller maintains that it is the activity which aims at bringing government to bear in a particular direction to secure particular results. The definition of politics in recent years has widened considerably from merely denoting the area of formal government in its widest sense, including all processes directly or indirectly associated with it and in which, in a democracy every citizen has a share .[21]

The concept of politics in terms of objectives and activities has evolved much further than this. Theorists have now accepted that movements, protests, and struggles are legitimate expressions of political behaviour. The political sphere, thus, includes the "spheres, in social relations," where power relations are generated, institutionalised and used to encourage, control or move people's behaviour, attitudes, beliefs in a specified direction to control and regulate the distribution of resources.

This broader definition was drawn up by a group of women scholars and activists, who participated in the UNESCO seminar in Lisbon in 1983. In 1985, this definition was endorsed by a non-aligned ministerial level conference on Role of Women in Development in 1985.

Feminist scholars have been very concerned about what constitutes politics—that it is basically "male activity". Feminist scholars have challenged the dominant hypothesis of the discipline of political science that politics is confined to public sphere. They are critical of the "sexual definition" of politics and of the manner is which the discipline of political science perpetuates this definition.[23] Traditional politics legitimises women's exclusion or absence from power spheres and also, depoticises and, thus, devalues women's concerns.[24] Feminists, therefore, question the rational behind the rigidly dichotomies 'public-private' spheres of activities, and assignment of the spheres on the basis of gender. Traditionally, political science has been built on the recorded knowledge of what has been basically male activities in a sphere designated as public. Feminist scholars have been critical of male lias in research, which accepts male as the norm.[25]

The feminists argue for a redefinition of politics. An important feature of the feminist efforts has been to proclaim the political nature of private life, and the relation between the sexes which has brought traditional politics into question. It has forced the authorities to take account of problems hitherto regarded as belonging to private life. Suggestions have been put forward to bring politics to home rather than trying to bring women to political structures.

Women's political behaviour and their activities in the political arena are severely conditioned by the considerations of gender and patriarchy, Gender could be understood in terms of sociocultural norms, which decide the spheres of action of both the male and female gender. A preconceived notion of the nature and attributes of men and women operate in the society. Culture affects women's political behaviour by depriving them of the self-esteem necessary for political leadership. In a culture which values the male more highly than the female, women may never acquire the confidence and autonomy required to seek power and wield it effectively. This observation made by Jeene J Kirkpatrict[25] on American women can very aptly be applied in almost all societies. The cultural factor sees the personality of women as the principle cause for the scarcity of women in politics. Culture decides role choices. The transition from the roles of housewife and mother to the role of political decision-maker is not easy and has not been frequently attempted. The roles of housewife, mother, law-makers etc, do not have what Eulau and Spranger have called professional convergence.[27] The traditional role system does make it difficult for women to begin a political career before middle age; to change her place of residence, to develop the skills and acquire the experience needed for political career.[28]

Kirkpatrick refutes the established relationship between power, politics and maleness. According to her, female psychology is no more a necessary disqualification for politics. She maintains that in the ultimate analysis, to many radical feminists "culture, ideology social structure is conspiracy, the enemies are males, and females are the most oppressed political caste in history."[29]

Patriarchy as a concept implies that power is operative in gender relations and in maintaining the *status que* some way or other. It is a structural system of male domination over the female, and this relationship is a political relationship. Thus, to Kate Millet, "our society is a patriarchy". Hartman Heidi maintains, the personal is political means for radical feminists that the original and basic class division is between the sexes, and that the motive force in history is the striving of man for power and domination over women."[30]

It is with this backdrop that an attempt has been made to study and asses the participation of Indian women in Politics — in its structures and in its processes and also in sociopolitical movements. The next chapter will present a synoptic view of the political environment in India; the criminalisation of politics through the use of money and muscle power, which affects the entry of women in politics in a very negative way.

References

1. Rubin Gayle, '*The* Traffic *is Women*: Motes on the Political Economy of Sex' in Reter's *Towards an Antropology of women*, 1975.

   Engels *The origin of Family, Private Property and the State*, Moscow, Progress Publishers, 1977.

2. *Ibid*, Rubin
3. Barrett Michels, *Women's Oppression Today Problems in Marxist Feminist Analysis*, London, NLB Verso Books, 1980.
4. *Ibid*.
5. Maithreyi Krishnaraj, *Feminist Concepts Part III*, Research Centre for Women's studies, SMDT University Bombay, *Introduction*, p 4.

6. Eisenstien Zillah, *Capitalism, Patriarchy and the Case for Socialist feminism*, New York, *Monthly Review Press*,
7. *Op. cit.*, Feminist Concepts.
8. Kate Millet, *Sexual Politics*, New York Doubleday, 1970.
9. Mackinnon Catherine, *Feminist Marxism, Method and the State: an Agenda for Theory*, Signe, Spring.
10. *Op. cit.*, Feminist Concepts.
11. *Op. cit.*, Eisentien.
12. *Ibid.*
13. Hartmann Heidi, *The Unhappy Marriage of Marxism and Feminism: Towards a More Progressive Union*, Capital and Class and Summer Issue.
14. *Ibid.*
15. *Op. cit.*, Feminist Concepts.
16. *Op. cit.*, Rubin.
17. Rowbothoms, The trouble with Patriarchy in Samuel R (ed) *Peoples History and Socialist Theory*, London Routledge and Kegan Paul, pp. 360-70.
18. *Opcit* Eisenstien.
19. Coward R (1983), *Patriarchical Precedents, Sexuality and Social Relations*, London, Routledge and Kegan Paul p. 259.
20. Hartstock. N. *Money, Sex, and Power: Towards a Feminial historical Materialism*, New York, London, Longman, 1983.
21. Nettle JP, *Political Mobilisation: A Sociological Analysis of Methods and Concepts*, Faber and Faber Ltd, 1967.
22. Report of the UNESCO meeting of experts on the participation of women in political life, and the means for increasing their participation Liston, Portugal. Dec. 13-16, 1983.
23. Simon C Bourque and Jean Grossholt, 'Politics and Unnatural Practice: Political Science Looks at Female Participation' in *Politics and Society*, pp 225-26.
24. Sapiro, Verginia, *What Research on the Political Socialisation Tell Us* 9. 163.

    Carol Patemon, *Women and Political Issues* in *Politics* Vol 17, No I, p. 45.
25. Sapiro, *The Political Integration of Women*, p. 59.

26. Jean J kirkpatric, *Political Women*, Basic Books, INC Publisher NY 1974, p. 15.
27. *Ibid* p. 18.
28. *Ibid* p. 19.
29. *Ibid* pp. 12-13.
30. *Ibid* p. 20.

3

WOMEN AND POLITICAL PARTICIPATION

Susheela Kaushik

This chapter aims at a definition of the term 'political participation' from the vantage point of women's studies, its various manifestations and components, significance in terms of its effectiveness and limitations.

The concept of political participation is closely involved with the concept of power. Since politics is a study of an exercise in power, any political participation should mean a participation in this exercise of power, the power to effectively influence decision-making processes and policies, to reverse the existing situation wherever they are disadvantageous and to bring about the necessary social changes. Hence, political participation is much more than a physical participation in formal institutions and structures, though physical participation in formal political institutions is very much necessary for itself and as a means for influencing decisions. Direct and visible participation helps to enlarge freedom of the social group and accelerate the pace of its advancement, but this is not enough. Even an enlarged participation by way of numbers may not lead to the advancement of the cause of that social group. It is, hence, untenable to argue that a substantial increase in the representation of women will automatically lead to greater promotion of women's interests. Further, it is one thing for more women to hold political positions, and it is another thing for them to use such positions and power for women's ends. This would also imply that it is lack of sufficient representation of women in various positions at present, which is responsible for their low status or share in the development. It is very much the reverse. A sexual division of labour, the exclusion of women from certain positions and levels of power, and their poor representation at decision-making machineries, are themselves the result of their poor status.

There are further, instances of women when put in positions of power, have been the first ones to cut off policies and schemes specially helpful for women. One also finds there is no correlation between extent of participation in formal institutions and the extent of development of women in society. There have been instances where the socially backward regions in India have sent more women into Assemblies, where women have gone in greater numbers to vote (as in Utter Pradesh). In fact, the first woman Chief Minister as well as the first woman Prime Minister in India belonged to this state, even though from the point of view of all development indicators for women, Utter Pradesh is one of the lowest.

It is thus necessary to ask the question as to whose benefit is this participation directed. What impact has this participation made on the policies and the system over a period? For effecting this impact, it is equally necessary to assess as to the levels at which this participation is taking place. Mere number is not enough; it has to be situated at levels which are significant and effective for exercising power. Massive mobilisation and numerically impressive participation in political processes, formal or informal, are not goals in themselves. They are a means and a strategy for achieving something more fundamental, which the group can do, only when its participation touches at the structure of politics itself. One has to, therefore, identify the broader processes of the political structure, and the way power is arranged in a particular society. The ideology of the state, the interrelationship between the important components in its structure, like class, caste and gender, and its basic development goals are essential in understanding the repercussions of participation. Often, a vastly expanded participation and wide mobilisation of a socially weak community — in this context women—has led to the strengthening of the present pattern of development rather than directing this pattern to their own development. Even values like equality (constitutional, political and economic), rights (property, access to resources) etc, may be meaningful only when women possess and exercise them for bringing about a change in their own position as well as of the society; otherwise they will merely add up to strengthening and reinforcing the existing social system by operating within the framework of patriarchy. Values like equality and rights, and concepts like participation and mobilisation need to constantly keep before them the objective of the client group. Above all, it should be related to and tested against another equally important value justice.

Any assessment of the political participation of women in India, then, has to start by asking questions like whether such participation has led to bringing about or moving towards improving the quality of life for them or simply making it more liveable for women? Whether such participation, by women, either as individuals or as group, has meant developing alternate strategies for development as well as structures of power? Whether political interventions, which women seek to make, start with women as points of departure or merely help women to infiltrate systematically in the existing hierarchies of power, thereby lending themselves to becoming women performers or even worse, careerists? If increasing political participation has to have any meaning for women, such participation should be based on a widespread and well orchestrated mobilisation of women on the central issue of women's oppression and subordinate status in society and family.

Any analysis of political participation of women in India, hence, would have to combine a few components like (a) the extent, level and nature of women's participation in the political processes of India, by way of both formal and informal institutions; (b) the impact and significance of such participation for women's rights and living conditions; and, (c) types of feminist issues that were raised in the course of this participation.

With the above three criteria in view, one can assess the nature and extent of women's participation in some of the significant formal and informal processes of Indian politics. The Freedom Struggle, peasant and trade union movements, electoral and legislative institutions, the local government (Panchayat Raj system) and administrative and judicial functioning are some of these formal processes wherein participation of women can be evaluated. There are also institutions like political parties; interest and lobby groups; and, regional, linguistic, religious and casteist, movements, where women are participating increasingly. Finally, it is the women's movement, with various women's groups and organisations.

This chapter cannot aim to examine all of these. To illustrate the main argument of this chapter on how to assess participation of women, I might take up a few examples.

(a) Participation in Freedom Struggle

The Freedom Struggle in India is one of the few liberation movements in the world, where women had participated in great number. Ever since the formation of the Indian National Congress in 1885, the participation of women in its activities grew steadily, but slowly. The years of social reforms for women from the second quarter of the 19th century, had helped to make them come forward and participate in many ways, both directly and indirectly, formally and informally, with support and backup or many which are now been unrecognised. The huge increase in women's participation following the clarion call of Mahatma Gandhi is, however, well documented.

What was the impact of such participation on society, family and on women themselves? The mobilisation of women in large numbers weakened the bondage of traditions and helped them to develop a perspective on wider sociopolitical problems. Their close link with the national movement helped them acquire the right to political participation, to franchise and to other constitutional rights. There developed a tacit acceptance of women occupying various positions, both in the political and professional spheres. It gave them the space, as well as the power to claim rights and question its noncompliance. It, thus, helped in bringing about significant changes in the way of thinking and attitude to life of women. Women were initiated in politicisation, and the effect of it could be seen in the gradual but a definite change in the bringing up of the next generation of girls.

Impact on Women

The net gain in the process was a heightened political awareness, and a much greater social consciousness among women. There were, of course, very few instances of women having defied the family to join in the nationalist movement, or of having given up her traditional values and roles. But the fact that many women, of all classes and walks of life, even housewives and the uneducated joined picketing, moved from house to house collecting clothes and donations, courted arrest and were imprisoned in distant jails, showed that there was nothing which could really prevent them from moving beyond traditional roles. The prevailing political environment and values, seem to have accepted and even positively encouraged such activities on the part of women. The Freedom Movement and Indian women's widespread participation in it, thus, brought out a conducive climate for perceptible changes in many areas. Women's education and participation in work outside home and in the income generation, were some of the changes which come about. The nationalist movement under Gandhi stressed on the simple ways of living, giving up of ostentation in daily lives as well as marriages, in eating habits as well as in women's relief from daily chores so as to give time to picketing, spinning, etc. These broader changes, undoubtedly, led to a changed attitude towards life and women's position. Marriages became simple: dowry system got weakened; education of girls went up; potentialities of girls were identified, tapped and encouraged; widow remarriages and singleness of girls definitely showed an upward trend. More and more women gave up *purdah*.

The impact of women's participation was immediate and visible on the Congress leadership. Gandhi and Nehru recognised the women's valuable contribution to the nationalist movement, and felt the need for improving their situation. Gandhi said, "I am uncompromising in the matter of women's rights ...she should labour under no legal disability not suffered by man".

The liberal egalitarian legacy of the Indian National Movement, in turn, had led to the Constitution of free India granting a position of equality to women by way of political rights. The provision of Fundamental Rights to women as equal citizens of India, it was believed then, would automatically provide a status of equality in actual political life. It was assumed that such a constitutional provision would take care of the various issues that had been bedevilling women for centuries and pave the way for their development much in the same way as it was viewed earlier that women's upliftment would come once freedom was achieved.

However, from the point of view of women's studies, it would be interesting to see the impact of women's participation and contribution on (a) cultural institutions in society, whether it could break some of the shackles on women and mitigate the social oppression by way of illiteracy, economic dependency, social movement, etc; (b) on the family and its patriarchal structure and values. Did women's role and contribution increase her status in the family to one of equality? Did the nationalist movement then, and the policies and programmes of independent India reflect the recognition of women's contribution and potentialities? While Gandhi's clarion call to women helped them to come out of the four walls of their houses and join the ranks of soldiers for freedom, he could not deliver much to women by way of right or policies. His economic policies for women by way of *charkha* or spinning wheel, did not find a place in the future economic plans. It is only of late that such questions are being pursued. Studies on women in the Freedom Struggle is gradually moving away from women in history to one of women's history.

There is also the question as to how far this promoted a feminist consciousness in them – whether the women were able to perceive and analyse their own position and work to promote their own rights, within or outside the context of India's freedom. The struggle against a common enemy (the British rule) seemed to have diverted the women, by and large, from their own specific oppression. The questions of women's rights within the family, protest against their traditional roles as wives and mothers, against the traditional power relations within the family or to the male defined values etc, did not seem to have figured in a big way. The Freedom Movement was born, the movement did not seem to feel concerned with the women's rights issues so as to face them squarely.

This also leaves us with another nagging doubt – did this (if so, how far) massive participation of women make any impact on the Indian nationalist movement itself? Did it affect the stances of the leaders, as well as bring forth any type of policy decisions or programmes for women? Obviously, the concern for women's rights and social position did not pervade the whole of national movement, nor did it have any impact on their policies and perspectives. Those like Gandhi and Nehru who recognised women's valuable contribution to the nationalist movement, believed in the need for improving their small proportion.

Nothing really happened or was undertaken for emancipating the women from their various disabilities. There was never any such well articulated organised campaign for women's emancipation, in the same way as there was for Harijan reforms or communal equality. Not that much success could be achieved in those areas either, but at least it led to much social awareness. This was evident from the fact that when (soon after Independence) the resurrected report of the BN Rau Committee on the Draft of Hindu Code called the Hindu Law Bill was placed before the Constituent Assembly, it was opposed by many traditionalists in the assembly. Apparently, the Fundamental

Rights and the equality that Congress had talked about, related only to the political spheres – not to the private and familial spheres. It took more than seven years before the Parliament could finally adopt one small portion of the original draft, viz with regard to marriage, divorce and maintenance. One had to be happy with the mere inclusion of the Uniform Civil Code in Article 44 of the Directive Principles of State Policy of the Constitution. Obviously, the voice of women was not loud enough to shake the leadership nor their participation in the decision–making was strong enough to demand their rights effectively.

(b) Participation in the Democratic Process

In any modern political system, elections occupy the most central place. The nature, periodicity and rate of participation by the masses in elections, is viewed as the touchstone for the representative character of democracy, and hence, democracy itself. Almost all nations in the world have adopted universal adult suffrage, wherein every adult, without any additional qualification or conditions, has the right to vote in general elections held periodically. How regular are these elections? What is the percentage of participation in voting by the people? How organised or peaceful the polls are? These, in turn, indicate the health and strength of democracy.

Elections being a forum for and method in self-government and democracy, occupy a significant place in drawing the attention of the nation to the problems and needs of the disadvantaged sectors. The party manifestoes, campaigns, individual candidate's promises, track records and future course of action, are indicative of the national concerns, as well as, mandates for action. As the instrument that brings into being the national Parliament and state Assemblies, the outcome of elections in terms of parties and individuals are significant for the adaptation of policies and measures for women's development.

Democracy does not, and cannot operate by proxy. Every citizen, conscious of his and the national movement's development, and aware of the value and utility of the vote to fetch the same, needs to correlate this right with development. This, he can do only by exercising this right (or by participating) in elections. The participatory theory of democracy believes that direct participation in decision-making would be the ideal of citizens ruling themselves. In a modern state whose size and population are large, whose problems are complex, and the art of governing almost a managerial technique, the next best would be a representative democracy. It is then that a psephologist worries about the voting percentage of the population in general, and of the depressed sections in particular. The proper selection of a correct party/candidate in an election is vital, if this representative democracy has to function in the interest of a majority of the population, which are depressed and disadvantaged.

Many studies believed that (i) women are not independent voters; (ii) that a majority of them are illiterate; (iii) that a majority of them make their choice on the basis of suggestions given by male members of the family - husband and sons, (iv) that women lack information and political awareness; and, (v) women were not politically conscious. However, these studies defined the words political participation very narrowly. Despite these limitations, one way make a general analysis of the voting pattern of women. A quick glance at their participation in elections over the past four decades will confirm the initial hopes placed by the founders of the Constitution. The extent, nature and level of Indian women's participation is much greater than in many other countries—developed or developing, except possibly in the countries that were going through radical revolutionary wars. A certain cultural background as well as the freedom struggle could be the main reasons for this. This participation has been more or less expanding steadily over the years, through the various elections—by way of voting, as candidates and participation in campaigning etc. The gap in the turnout between men and women is getting more and more narrowed. The number of women getting elected to the representative bodies is slowly increasing.

This increase in the turnout of women voters,

particularly of the lower class and castes, may be attributed to a high degree of mobilisation, rather than of one's own political consciousness. In India, one can talk in general of high level of awareness of the value to vote, which is possessed and cast eagerly by the poor and the Scheduled Castes, at times very pragmatically and rationally. They are politically sensitive, well aware of their interests and even the political issues. But this awareness, in order to be translated into a political exercise like voting, needs tremendous mobilisation. This is all the more in the case of women, as poverty and daily work, household chores and care, patriarchal and family norms, act as great disincentives. Distance of booths, possibility of violence, health and other factors further discourage them. The linkage between the 'personal' and 'public' is missing, and women do not feel automatically impelled.

Recognising the significance of the women voters, many political parties have, of late, been exerting themselves to devise various methods. Mobilisation in the past have been mainly at the time of decisions in the form of adhoc promises made on populistic and opportunistic short-term basis, rather than on long-term goals of a social change for women.

To the extent there was any correlation between the campaign promises and voting support, it also reflected on the low impact that the women's movement had made in educating their lot, as well as in making a dent on the patriarchal politicians. The Congress Party too, was not far behind. In 1984, much of the victory of Congress (I) could be attributed to a sympathy vote by women for the young Prime Minister and against the slaying of the women Prime Minister Indira Gandhi on a woman-to-woman basis.

The increase in the number of women voters since Independence, and their eager participation in voting, has made almost all political parties pay special attention to organising themselves, campaigning among themselves, and choosing them to contest elections. Definitely in the earlier years such campaigning among women and soliciting their votes were done rather casually. More recently, the parties have organised regular party forums, cells and front organisations, specially for women. These women's cells not only mobilise and campaign among women, and seek their support and membership for party issues during elections as well as normal period, but also quite often take up issues concerning women. Of late, parties are also taking stand on women's issues, organise rallies and demonstrations, pass resolutions, lobby with and pressurise the government for specific policies. Women are participating in them in great numbers and have even courted arrest on issues like *sati*, Muslim Women's Right to Maintenance, rape incidents, violence, police excesses on women, etc.

Women in Party Positions

But in this context there are many important questions to ask. In view of the extent of the recognition of the need for women's support, both for image building as well as electoral successes, how many women have been able to occupy important positions in the party? There have been many important political personalities among women at the helm of various parties. There have been a number of women who were members of the highest executive committees of their parties and have functioned as office bearers. The Congress Party, particularly, has taken care to give representation to women among its office-bearers. In fact, it has almost become axiomatic in India that the highest decision-making bodies of the various parties need to have definitely at least one or two women members. It is, however, necessary to ask the question whether it is a mere tokenism. Such representation by being very limited in number, as well as often occupied by weak and colourless personalities, does become more a symbolism rather than real power wielding. There are, of course, some exception to this.

Despite the increase, the number of women contesting the elections still constitute only 1 to 2 per cent. Even where seats are reserved as in the Panchayats, they do not come forward so easily. Out of these contestants, the ones who get elected constitute still smaller percentage. While those who belong to the major political parties stand a better chance of success, the non-party candidates and those who belong to minor political parties, are hardly successful. Despite this, many women contest as independents. This perhaps implies that political parties are, by and large, reluctant to choose women as candidates. The maximum number of candidates being from the Congress Party. But even this party allotted only 3 per cent of seats in 1977 to women. Obviously, this is much more in the nature of a tokenism rather than an acceptance of women's equality or capability. Often women candidates are viewed as depriving men in their chances. Even the small number of women who contest, gain their candidates by their birth and close relationship with already established party leaders. Almost all the women who figure in electoral politics are invariably someone's wife, daughter, daughter-in-law or other close relations. There are exceptions only among the Left parties, where a few of them can claim as having worked with the working class. Most of these women, thus, come from urban, middle class, with educated elite, background and cannot claim a stage-by-stage growth or participation in their political career. Apparently, there is no correlation between female population's voting percentage and their number in the elected assemblies. The subordinated position of the 'ordinary' women in families, their routine and normal duties of looking after the family, bringing up children, performing both the unpaid and paid work, do not allow them much scope to participate freely in public-political activities. To this must be added the economic factor. Elections in India as in all other modern democracies, has become very complicated, violent, dirty and expensive, inviting thereby very many legitimate and not so legitimate ways of finding and managing them. Women cannot obviously fit into this matrix of election. The participation costs in formal politics is at present too high for women. Political participation of women, by the conventional and formal yardstick, thus is low, and lower than men of even weaker sections. In the case of Scheduled Castes and Tribes, due to reservation of constituencies, the number of representatives is proportionate to the population. But it is ironic, if not cruel that only one of these seats had gone to woman. No study has yet been undertaken on an all India basis, on the nature and extent of women's participation in the legislative business. In the early years after Independence, the Parliament did witness many women like Renuka Ray participating vigorously in the Hindu Code Bill, etc. More recently, many women members of Parliament (MPs) belonging to different parties are drawing attention to issues like atrocities against women, women's right, social crimes like *sati*, dowry, rape, etc. Still by and large, such participation are confined repeatedly to few women. A majority of them are silent on many issues, particularly on the general, political concerns. On the whole, it looks like those who are good and articulate and participate often. Others who are dormant, are invisible and silent on most of the issues. Political parties must exercise more care in choosing the correct type of women who are knowledgeable and can represent the majority of the poor and rural women. More presence of women in Parliament, even if of a greater number, will mean very little by way of women's development.

Conclusion

The above two processes have been taken up merely to point out some of the possible dangers involved in analysing the participation or pleading for increased participation of women in political developments and institutions. This is not attempted in order to discourage such pleas nor in a mood of cynicism nor negativism. The visible participation of more and more women in the public sphere, their greater representation at the decision-making and managerial level, are definitely important for more than one reason. Apart from their own possible contribution to women's development with a degree of empathy and understanding, they also would be able to project and sensitise fellow workers, politicians and executives on women's perspectives, and help adopt mid-term corrections in policies and their implementation. It acts further as role models for younger and other women with political and personal ambitions. May be it is too much to expect every woman to have cultivated a perspective on "correct" women's studies on every issue, but one can hope at least some women to have images or acquire it in the course.

As women's studies is gaining deeper roots in India and as women's development is getting increasing attention, it is prudent that the women's studies scholars take stock of some of the developments and attempt conceptual clarification. It is in this spirit that this chapter is presented.

Development Indicators (1981)

Political Participation Indicators (1984)

States	Literacy		Percapita Income		Sex ratio	Age of Marriage		Female Mortality rate			Women Contes.		Women Members elected		Total	Voters F
	Male	Female				Male	Female	Male	Female	1983	LS	Ass.	LS	Ass.		
Kerala	75.26	65.7	70.4	1379	10.32	27.2	21.9	5.8	7.8	33	7	17 (82-83)	—	4 (82-83)	—	—
U.P.	38.8	14.0	27.2	1280	885	20.9	17.8	16.6	15.0	155	45	94 (79-80)	9	24 (79-80)	—	—
Bihar	38.1	13.6	26.2	927	946	21.5	16.5	13.6	12.4	99	16	77 (79-80)	10	12	—	—
India	46.8	24.8	36.2	—	933	23.3	18.3	12.0	11.9	105	164	241	46	44	63.61	58

Note: The above table confirms the findings. Kerala one of the more advanced State of India from the point of womens development, sends in the least number of women to Parliament and State Assembles. The state of Uttar Pradesh and Bihar which are backward from the point of view of female development indicators has the maximum of women participants in politics.

4

WOMEN'S PARTICIPATION IN NATIONAL FREEDOM STRUGGLE

Niroj Sinha

Women have been known to participate in national liberation movements throughout the world. Although they have not been found to be politically very conscious or involved in day-to-day political issues, women have mobilised themselves during crisis situations. In India, women have participated in the National Freedom Struggle. However, a clear picture has not emerged. There have been debates and counter–debates about the magnitude of women's participation in national struggle as to: (a) Which section of women did participate? (b) Did it help in the emergence of female political leadership? (c) Were women able to create some niche for themselves in the political sphere? (d) Was their participation in some way a reinforcement of patriarchy or it created and acknowledged the separate identity of women as individuals?

In attempting to analyse the role of women in Indian Freedom Struggle, one is beset by a series of problems at the very outset. For, one, the political role of women as a subject of research is of recent origin in India.[1] There are very few comprehensive studies on women's participation in the Freedom Struggle. Studies published between 1968-88 do touch upon various aspects and dimensions of women's participation. Some date has also been generated, some factual accounts made such as most standard histories of The National Movement mention women's participation and role in the Civil Disobedience Movement. Women in revolutionary terrorism have also been described. Some accounts of contemporaries who participated in the movement refer to the strength and broad base acquired by it as a whole through women's participation.

However, information on women in the writings prior to 1975 have been mainly on women of elite sections of society. Large majority of women have not figured in these accounts, and their role has remained unexplored and marginalised.[2] Except some autobiographical accounts by some elite women participants, not much is known about the lives or the social background of the mass of women, who entered the movement in different regions of the country. But recently some work has been done in this area.

Further, most of the accounts of women's participation have been mainly descriptive and not analytical. They do not examine either the reason or the implications of this spontaneous upsurge of political activity by women of all classes. The elite perspective is dominant, which relates women's participation to reform movement and education but ignores the role of peasant women. Women from different sections including even prostitutes or thousands of housewives, who directly or indirectly supported the freedom fighters by shouldering family responsibilities, have not been discussed. The impact of colonialism on women's lives and believes, created a source for radicalism among Bengali youth. Strangely, it was recorded by an English administrator as early as 1907, and repeatedly mentioned by Mahatma Gandhi.[3]

Some have described existing research on women's participation in national struggle as non-comprehensive, cursory in nature and generally a history from above.[4] Thus, one has to start with caution and carefulness in recording and analysing women's participation in national liberation movement.

Generally, one starts with the presumption that the social reform movement from the mid-19th century prepared the base for women's awakening and their entry in the movement later on. The elite class-led social movement of the 19th century, was a movement run by men on women's issues. Pandita Ramabai stands solitary in the galaxy of names like Raja Ram Mohan Roy, Agarkar, Ishwar Chandra Vidyasagar and Veerasalengam. Their efforts rallied round issues affecting women's life adversely such as the practice of *sati*, female infanticide, plight of the widow, child marriage, polygamy, etc. Raja Ram Mohan Roy championed the ban of the practice of *sati*. His campaigns resulted in the governmental resolution of 1829, banning the practice of *sati*. Raja Ram Mohan Roy was trained in western liberal education. He founded the Brahmo Samaj in 1929, which by the second half of the century practiced a Christianised version of Hinduism. The Brahmo Samaj split in 1886 into Adi Brahmo Samaj led by Devendra Nath Tagore, and Brahmo Samaj of India led by Keshav Chandra Sen. This faction opened schools for girls, started a women's magazine in 1863 and founded the Brahmitra Samaj in 1867. This Samaj taught Brahmo religion, handicrafts and social skills to the female relatives of the Brahmo Samaj members. Keshav Chandra Sen exhibited a mixture of reformist, revivalist and traditional ideas about women. On the one hand, he pressed for a law to legalise cross-caste marriage within the Brahmo community, and to raise the minimum age for marriage of girls to 14, on the other hand, got his daughter married at the age of 13. The Brahmo Samaj was further split in 1878 into liberal and conservative factions. The liberal Sadharan Samaj sponsored women's education, but the Nava Vedhan Brahmo Samaj did not favour higher education for women. Vidyasagar took up the cause of widows, and started a movement in support for widow remarriage in the 1850s. It resulted in Hindu Widows Marriage Act of 1865, but in actuality not much was achieved. It met with strong opposition from the Bengali orthodoxy. There were signature campaigns but most effective was the social pressure from the reform leaders, ranging from social outcasting to threats of violence.[5]

The real explosion came with the campaign against child marriage and the debate over age of consent bill, initiated by Behramji Malabari in 1884, who started a nationwide debate. It met with strong opposition from the orthodox. The attack was spearheaded by Lokmanya Tilak, who defined the legislation as an attack on religion. The orthodox were not wrong in connecting the issues of reform and religion. Throughout the 19th century, the conservative Brahman elite class was making a very successful attempt. It remains the major factor in Indian politics even today to define Indian culture and Indian nationality in terms of reconstituted Hinduism. There was no way the reformers could avoid the issue. This 'Hindu identity' had to be challenged to make active even a consistent democratic liberalism or liberal feminism because it had remained casteist and patriarchal. Numerous low-caste radicals were willing to meet this challenge, but only few of the elites were eager. As a result, the movement was almost totally overwhelmed by Hindu revivalism by the end of the 19th century.[6] The new revivalism was embodied in powerful organisations such as Dayanand Saraswati's Arya Samaj (1875), Vivekananda's Ramkrishna Mission (1897) and Annie Besant's Madras Hindu Association (1904). These new organisations attacked the reformers, but supported some reforms of the Hindu society. They did incorporate a good deal of the programme of reformers such as educating women, raising the age of marriage, remarriage of child widows etc, but all this was to be done within the framework of Hinduism. The ideal of Sita, the subordinate and oppressed 'Pativrate', defined the limits of Indian women's advance.[7]

Barring a few exceptions, the modernists and the revivalists were not really concerned with gender equality, women's own desires or their perspectives on dignity and justice. Nor were they aware of the interrelationship between patriarchal control over women's freedom, roles and behaviour and the carefully preserved pluralist hierarchical organisation of the Indian society.[8]

Some regard the reform movement as a failure, but Gail Omvedt maintains that it helped to lay some of the foundations for the women's movement that emerged in the 1920s. Though men kept control within the family and within public life, the slow movement of women out of the home and the women's groups sponsored by male reformers and later the nationalists helped to 'extend the female space' for action.[9]

One generation later Jyotiba Phule spearheaded the middle class and low caste movement for their rights all over India in the mid-19th century. He pushed the analysis of the interrelationship between women's sub-ordination and maintenance of caste hierarchy far beyond the point that Vidyasagar had managed to articulate. Phule identified women's subordination as an instrument to perpetuate existing models of hierarchy. Periyar called for rejection of the *mangalputra* and wrote, "our ladies must come forward to compete with males in all spheres."[10] The main social organisations founded by men centred round ceremonies. 'Satyashodhak marriages' dramatised the defiance of caste ideology by refusing the use of Brahmin priests or traditional rituals and by institutionalising women's equality. The ceremony concludes with the *mangalashataka* and garlanding. Periyar also emphasised garlanding and equality. In this respect, both were ahead of even the best laws of today — the reformed 'Civil Code' includes the patriarchal *saptapadi* ritual and even registered marriages make not even a rhetoric mention of women's equality.[11]

The ideology of Phule and Periyar had a strong feminist element in it. They definitely connected women's oppression and exploitation with other forms of social inequality and called rigorously for a fully liberated society.

However, in the long run, the reform movements strengthened women's "socialisation for inequality" within the middle class as a whole and heightened the growth of institutions like dowry and the supremacy of the patriarchal family in women's lives. Instead of its expected liberating influence, education became a powerful force in strengthening the sanskritisation process, which manifests the integral links and mutually supportive relationship between patriarchy and heirarchy.[12]

Women's participation in the Freedom Struggle dates back to 1905. The Swadeshi movement, which was triggered by the British decision to partition Bengal in 1905, saw women's entry into the movement, and the skilful tactics of several women leaders contributed to increase the participation of women in public life. Attempts at mass-mobilisation also facilitated this participation.[13] Pamphlets were written in Bengali and widely distributed. One of those was a pamphlet by Ramendrasundari Trivedi entitled 'a vow for Bengali Women', which tried to explain the Swadeshi movement in simple language for a village woman to understand. The pamphlet called upon women to participate in the ritual of *Rakhi bandhan* and *arandhan* (not lighting cooking fires), and to boycott foreign goods. Nirod Choudhary reported that the Swadeshi movement aroused a strong sense of patriotism in his mother who smashed the family's foreign made cooking pots. The traditions of Hindu *mela* were revived and exhibitions became a regular part of Congress meetings. Meetings were regularly held by women, although there was strong opposition, especially against the young unmarried girls in the leadership. Sarla Devi, daughter of Swarna Kumari Devi, started physical culture clubs, began a Swadeshi store for Women's work and organised festivals which celebrated Bengali traditions. She played an important role in the Swadeshi movement until she moved to Lahore in 1905 after marrying Arya Samaj leader Ram Bhoj Dutt Choudhary. Some British women who made Indian nationalism their own cause, played important roles as helpers as well as 'catalysts' such as Annie Besant, Dorethy Jinaragadasa, Margaret Cousins, an Irish feminist and Sister Nivedita.[14]

The Swadeshi movement also marked the formation of several women's organisations. Mahila Shilpa Samiti (1906-1908) was clearly inspired by the Swadeshi movement. Earlier, in 1901, Sarla Devi Choudhrani had formed the Bharat Stri Mahamandal after serious differences with the male leadership of the National Social Conference (NSC). In fact, women's associations had started coming up in the latter half of the previous century. In the Presidency of Bombay a women's magazine 'Stress Bodh' was started in

1857 by the Parsies. The 'Prasthana Samaj' which had organised Arya Mahila Samaj in 1882 under the leadership of Pandita Ramabai Ranade, associated with the modern faction, sought government funds for a girls' high school and legal authority to discourage child marriage. She formed NSC to provide an all-India forum for discussion of social reform after the leaders of the National Congress had decided to eliminate this subject from their agenda in order to present a united front to the British. Tilak was bitterly opposed to Ranade's action. In 1895, Tilak's opposition to NSC forced the holding of separate sessions by the Congress and NSC.

Female relatives of the reform oriented leaders began forming local women's organisations, justified by revivalist ideals, and there were no campaigns for social legislation. The Hindu ladies social and literacy 'cell' was started in 1902, Gujarati Street Mandal in 1903 and Women's Zoroastrian Association in 1903.[15] In 1908, Seva Sadan was started by the reform oriented leaders of the different communities. In 1904, the leaders of Maharashtra Social Conference (MSC) organised a women's section which held an annual conference during MSC sessions. This conference, the Bharat Mahila Parishad (BMP) organised educational and inspirational programmes in which women of distinction — Ramabai, Annie Besant, Sarojini Naidu and several others — gave speeches before women.

In the Madras Presidency, a women's magazine was started by Kamala, wife of Indian Christians' social reformer Satlinadhan.[16] A Brahmin widow's home was founded in 1913 by Subhalakshmi Annal, and a Mahila Seva Samaj in Mysore in 1913.

Local Muslim women's associations were found in the early 20th century by upper class Muslim women in several cities. In 1916, the Begum of Bhopal formed the All India Muslim Women's Conference, at which papers on social reform and education were read and resolutions passed. In 1917, Abu Begum proposed a resolution against polygamy that provoked opposition from Muslims. However, Gail Minault points out that in other cases Muslim women skilfully utilised religious themes and anti-British feelings to justify there activities during the Khilafat and Non-cooperation Movement.[17]

After 1910, women experienced in organising and working in local women's associations, and convinced that women should take the leadership into their own hands, started provincial and national women's organisations. There associations were inevitably elite, bourgeois and urban, consisting of women from the upper class with the advantage of social status, education and privilege, but redeemed by their desire to serve all women. The Young Women's Christian Association of India (YMCA) had become national in 1896. The Women's India Association (WIA) was formed in 1917 in Madras (now called Chennai). In the same year, Sarojini Naidu led a delegation of women formed by Margaret Cousins to the Constitutional Reforms Committee, demanding universal adult franchise women.[18]

The National Council of Women in India (NCWI) was formed in 1925, All India Women's Conference (AIWC) in 1927. By mid-1935, WIA and AIWC claimed membership of over 10,000 women.[19] NCWI developed eight provincial councils by 1934 and had 180 affiliated societies with a membership of over 8000.[20] WIA did not limit itself to fund raising, social service and women's education, but also sought to influence government policy on equal rights for women in some areas, and was involved with the issue of suffrage, education and social reform. WIA founders included women like Margaret Cousins and Annie Besant who were not only suffragists, but political radicals and critics of imperialism in their own country.

AIWC, which had originally convened only to discuss women's education, became a permanent body which succeeded in developing branches all over India. It called itself apolitical, even had a clause in its constitution prohibiting its engagement in party politics. But by 1932, however, AIMC had involved itself with political rights of women. Although its major focus and priority remained women's question and elimination of women's backwardness, the future of India gradually became and important concern.[21] From the beginning, WIA had an interest in home rule and women's suffrage, which was clearly patriotic. Yet, even in troubled time of 1928-29, he WIA insisted that their policy was to work for reform through the Legislative Council. They were not prepared to accept Civil Disobedience, for this would jeopardise the relation they had so carefully worked out with the government to secure for women, positions of magistrates on various councils and committees and to urge the legislation for the improvement of women's status. However, when the Civil Disobedience Movement started in 1930, WIA was faced with a dilemma. Dr Muthulakshmi Reddi, a founder member of WIA and later as Vice-President signed a protest in 1928 against the all British Composition of the Simon Commission. The choice was between aligning with the national movement or adopting an apolitical stance. Situations caused leaders of these organisations to redefine their aims, amend bylaws, argue with each other, and finally end up with organisations which were somewhere between autonomous women's associations and women's auxiliary of the Indian National Congress.

Kamala Devi Chattopadhyay observed, though the Women's Conference had originally stated it would not participate in politics, it realised that it would have to concern itself with public in its wide term, without alignment to any particular political party. It also accepted as members women from any party. It took a strong nationalist stand, and demanded equal rights for women to enable them to play their full and legitimate role in the national affairs. Otherwise, all other rights might become illusory.[22]

Many members of WTA were also members of AIWC, and many such members were members of the Indian National Congress, and leaders in the National movement as well. This factor led to close relations between women and the national movement.

Although women's associations could never decide their stand on the involvement of women in politics, the women in general were ultimately drawn into the vortex of the Freedom Struggle by Mahatma Gandhi. In South Africa, his *stayagrah* 'army' had women in it. With his experience of South Africa behind him, Gandhi was aware of the potentialities of women as passive resistance. As he experimented with his weapon of *satyagrah* in India, he realised that women could participate in it together with men.

With the belief that for the Freedom Movement to be successful it had to be a movement of masses, Gandhi felt that *swaraj* would be meaningless without reform of social structures and upliftment of the weaker sections, namely the women and the lower social strata, to a position of equality with others. While lending support to the cause of improving women's condition through education and reform of marriage laws, he declared himself to be uncompromising in the matter of women's right.[23] He remarked, "woman has been suppressed under custom and law for which man was responsible and in the shaping of which she had no hand....Woman has as much right to shape her own destiny as man has to shape his....It is upto men to see that they enable them to realise their full status and play their part as equal of men."[24] He differed from the early reformers by his revolutionary approach to women's role in society and their right to personal dignity as individuals. Without belittling their roles as mothers and wives, he insisted that they must play an equal role with men in the achievement of freedom and social justice. In his opinion, women had natural abilities to lead in a non-violent struggle for human liberation. The most significant aspect of Gandhi's ideas lies in the remarkable similarity between them and the demands now voiced by the women's liberation movement all over the world — equality in the family and society, the right to one's own body; the opening of wider opportunities for self development; and, a refusal to be treated as sex symbol.[25]

As president of the Indian National Congress in 1931, Pandit Nehru accepted equal political and legal rights of women, and introduced the concept of equal obligations along with equal rights in the Fundamental Rights resolution passed by the Congress that year. Along with adult suffrage, the resolution emphasised the need for protecting women workers, particularly granting them maternity leave. He asserted that "women must be trained to participate in every department of human activity and play an active part in all professions and sphere. For this purpose, they must fight social institutions like *purdah*, untouchability, caste system and marriage laws. But above all, they must participate in the struggle against the root cause of political subjugation and the economic system. The women's movement would suffer set back if it remained isolated from the general political and economic struggle for liberation in the country.

Some historians of the social reform movement have held that this merger of the women's movement in the political struggle diluted its strength, though perhaps it gained in legitimacy by the championship of national leaders.[26] Some others, however, claim that the India perspective gave the women's movement in India an identity distinct from similar movement in other countries.[27]

Thus, women and their associations were drawn inside the vortex of national struggle for freedom under the inspiration and guidance of national leaders like Gandhi and Nehru. During the Non-cooperation Movement, women in different parts of India joined processions, propagated the use of *khadi* and *charkha*; some of them left government schools and colleges. Renuka Ray in Calcutta gave up her studies along with her friends and joined the movement. So did Vijayalaxmi Pandit.[28]

Basanti Devi, wife of C R Das, accompanied her husband in his tour of Bengal and asked women to boycott foreign goods. She was arrested on December 7, 1921, on the charge of obstracting the gentlemen of Calcutta, by selling *khadi*. She presided over the Bengal provincial conference of Chittagong in April 1922, and Kasturba Gandhi presided over the Gujarat provincial conference appealing to women to take to spinning and weaving *khadi*. In Allahabad, Rameshwari Mehra formed a *kumari sabhar* to encourage girls to take part in public discussions. There were women like Hemprabha Majumdar, who received *lathi* blows. Bee

Amman, mother of the Ali Brothers, discarded her veil and addressed meetings all over India, advocating the use of *khadi*, supporting Hindu Muslim unity.[29]

In Borsad *satyagrah* of 1923-24, women turned out in large numbers. It is on record that women displayed greater courage than men, when police confiscated their house, buffaloes and other property.

In the Bardoli *satyagrah* of 1928, the women gradually outnumbered men in political gatherings. Sardar Patel commented that in stead-fastness of purpose, simplicity and purity, they were better than their men. Maniben Patel and Bhakti Desai fixed their tents and huts on the land declared to be sold by the government.[30]

The salt *satyagraha* launched by Gandhiji in March 1930, was extended to a mass campaign at the beginning of April 1930. Gandhiji had initially exclude women from participating in 'salt *satyagraha*'. This was not taken lightly by women. Margaret Cousins sent a spirited reply on behalf of WIA, protesting against the division of work by sex, as women had been left in charge of the *ashram* of Sabarmati while men were to accompany Gandhi in the march to Dandi. Kamla Devi Chattopadhyay met Gandhi and expressed her desire to be involved in the *satyagraha*. Durgabai Desmukh met the local leaders of Madras and suggested that they be included in the movement.[31]

On April 6, 1930, the salt laws were ceremoniously broken by Gandhi. Sarojini Naidu and Muthuben Patel were with him. Many women had walked to Dandi and the awakening in the villages was astonishing. Gandhi was arrested and in a statement to the press on 7 April, 1930. Gandhi said that he was becoming increasingly certain that in the struggle for *swaraj*, the women of this country could contribute a greater share than men.[32]

Gandhi had nominated Sarojini Naidu to lead the raid on Dhasana salt fields. She declared that the "time has come when women can no longer seek immunity behind the shelter of their sex, but must face equally with their male comrades all the pains and sacrifices for the liberation of this country."[33] Lilavati Mushi and Sarojini Naidu organised women and led them in different parts of Bombay (now called Mumbai) to make salt. Kamala Devi Chattopadhyay stood outside the law courts and sold salt at high prices.

Women's role in salt *satyagrah* was significant in two ways. First, among Congress women, this represented a shift from role of supportive auxiliaries to direct participation in the struggle, even when it involved defiance of the leadership. Secondly, the impact of the women's role resulted in the conversion of a section of the leadership, especially Gandhi and Nehru. Kamala Devi Chattopadhyay commented, "ancient prejudices melted, walls of tradition cracked and rays of new hope is creeping in."[34] Nehru remarked, "our women came to the forefront and took charge of the struggle. Women had always been there of course, but now there was an avalanche of them which took not only the British government, but their own men-folk by surprise. There were these women, of the upper or middle classes leading sheltered lives in their homes, peasant women, working class women, rich women — coming out into tens of thousands in defiance of government orders and police *lathis*. It was not only the displays of courage and daring, but what was even more surprising was the organisational power they showed."[35] Thus, the women had turned this struggle into a beautiful epic.[36]

In July 1930, when Lord Irwin was to address the Central Assembly, it was decided that there should be picketing by a group of women volunteers on the first day, and 27 women from Lahore, Ambala and Simla were chosen for this purpose. Women went in groups of twos and threes and stood outside the Central Legislative assembly Hall. They had black flags hidden under the fold of their sarees. As soon as the viceroy came and got down from his car, they took out their flags and shouted "Irwin, go back". In Lahore, Manmohine Sehgal organised picketing in front of college gates and also students strikes. Arrested women in Lahore jail were Zutshi, Kamala Nehru's mother Raspati Kaul, Parvati Devi, Asaf Ali and Satyavati from Delhi.[37]

Same happened in Bihar, where a number of women

were arrested. Hasan Imam addressed several meetings of students in Patna and Barh. Together with her daughter Sami, Smt. CC Das and some other women, she organised a procession of women in Patna on July 15 to inaugurate an intensive campaign of boycott of British goods. During the week ending July 25 Patna witnessed two demonstrations,. in which nearly 3000 women took part. Hasan Imam, Sami, Smt. CC Das, Gauri Das and Vindhyavasini Devi were summoned to court. Imam formed a committee of women in Muzaffarpur to propagate spinning. Women leaders were also advocating non-payment of chowkidari tax.[38]

In Karnataka women who took part in the struggle were Kamala Devi Chattopadhyay, Umabai Kundapur, Krishnabai, Panjikar and Ballasi Seddama. Gowramma and her co-workers offered *satyagarh* in front of the house of the Patel of Akoriji in north Kanara. The police dragged women, beat them with canes and harassed them. Women gave food and shelter to Congressmen, often acted as messengers carrying secret information from one camp to another, and when the call for *satyagrah* came they to be proved fervent *satyagrahas.*

Women in princely states did not keep aloof. In Viramgam *satyagrah* in May 1930, 700 women were lathicharged.[39] In the Rajkot *satyagrah* of 1938-39[40] and the movement in Linodi, women were active. In Rajkot, Kasturba was jailed along with Manibehn Patel and Mridula Sarabhai. Kamala Devi organised agitation in Ram Durg state in Karnataka in 1930.[41]

In the Civil Diobedience Movement inaugurated by Gandhi in October 1940, women courted arrest in large numbers. One of the first to do so was Sucheta Kripalani, who had been in charge of the women's department of the All India Congress Committee since 1939.

In the 1942 Quit India Movement' almost all the top leaders were immediately arrested, and the movement was practically leaderless. However, women joined in taking out processions, holding meetings and demonstrations and organising strikes. In Assam, a young girl, Kanaklata Barua, led a procession of 500 and was killed in the police firings. In Midnapur, Bengal, women played a notable role and were victims of police atrocities. In Bombay, Usha Mehta operated an underground radio station. The Congress Radio, broadcasted news at 7.30 pm from August to November 13th, 1942, till Usha Mehta along with her colleagues were arrested. She were sentenced to few years rigorous imprisonment and was sent to Yeraveda jail, where she found herself among 250 women political prisoners.[42]

Aruna Asaf Ali was one of the most important figures of 1942. For four years she remained underground, avoiding arrest. She published bulletins and edited along with Ram Manohar Lohia '*The Inquilab*'. A price of Rs 5,000 was announced as a reward for her capture.

Besides the women who joined the Freedom Movement on the call of Gandhi, there were a few who could not believe his creed of non-violence. They were revolutionary and in the 1930s such organisations sprang up rapidly. They were active in Bengal, Dakha, Commilla and Chittagong were the storm centres. Young college girls joined these secret societies. Kalpana Joshi, Preeti Waddadar were associated with Chittagong armoury raid. Preeti led a raid on the Pahartali railway officers' club. She later committed suicide. Shanti and Soniti shot dead Stevens, the district magistrate of Commilla in December 1931, and were given life sentences.[43] The Chchatri Sangh started in Calcutta in 1928 was an important training and recruiting ground for future revolutionaries. In Delhi, Roopvati Jain, at the age of 17, was in charge of a bomb factory under Chandrashekhar Ajad. Sushila Devi cut her finger and put *tilak* on the forehead of Bhagat Singh and Batukeshwar Dutta on April 9, 1920. She was arrested and imprisoned. Durga Devi played the role of Bhagat Singh's wife. She shot a police sergeant at Hamilton Road, Bombay. She was elected president of the Delhi provincial Congress Committee in 1938.[44]

In January 1942, the Indian Independence League was formed in Kualalampur and Indian women in Southeast Asia worked for the cause of India's freedom. In March

1943, a women section of the league was started and Indian women in Malaya, Thailand and Burma, enlisted as volunteers on the call of Subhash Chandra Bose. In July 1933, a women's regiment—the Rani of Jhansi Regiment—was formed with Lakshmi Sahgal as the captain.

The general idea or myth circulated for quite a long period has been that women's role in the national movement(s) against imperialism was male-dictated or male manipulated. Uma Rao and Ishani Mukherjee in their writings offer enough evidence against it.[45] Various writings in recent years indicate that once mobilised, women moved on their own, acquiring new confidence and articulating new priorities. The number of women directly involved in revolutionary movements in Bengal, Maharashtra, Punjab, in Uttar Pradesh and the erstwhile Madras Presidency in the turn of the century may have been small, but the inspirational support base of the revolutionaries included more women whose names will never feature in dictionaries of freedom fighters. The women who provided shelter and food, carried messages or arms, or instilled a passion to 'serve their country' among their children, telling them about the 'heroes' and 'martyrs' who sacrificed their lives for the country's freedom, did not belong to the elite class only. Many were uneducated and poor. They played such roles without waiting for any social sanction. They provided a communication channel for the message of nationalism when nationalist literature was under severe control. The stories continued to spread and the songs and poems were eagerly observed by young people, often from women in their homes. Women's invisible role, which provided greater force, has received little formal acknowledgement.[46]

Similarly, women's active and even militant roles as participants and leaders in quasi-national peasants and workers' struggles remained strongly invisible till recently. Recent attempts to reconstruct life stories of women activists and to obtain oral history from surviving women freedom fighters provide little substance to the theory of male direction, guidance or manipulation.

Some find it difficult to believe that leaders of the

national movement were not aware of the growing base of women's support and feelings of national cause, and were 'surprised' at the intensity and the degree of their response to the Civil Disobedience Movement. The history of national movement records various instances when women defied the national leadership. It was evident during the salt *satyagrah* of 1930. Sarojini Naidu was defiant, Margaret Cousins wrote a spirited letter to Gandhiji, protesting against the division of work by sex, as women had been left in charge of the 'ashram' and Sabarmati, while men accompanied Gandhi in his famous Dandi March. Despite the reluctance on the part of Gandhi, women participated in a big way in the *satyagraha.*[47]

By and large, the leaders of the national movement envisaged a supportive role for women. They did not want women to involve in direct action. Gandhi himself described the difference between men and women as follows. "She is passive, he is active. She is essentially the mistress of the house. He is the breadearner.[48] This sexual division of labour was perpetuated even during the National Freedom Struggle. In fact, Gandhi inducted women in the Freedom Struggle because they were considered to be self-sacrificing, able to endure pain, and were essentially non-violent in nature. Gandhi did not visualise any fundamental change in the sexual division of labour, or any departure of women from their normal social roles as wife and mother. Madhu Kishwar remarks: "The symbols put forward to draw the into public life are those of ideal wives whose chief qualification was that they spent their lives in self-less service and unending devotion of husbands, following them to the end of the World."[49] There was some inherent dichotomy in Gandhiji's thinking on women. On the one hand, he asserted that women had the same rights of freedom and liberty as men.[50] On the other hand, he kept reforming to the mythical figures of Sita and Damayanti and their devotion to duty despite sufferings.[51] The deduction-"participation in politics would be simply an extension of this duty." This approach has been criticised by Gail Omvedt and Maria Mies. Mies claims that Gandhi created a new myth of Indian womanhood, Sita-like in her devotion to service and self-sacrifice, weather to her family or her nation. As a consequence, Gandhi attracted women from well-to-do classes with "good education, well placed husbands and servants". For these women, family came first and concern with sociopolitical issues after wards.[52] May be Gandhi was not prepared for radical changes at the structural and institutional level. The status of women had to be improved, but institutions which impinged on and curtailed their freedom were to be retained.

However, in all fireness to Gandhiji, it has to be accepted that he has a broader vision in comparison to other leaders of the movement. Unlike social reformers, Gandhi had realised some of the negative consequences of colonial role on women's economic status. He decided to launch the *khadi* movement which would offer to the masses of women an immediate open channel for their participation in the national struggle. Even more, Gandhi used women's role in the *khadi* movement to convince men that women's participation as equals was essential if the *swadeshi* or boycott movement was to succeed — an argument that he extended later to the winning of full freedom for India and nation building. For women to provide leadership in the movement was not enough. They had to understand the dignity that came from being productive and independent. Such an understanding would help them to identify with poor women, emancipate themselves and achieve the new identity necessary for nation building.

Nahru's understanding of women's subordination was both limited and static. Though fully aware of the problems of building a democratic and eqalitarian society on the foundations of a social and cultural structure divided by multiple allegiance (or identities) — religious, linguistic, caste and tribal and hierarchical beliefs that prevented a "sense of equality", he did not understand the "critical connections between the control over women and the maintenance of that differentiated and hierarchical social structures.[53] While he certainly accepted the emancipation of women as a value in itself, and claimed improvement in Indian women's status as his greatest achievement, some argue that his approach to women reflected the elitist vision of social reformers, relieved to some extent by his fascination for socialism, with little or no understanding of the deeper causes of women's subordination in India. While he introduced the emphasis on women's rights in the constitution, he did little to reduce the controls of the collectives that determined the boundaries of women's lives and behaviour — the family, community, caste, class, and religion.

Some argue that the issue of gender equality was given a back seat, and women's issue lost its appeal and fervour by being subsumed within nationalism. The new politics of nationalism glorified India's past and tended to defend everything traditional Nationalism in this phase fostered conservatism in social beliefs and practices. Partha Chatterjee maintains, "the new patriarchy of nationalism gave women 'a new social responsibility' not to alienate men, but "to maintain the cohesiveness of family life and solidarity with the kin group. In addition, by associating the task of 'female emancipation' with 'sovereign nationhood', nationalism "bound them to a yet entirely legitimate subordination." Partha Chatterjee also explains the "disappearance of the women's question from the political domain by the end of the 19th century as the result of nationalism's "refusal to make the women's question an issue of political negotiation with the colonial state."[54]

Some feel that this analysis suffers from the basic problem arising out of a tendency to find a linear connection between the reform movement, growth of nationalism and the roles prescribed for, or played by women in the Freedom Struggle. It neglects the fact that of women's own response to the challenges of colonial rule. Gail Minault and Geraldin Forber argue that women adapted the institution of *purdah* or seclusion, to form their own institutions. *purdah*, otherwise a hindrance to women's advancement, helped them through women's forums in which they could voice their concerns. Despite the restriction of *purdah* and without challenging patriarchal structures, it was possible for this rudimentary women's movement to acquire a unique strength.[55]

Some opine that women's involvement in the national movement or the merger of women's movement with the Freedom Struggle diluted its strength, though perhaps it gained in legitimacy by the championship of national leaders. It has to be accepted that gender equality was not the main thrust either of the social reform movement nor the National Freedom Movement. The social reform did help to improve the status of Indian women and placed great importance on education as the emancipator of women. However, education never became the sole agent for gender equality, it suffered from the basic contradiction between upliftment of women and limited vision of that upliftment. Everything had to be done within the framework of patriarchal family. Women were not seen as individuals. Similarly, the national movement leaders envisaged an auxiliary role for women in the movement. It was by sheer hardwork and readiness for come what may, that women were able to prove their worth during the Civil Disobedience, salt *satyagrah* and the Quit India movements. The so-called extremist movement of Bengal witnessed a galaxy of brave young girls, who readily scarified their lives for the freedom movement. Innumerable number of women provided support to freedom fighters, looked after their families in the absence of their fathers, husbands and sons. Participation in the national movement was not limited to elite class women only. They did provide organisation base and ideas and vision to the masses of women. But once aroused, the common women surged forward and became the most solid base of the National movement, we salute those masses of invisible and unnamed women who added strength to the movement, which by many is termed as the 'elite agitational politics'. Recording the participation of such women is a mammoth task. Efforts in this direction are commendable. It is hoped, someday a new history will be written about the national struggle, which will place women at the helm, and truly acknowledge their contributions.

References

1. Kalpana, Dasgupta 1976, *Women on the Indian Scene*, New Delhi, Abhinar Prakashan p. 16.

2. *Ibid.*, p. 5.

3. Gail, Pearson 1981, 'Nationalism, Universalization and Extended Female Space in Bombay City,' in Gail Mirault (ed.) *The Extended Family: Women and Political Participation in India and Pakistan.*

4. Rajani, Alexander 1984, *Participation and Perceptions* Women and the Indian Independence Movement, Samya Shakti, Vol. I, No. 2, pp. 1-5.

5. Gail, Omvedt *Feminism and the Women's in India.* Unpublished Paper, SMDT. University Research Centre for Women's Studies, Bombay 1987, p. 14.

6. *Ibid.*, p. 18.

7. *Ibid.*, pp. 18-19.

8. V Majumdar and Kumud Sharma, 1990, Sexual Division of Labour and the subordination of Women: A Reappraisal for India in Irene Tinker (ed.) *Persistent Inequalitites*: Women and World Development, New York, Oxford University Press.

9. G, Minault 1981, *Introduction*: The Extended Family as Metaphor and Expanison of Women's Realm.

10. *Op. cit.*, Gail Omvedt. pp. 10-17, 24.

11. *Ibid.*, p. 24.

12. CSWI Report, Majumdar & Pandey Chapter II, pp. 234-35, 261-63.

13. Nirad, Choudhuri, *The Autobiography of Unknown Indian.* University of Calofornia Press, 1968, p. 225.

14. Barbara Ramusack, 1981, 'Catalysts or Helpers'? in Minault (ed.), pp. 3-15.

15. MS Vedwas, The Life Work of Ramabai Ranade in Ranade-His Wife's Remenisienes (New Delhi), 1963, p. 221.

16. Padmini Sengupta, The Portrait of an Indian Women (Calcutta, 1956).

17. Gail Minault, Pards Politics - The Role of Muslim Women in Indian Nationalism 1911-1920, Paper

presented at the AAS Meeting April 2, 1974, Modern Review 1926, p. 257.

18. Jana Matson Everett, *Women and Social Change in India* Heritage Publishers, 1979, p.103 & Aparna Basu, 1976, The Role of Women in Indian Struggle for Freedom in BR Nanda (ed.) *Indian Women from Purdah* to Modernity, New Delhi, Vikas Publishing House, p. 20.
19. Geraldin Forbes, 1981, The Indian Women's Movement: A Struggle for Women's Rights or National Liberation?' in Gail Menault (ed.), *op. cit.* p. 54.
20. Everett, *op. cit*, p.73.
21. Ashok Mitra, Lalit Pathak and Shekhar Mukherjee, 1980, 'Introduction', in *The Status of Women, Shifts in Occupational Participation 1961-1971*, New Delhi, ICSSR and JNU, Abhinav Publications.
22. Kamala Devi Chattopadhyay, Indian's *Women's Struggle for Freedom*, Abhinav Rubhcations New Delhi 1983.
23. *Young India*, October 17 1929, quoted in MK Gandhi, The Role of Women, Bombay 1964, p. 71.
24. 'Constructive Programme', 1945 in *Ibid.*, pp. 1-2.
25. Vina, Majumdar, 'Towards Equality' in '*Women of the World*: Allusion and Reality (ed.) Urmila Phadnis & Indira Malani, Vikas Publishing House, New Delhi, pp. 20-21.
26. S Natrajan, *A Century of Social Reforms in India*, p. 204.
27. Dasgupta & IN Tiwari, Women's Emancipation in India, A Sociological Analysis, unpublished Paper, Prepared for CSWI.
28. *Op. cit.*, Basu, p. 21.
29. *Ibid.*, p. 22.
30. Quoted by Basu from Manibhen Patel's '*Board Satyagraha Guzarat Ahmedabad*, 1972, p. 101.

31. P Thomas, '*Indian Women though Ages*', Asia Publishing House, New York, 1964, p. 330. Kamala Devi Chattopadhyay, Women in India also Geraldin Fores Votes for Women in Vina Majumdar (ed.) *Symbols of Power*, Allied Publishers, New Delhi, 1979.
32. Radhakrishna Sharma, *Nationalism, Social Reform and Indian Women*, Janki Prakashan, Delhi 198, p. 66.
33. *Ibid.*
34. Kamla Devi Chattopadhyay, *Awakening of Indian Women*, Madras, 1939, p. 30.
35. Jawahar Lal Nehru, The Discovery of India, Allen & Unwin, 1947, p. 27.
36. Tata Ali Baig (ed.) *Women of India*, New Delhi, Publication Division, 1958, p. 19.
37. *Op. cit* Basu, p. 28.
38. K.K. Dutta, *History of Freedom Movement in Bihar*, 1928-41, Vol. II, Patna 1957, pp. 114-16.
39. Thomas *Op. cit.* p. 331.
40. Basu *Op. cit.*, p. 30.
41. *Ibid.*
42. *Ibid*, p. 31.
43. *Ibid.*
44. *Ibid.*
45. Uma Rao, 'Women in the Frontline: The Case of UP' in Leela Kasturi & Majumdar V (ed.) *Women and Indian Nationalism (1994)* Vikas Publishing Huse, New Delhi, pp. 28-49 and

    Ishaance Mukherjee in Kasturi & Majumdar (ed.) *Women and Indian Nationalism* 1994, pp. 53-69.
46. Kasturi & Majumdar, *Women and Indian Nationalism:* Vikas Publishing House, New Delhi 1994.
47. *Op. cit*, Thomas p. 330. Also, Geraldin Forbes 'Voted for Women', in Vina Majumdar (ed.) *Symbols of Power*. *Allied*, Delhi, 1979.

48. Madhu Kishwar 'Gandhi and Women' (unpublished MSS, 1976, p. 19.
49. *Ibid.*
50. MK Gandhi, Young India February 20, 1918 Collected Works Vol. XIV, GOI.
51. *Op: cit.*, Kamla Devi Chattopadhyay (Women's Battle for Freedom).
52. Maria Mies, *Indian Women and Leadership*, BCAS VII Jan-March, 1975, pp. 58-59.
53. V, Mukherjee 1989 'An unfulfilled or Blurred Vision? Jawahar Lal Nehru and Indian Women', Paper presented at the International Seminar on Nehru and Non-alignment, University of Sydney, Australia, Dec. 13-15.
54. V, Majumdar (Ibid.) Lolika Sarkar 1977 'Nehru and Gender Justice, Paper presented at the National Seminar on Nehru and Constitution, Indian Law Institute, Dec 30-31 & Sarkar 1989, Empowering Women in Seminar.
55. G. Menailt *Purdah Politics, op. cit*, in Hanna Papanak & Gail Minault (ed.) Forbes G in the same volume.

5

THE POLITICAL SCENARIO IN INDIA AND WOMEN'S ROLE

Rashmi Srivastava

Introduction

The political scenario in India today is characterised by a rather curious feature with most of the political parties and combination of parties accusing one another of striving to subvert democratic institutions. The Narora document has done the right thing to focus on the central fact that politics in India today faces grave threats. It is also correct in underlining the fact that most of the political issues the country is agitating on are directly or indirectly related to this central fact.[1]

For a proper understanding, however, of the current turmoils and conflicts in this vast country of nearly 900 million population, into which gigantic social forces are being inexorably drawn, it is necessary to start with an analysis of the real nature of politics in India, and its active role in the course of sociopolitical development. Only an examination of the nature and role of the existing political institutions can lead to an understanding of the nature of subversive attacks on them and, consequently, of the imperatives for overcoming them. The debate on women's entry into politics in India is closely related to this analysis, In order to start this debate, one has to look at the nature and working of politics in India.

Nature of Political Power in India

The basic nature of a political system is judged not by the speed of its ways, nor even by the proclamations it may have chosen to make, it has to be judged by its actual working—by the resultant of the social processes it seeks to encourage, control and repress. Earlier, even before the transfer of power, on January 22, 1947, a resolution moved by Jawaharlal Nehru in the Constituent Assembly of India, which set the objective of framing a Constitution—"wherein shall be guaranteed and secured to all the people of Indian justice, social, economic and political; equality of status, of opportunity, and before the law; freedom of thought, expression, belief, faith, worship, vocation, association and action, subject to law and morality".[2] The Preamble of the Constitution proclaims the resolution on the same lines. Devices like confided Fundamental rights, Directive Principles of State Policy, special safeguards for minorities, Scheduled Castes and Tribes and so on, have added to the attractive look of the Constitution. The democratic and egalitarian appearance of the political power in India has been further reinforced by the adoption of the socialistic pattern of society as the goal, still later by the full-threaded declaration of war against mass poverty—'*garibi hatao*' and, finally, by the 42nd amendment of the Constitution to declare the Indian Republic as a socialist and secular state. However, observers within the country and from abroad have refused to take these proclamations at their face value. They have clearly and categorically characterised the existing political power structure in India as exclusive and elitist.

For instance, Professor V K Rao, a former Union minister, identifies the locus of political power in India in "a political alliance of the intermediate classes with the upper classes, resorting to socialist ideology only to win mass support but using all levers of power to facilitate a type of capitalist development in the interest of a narrow section of Indian society".[3] Another Indian analyst says, "whether in agriculture or industry or infrastructure or even scientific research, the advantage has invariably gone to that segment of power elite, which holds the political levers of parliamentary democracy. The present power structure constitutes the greatest stumbling block to any successful effort to relieve the poverty of the poor."[4] According to Gunnar Myrdal, "India is ruled by a select group of upper class citizens who use their power to secure their privileged positions".[5] He defines the elite groups as the product of a linking up of the vested interests of business, permanent officials and political leaders.

Caste Politics

The process of politics is one of identifying and manipulating existing structures in order to mobilise support and consolidate positions. When the caste structure provides one of the most important organisational clusters in which the population is found to live, politics must strive to organise through such a structure. The alleged casteism in politics is thus no more and no less than the politicisation of caste. Caste in contemporary Indian politics plays a very important role behind the facade of parliamentary democracy. The political behaviours of people is influenced by caste considerations as is quite evident at the time of distribution of tickets by political parties for elections and composition of ministries.[6] As far as possible and practicable, the people prefer a candidate of their own caste, irrespective of his merits and demerits. Similar regard is paid when the list of party's office-bearers is prepared. When a single party is not in a position to have its own candidates, alliances are formed on the basis of caste to recommend the name of a person after arrangements of 'give and take' are made to the satisfaction of the constituents. The central discovery is that politics is more important to caste and castes are more important to politics than before.[7] There is a widespread impression among educated Indians that caste is on its last legs and that, educated, urbanised and westernised members of the upper classes have already escaped its bond. Both these impressions are wrong. These people may observe very few dietetic restrictions, marry outside caste and even religion, but this does not mean that they have escaped the bonds of castes entirely. They show caste attitude in surprising context.[8] That is the reason no political analysis of Indian politics that neglects caste is worthwhile.[9] In fact, caste has become a factor to be reckoned with and none of the political parties, including Congress, Bharatiya Janata Party (BJP) and Communist, can ignore it. Some of the political parties are organised purely on caste basis. For example Dravida Munnetra Kazhagam (DMK) and All-India Anna Dravida Munnetra Kazhagam (AIADMK) are anti-Brahmin parties,[10] National Democratic Party of Nair community, Socialist Republican Party of Ezhava community, Kerala Congress of Catholic community and Bahujan Samaj Party (BSP) of lower caste communities are purely casteist parties.[11] In Madhya Pradesh, it is a general observation that whenever there was Thakur Chief Minister, the Yadava, Kurmi and Brahmin legislators felt themselves neglected. Thakur officers were being promoted out of turn, despite the fact that some of them had adverse service records and inquiries were pending against them. Furthermore, few of the senior IAS Brahmin officers have been suspended.[12] More or less, this has been observed all over the country.

To a limited extent, caste system was recognised by the framers of the constitution when they reserved seats for Scheduled Castes and Scheduled Tribes in the House of People and Legislative Assemblies of the states[14], made a provision for the appointment of a special officer for Scheduled Castes and Scheduled Tribes to investigate matters relating to the various safeguards provided for them in the Constitution[15], and also by providing for a minister in charge to look after the welfare of Scheduled Castes, Scheduled Tribes and other backward classes in the states of Bihar, Madhya Pradesh and Orissa.[16] There is also a provision which empowers the President/Parliament to indulge/exclude certain castes or groups therein in the category of Scheduled Castes.[17] Subsequently, the Constitution was amended in 1951, and a provision was also made for protective discrimination in favour of Scheduled Castes, scheduled tribes and other socially and educationally backward classes of citizens in services.[18] Keeping in view the social hierarchical caste based-structure, which exploited the weaker sections of society, there was and is a justification for such a provision in the Constitution,[19] but only to limited extent for a limited period. However, while doing so efficiency of administration should also not be blindly ignored,[20] otherwise, their condition would become more miserable. It is important to note that the expression 'Scheduled Castes and Scheduled Tribes' as used in Article 338, include "such other backward classes as the President may, on receipt of the report of a commission appointed under clause (I) of Article 340, by order specify and also the Anglo-Indian community". About reservation, it should be remembered that reservation can neither be made on communal considerations nor more than 50 per cent seats be reserved. While caste has been politicised, in the process it has provided the Indian politics with processes and symbols of political articulation.[21] Thus, within the new context of political democracy, caste remains a central element of Indian society even while adapting itself to the values and methods of democratic politics.[22]

Class Conflict in Politics

In a literal sense, castes and classes have different implications. But in the politics of our country, they have come to be identified with each other. Even courts have accepted the view that in certain situations, the class as a whole may be taken as a caste and thus, caste may be entitled for the benefits of reservation that are available to a backward class.

We find that most of the tensions and conflicts have their source in social stratification and, for this reason, a possible solution to such political problems should be discovered in the rectification of the balance between different classes. The dialectics of Indian politics demand grappling with complex and contradictory trends in the country, which has shown many positive and negative features during the past few years.[23] Simply stated, the term 'class' signifies an aggregate of persons within a society possessing approximately the same status. It is a set of relationship constituted by the granting of deference of individual roles and institutions in the light of their place in the system of power and occupation.[24] What really makes a class is the factor of economic interest. The factor of economic interest is so deep that, as suggested by Karl Marx, it differentiates between the rules and the ruled, the exploiters and the exploited. Marx, however, makes the meaning of the term 'class' very rigid by applying the criteria of ownership and control over the means of production and distribution of goods.[25] It may also be added that in common parlance, this term is used in greatly varying senses as upper or middle classes, propertied and non-propertied classes, educated and uneducated classes, even productive and unproductive classes. Liberal writers dwell upon the doctrine of three broad strata of society—upper, lower and middle—living in harmony and peace. Max Weber takes a middle view in this regard and, while dealing with the objective and subjective dimension of this important issue, builds the concept of class on three factors—possession of economic means, external standard of living, and cultural and recreational possibilities.[26]

The struggle of the members of different classes, for the sake of protecting and promoting their specific interest, leads to the creation of conflicts and crises that demand their solution, sooner the better, and thereby the relationship between social set up and political system is established. In the context of Indian politics, class cuts into caste and is also cut into sub-caste by it. Low standing in the social hierarchy has been commonly taken as a sufficient indicator of backwardness.[27] The cause of most of the social conflicts and tensions lies in the want of economic justice.

Illiteracy and Backwardness

The socioeconomic analysis of educational advance in the post-Independence period is available from a number of village surveys. From these, it is clear that the spread of literacy and education is much in evidence among the more affluent and socially advance sections of society than among the poorer and more backward sections. The traditionally upper castes are almost all literate and have progressed much further in higher education; the middle castes have registered significant educational progress; but the lower and other backward sections of the population are lagging considerably behind. Literacy is crawling at snail's pace, and female education has not even touched these sections of society, particularly in rural areas. Thus, backwardness in education is closely related to the economic and social backwardness and bears the same hallmarks of a society divided against itself. The benefits of high agricultural productivity have not trickled down to the lower castes, the majority of whom work as agricultural labourers. The rigidity of social customs and the relatively poor bargaining power have kept the lower castes in their caste-ordained position.[28]

The economic and political power essentially belongs to the propertied classes, mostly from the upper castes, who have continued to monopolise education and culture too. The vast masses at the base of the social pyramid are not only deprived of the real power, but the power mechanism so works as to perpetuate and intensify this deprivation of the masses lower down. Lower caste segments of population who have historically constituted the most oppressed and exploited mass of the Indian people, practically deprived of any share in the economic, political and educational cultural developments in the country, continue to live in almost the same socioeconomic conditions, some symbolic improvements in certain sectors notwithstanding. Can a nation of 960 million catch up with the rest of the world with nearly 48 per cent of its population totally illiterate? It cannot, if it does not take up bold measures to tackle the chronic problem within a timeframe. Though we have impressive statistics on education: 590,421 primary schools, 171,216 upper primary and 98,134 high schools, 6,596 colleges for general education, 1,354 professional colleges and 226 universities, For the 150.7 million children enrolled in the age group of 6-14 years, there are 2.90 million teachers. But India of 1999 is caught between the paradox of high technocrats. IIT professionals, MBA, graduates and other literate and another India overflowing with an illiterate population of more than 400 million.[29]

Money Power in Politics

Economic power has paved the way for capturing political power and thereby using state apparatus for suppressing the opponents belonging to the poor and backward class. For instance, it is the power of money that purchase the vote bank and thereby manages to have the induction of legislators and administrators, who protect and promote the interests of the rich and upper class. Likewise, in rural areas, the rich peasants have established linkages with the administrative apparatus that work against the rural poor, who are immensely vulnerable because they are non-owners and the power-wielders are supported by their ownership of land. Corruption breeds corruption. When it sets in, it grows like weeds in a garden. There is no known antidote for it except exposure and punishment.[30]

Due to expensive elections, degeneration of moral values, and the desire to be rich overnight, political corruption has now become a great threat to our political system. It has diluted moral and ethical standards over the years, has seeped into all walks of life, and hampered the economic development of the country. Since Independence, all the Prime Ministers not only ignored, but actively helped some of the politicians who were very close to them in the matters of financial improprieties. This approach of Prime Ministers of not only shielding but also promoting the corrupt politicians, had its adverse impact on the Indian political system because it encouraged political corruption and hence, corruption started spreading from top to bottom. It is interesting to note that on the one hand Prime Ministers refused to appoint a commission of inquiry against their ministers or chief ministers, belonging to their party, but were quick in appointing such commission whenever a minister or chief minister belonging to some opposition party was involved. This shows that all the Prime Ministers have dragged their feet in appointing commissions of inquiry when their own kith and kin or lieutenants were involved. With the passage of time, links with the underworld of gamblers, smugglers and FERA violators on the one hand, and further deterioration in moral and political standards on the other, has further increased corruption in political life. When politicians indulge in corruption on a large scale, bureaucracy cannot remain far behind. The selling of national secrets by officials occupying sensitive places is a sad commentary on the political and bureaucratic leadership of the country. Public Service Commissions and other recruiting agencies in some of the states have also become dens of corruption. One of the most disturbing developments which has encouraged corruption is that politicians have undermined the process of rule of law by withdrawing cases of corruption lying in the court of laws. It follows that when politicians who amass wealth by misusing their powers and position and are still not punished, then how can bureaucrats who are stunningly corrupt and serve their political masters, be punished? In fact, Indira Gandhi had once said that corruption is a worldwide phenomena.[31] She had also admitted that it is not true that the Congress alone gets the money or gives the favours.... We do collect money, but everybody does".[32] According to Viren Shah, the ex-president of the Indian Merchants' Chamber of Commerce, "Can we say that we have not contributed to corruption by bribing those in authority or making clandestine contributions to party funds?"[33]

It is important to note that the history of many Third World countries tells us that when corruption and crime jointly act upon economic and political institutions and state power is employed for partisan political objectives, the result inevitably is both massive violence and authoritarianism,[34] and this is exactly the direction in which Indian polity is now heading which is very dangerous and unfortunate.

The Nexus of Crime and Politics

Nani A Palkhivala, the eminent constitutional expert observes, "I do not think India, in its entire history of five thousand years has ever reached a lower level of degradation than it has reached now.... The picture that emerges is that of a great nation in a state of moral decay, of which crime, chaos and corruption are three of the several facets."[35] In order to protect themselves, citizens in some parts of the country have begun to organise private armies. Sooner or later, all developing countries become difficult to govern, and over the past two decades, India has been moving in that direction.[36]

The much talked report of the Vohra panel categorically points out that crime syndicates and mafia organisations have developed muscle and money power and established linkages with government functionaries, political leaders and others. The CBI has reported that the nexus between the criminal gangs, police, bureaucracy and politicians has come out clearly in various parts of the country.[37] There has been a rapid spread and growth of criminal gangs, armed *senas*, drug mafia, smuggling gangs, drug peddlers and economic lobbies in the country, which have, over the years, developed an extensive network of contacts with the bureaucrats/government functionaries at the local levels, politicians, media persons and strategically located individuals in the non-state sector. In certain states like Bihar, Haryana and Uttar Pradesh, these gangs enjoy the patronage of local level politicians, cutting across party lines and protection of government functionaries.

The big smuggling syndicates with international linkages, have spread into and infected the various economic and financial activities, including hawala transactions economy causing serious damage to the economic fibre of the country. The network of mafia is virtually running a parallel government, pushing the state apparatus into irrelevance. The cost of contesting elections has thrown the politicians into the lap of these elements.[38] Another feature in the political culture of the ruling class is the politicisation of crime and criminalisation of politics. Politicisation of crime involves of competitive use of anti-social forces for the mobilisation of party funds, for management's of elections, for organising meetings and conferences and even for recruiting workers at lower levels from among anti-social elements. It also means the misuse of criminal intelligence as a political tool for black mailing political opponents.[39]

Criminalisation of politics means direct entry of criminals into political parties and legislatures, including Parliament.

Today politics is no longer decent; holigans and hoodlums are gaining control of public life. The notorious criminals, history—shelters, smugglers and murderers are swarming into politics. Formerly, they were on the periphery of Indian political life; now they have moved considerably towards the centre to manipulate the gears and levers of political machine.

Kuldeep Nayer wrote that according to the Chief Election Commissioner, 180 out of the 425 members of Uttar Pradesh Legislative Assembly had criminal records and the last general elections in Bihar were contested by as many as 243 candidates against whom charges were pending.[40] According to *India Today*, "of the 424 members of the Vidhan Sabha, 132 are suspected criminals, 16 of them now actually sit in cabinet meetings.[41] Election Commissioner G V G Krishnamurty, while addressing press persons on August 20, 1997, said as per records, 40 members of Parliament has criminal cases pending against them while nearly 700 members of state assemblies out of 4,072 are named in criminal cases, though it was an international accepted norm that "law breakers cannot be allowed to be lawmakers", which India must also follow.[42]

In a historic judgement on March 20, 1997, the then Chief Justice of India, A M Ahmadi, warned the nation of the emergence of new crime syndicates with a very strong nexus with politicians, bureaucrats, media, personalities and even members of the judiciary.[43] It is unfortunate that no countermoving force to check criminalisation of politics is emerging. The historic resolution passed by the Lok Sabha at the special session of Parliament on the occasion of the golden jubilee of Independence, August 26 to September 1, 1997 observes: "The meaningful electoral reforms be carried out so that our Parliament and other legislative bodies be balanced and effective instruments of democracy and further that political life and processes be free of the adverse impact, on governance of undesirable extraneous factors including criminalisation."[44]

Women of India are paying a heavy price in terms of a rising tide of violence and assent on their honour just because of distorted social values, a band of politicians, hand in glove with criminals and anti-social elements, caste conflicts, etc. Crime against women are on rise despite all sacrosanct provisions in the Constitution, criminal law, Parliament, judiciary, police, media coverage, the National Human Rights Commission and the National Commission for Women. Perhaps every segment of India has to own the blame and should dip its head in shame for the continuing assault on womanhood in India.[45]

Indian Women in Present Political Scenario

The women of India have been exposed to greater insecurity, to poverty, illiteracy, casteism, orthodoxy, unhealthy living conditions, traditionalism, backwardness, corruption, criminalisation and male dominance in most of the fields. They have been affected by lack of opportunities and facilities owing to the innate discrimination prevalent in the society. In the last 20 years, there has been a global effort with a strong support from the United Nations to understand the discrimination and restore a status to women of the world. The slogan has been equality, development and peace.

The United Nations General Assembly declared the International Year of Women in 1975 followed by the International Women's Decade and organised three world conferences—Mexico in 1975, Copenhagen in 1980 and Nairobi in 1985. The Nairobi conference decided strategies for the advancement of women upto 2000 AD. The world has consciously marched forward with various instruments for eliminating discrimination against women during the 20 years. The fourth world conference on women held in Beijing in 1995, focused on the structural changes that are necessary in the society.[46] It emphasised that no enduring solution to society's most threatening social, economic and political problems can be found without the full participation and full empowerment of the women. India's strategies and action plans are to eliminate all discrimination against women; remove the chasm between legal status and defect status; create an environment of harmony and partnership of men and women.

There are countries like Sweden, Finland and Norway, where women make up almost half the national legislatures. Stories of smooth succession of power from husband to wife are in plenty. Commenting on how widows and daughters have been thrust into power by dynastic imperatives in Asian countries like Philippines, India and Indonesia. Rounaq Jahan, a Bangladeshi political scientist had observed, "they think that they can manipulate these women. But every time they were surprised that once in power, Women handled the men and mastered old style politics."[47]

But behind most successful women leaders in India, there has been the hidden hand of a man. Just as Jawaharlal Nehru groomed Indira Gandhi, MG Ramchandran did for his screen partner Jayalalitha and Kanshi Ram is doing for his acolyte Mayawati. Even Laloo Prasad Yadav is not far behind these veterans in propping up his wife Rabri Devi, who confidently faces the camera today instead of taking shelter in her kitchen. There may be a sharp variance in their life style, levels of political sophistication, in their dress sense, but they have one thing in common, that is, their valuable grooming in a political career by their mentors. Grooming includes training in developing their ethos, political issues and marketing them to their selected audience (voters). Many of them would be raw, without a political or famed godfather to lend support. Like one-third reservation for women at rural and urban local bodies, 33 per cent quota may help women in increasing their numerical strength to 181 in the Lok Sabha, it certainly may not be enough in attaining empowerment in the real sense, which would still remain a far cry. After all the road to empowerment is circuitous. Attaining political power may not mean enjoying or utilising it for the betterment of the country or her constituents, till they are trained to cross the rough and tumble of Indian politics.

Therefore, the present political scenario and demand for women's quota have generated a need for starting grooming courses for women politicians in India. Just as the path of empowerment became easy for the American women by mastering political skills, the Indian Women can also attain empowerment, if only they are groomed well. For women in the West, there are no reservations on the road to political empowerment. But they have the 'primaries' and other sundry opportunities to make themselves hard enough for the long grind in the political arena. Strangely, the idea has not struck us, where women advancement in the political domain is just a matter of time. A politically ambitious women in our country is just thrown in the thick of things, to fend for herself. As more and more women get into the thick of things there is an urgent need to evolve a system that will prepare them for this opportunity. Though there are many examples of women who have come through the system, they are seasoned, and experienced. But they have never been to any finishing school. What they have learnt is through sheer experience. There are no caucuses and no primaries where they can cut their political teeth. In effect, they have to behave, react and act as a politician from the word go. It is not an easy task. There are few women in public offices because few of them run for elections. The reservation in *panchayats* and municipalities will gradually bring more and more women into the political field. They will gather experience at a level, which will teach them the indispensability of a plural society. Among the women at the local institution level, those who want to adopt politics as a full-time career, will move up to the higher bodies in course of time, and their male colleagues will regard their ascent as a natural and legitimate progression.[48] The training institutions or organisations will teach these political women not only the finer things of decision-making and use their power properly, but also the awareness, understanding of outer world, public dealings and if required, literacy, can also be taught to them. Such a process will not cause any political or social upheaval. The benefits of empowerment would also come in due course without the element of confrontation with other groups.

At present, like other Asian countries, there is very slow rise in the percentage of Indian women in Parliament, central ministry, administration, higher education and technical institutions (see Table 1).

Table 1: Indian Women: Slow Rise up the Ranks (Percentage of Women)

Country	*Seats held in Parliament*	*Central ministers*	*Administrators and managers*	*Professors and technical workers*
India	8.8	9.0	2.3	20.5
Pakistan	3.4	4.0	3.4	20.1
Bangladesh	9.1	5.0	5.1	23.1
Sweeden	40.4	47.8	38.9	64.4
USA.	11.2	21.1	42.0	52.0
Iran	4.0	0	3.5	32.6
Japan	7.7	6.7	8.5	41.8

Source: India Today, Living Media, New Delhi, No. 30, July 21-27, 1998, p. 18.

The Union government obviously thinks this call for affirmative action as is evident from its decision to introduce the Constitution (81st Amendment) Bill in the Lower House. If passed by Parliament, the amendment will have a third of the seats reserved for women in the Lok Sabha and the state assemblies.[49] In this situation, the need for grooming institutions becomes very relevant.

Mohini Giri wrote, "the country is facing, as never before, a torrent of crime due to various socioeconomic reasons not to speak of infiltration of illegal migrants, besides other state sponsored terrorism...much of these kinds of heinous crimes and atrocities have their roots in the drug mafia, foreign patronage and other country strategies to destabilise civilian population."[50] Criminalisation is a big problem as most Asian cities are unsafe to live in despite the economic growth in the region. Compared to them, the law and order situation in Indian metros is better. The crime rate in Bangalore and Delhi is much lower than that in Seoul or Tokyo (see Table 2).

Table 2: Criminal Cases in Asian Cities

Asian city	*Cases per 10,000 people*
Seoul	303
Okasa	308
Macau	206
Tokyo	203
Kualalumpur	188
Singapore	159
Hongkong	125
Taipai	123
Bangkok	95
Colombo	72
Bangalore	35
Delhi	20
Mumbai	14

Source: Asian Week Research Survey, in *India Today*, July 20, 1998.

Apart from this situation, women's status in Asia is clearly in flux. Democracy seems to have helped by creating an environment in which autonomous women's groups could form, network, and develop some political influence. Progress in terms of formal political representation of women has been much more gradual in most Asian nations. The practice of reserving parliamentary quotas for women seems to be spreading, although this obviously is a lengthy process. Women in Asia, therefore, face substantial political challenges with significant, but limited resources at their disposal.

Fortunately, in recent times, women have awakened to the fact that in order to break gender-barriers and overcome social bias, women's participation in the political process is essential. Though women constitute nearly half of the total population, politics has all along been men's domain. A February 1997 report on inter-Parliamentary unions says that Indian women hold only 7.2 per cent seats in the Lower House and 7.8 per cent seats in the Upper House.[51] This can be called as token representation (see Table 3).

Table 3: Percentage of women MPs

Years	*Lok Sabha*	*Rajya Sabha*
1952	4.9	7.3
1957	5.4	7.5
1962	6.7	7.6
1967	5.9	8.3
1971	4.2	7.0
1977	3.4	10.2
1980	5.0	9.8
1984	7.7	11.4
1989	5.3	9.7
1991	6.7	15.5
1996	7.1	9.0
1998	7.9	9.0

The percentage of women MLAs in state assemblies is also not very encouraging. Though in comparison to 1952, the percentage in the years from 1993 to 1998, has been certainly increased but still it is insignificant, (see Table 4).

Table 4: Percentage of women MLAs in state assemblies

State	*1952*	*1993-98*
Andhra Pradesh	2.9	2.7
Assam	0.5	4.8
Bihar	3.6	3.4
Goa	-	10.0
Gujarat	-	1.1
Haryana	-	4.4
Himachal Pradesh	-	4.4
Jammu & Kashmir	-	2.3
Karnataka	2.0	3.1
Kerala	0	9.3
Madhya Pradesh	2.1	4.3
Maharashtra	1.9	3.8
Orissa	9.6	5.4
Punjab	2.2	6.0
Rajasthan	-	4.5
Sikkim	-	3.1
Tamil Nadu	0.3	3.8
Uttar Pradesh	1.2	4.0
West Bengal	0.8	6.8
Delhi	4.2	4.3

Source: *India Today*, Living Media, New Delhi, July 27, 1998, p. 28.

The truth is that except for mouthing political platitudes during elections, men are not prepared to give political space to women. One must realise that advancing the status of women is not only a moral imperative, but women's presence at the decision-making level is *sine qua* non for strengthening democratic traditions and fighting against injustice and oppression.

However, laws alone do not lead to social transformation unless followed by resolute action and socialite awareness of the wrong that have been perpetuated on women from time immemorial. But first of all there should be a revolution of consciousness in the minds of women—in the way they thought about themselves. Women must realise that gender deprivation is inconsistent with the basic human rights of women. They must realise that they have constitutional rights to equality, health care, economic security, access to education, employment opportunities, pay equity and political power. As India has celebrated more than 50 years of its Independence, this is an historic opportunity to invest in India's future. For when a women thrives, her family thrives, when families thrives, communities flourish and the nation reaps the benefits.

References

1. Alit Roy, *Political Power in India: Nature and Trends*, Naya Prakash, Calcutta, 1981, p. 1.
2. D Basu, *Introduction to the Constitution of India*, S C Sarkar and Sons, Calcutta, 1960, p. 49.
3. V K Rao, 'Some Fundamental Aspects of Socialist Transformation in India', Inaugural Address at the 56th Session of the Indian Economic Conference, December, 1973, Mimeograph copy, p. 25.
4. Vadilal Dagli, *Growth for Whom*, Commerce Pamphlet, No.62, 1973, Bombay, p. 6.
5. Gunnar Myrdal, *Asian Drama*, Pantheon, New York, p. 766.
6. J C Johari, *Indian Politics*, Vishal Publications, Jalandhar, 1996, p. 156.
7. W H Morris-Jones, *The Government and Politics of India*, Ed. 1, p. 65.

8. M N Srinivas, 'The Indian Road to Inequality' in *Economic and Political Weekly*, Bombay, Vol. XII, June 1960, p. 267.
9. A H Hanson and Janet Douglas - Indian Democracy, Weidenfeld and Nicolson, 1972, p. 5.
10. *The Hindustan Times*, August 4, 1980, p. 8.
11. J R Siwach, Dynamics of Indian Government and Politics, Sterling Publishers, Delhi, 1990, p. 705.
12. *The Hindustan Times*, April 28, 1982, p. 7.
13. Article 330, Constitution of India.
14. Article 332, Constitution of India.
15. Article 338, Constitution of India.
16. Article 164, Constitution of India.
17. Article 341, Constitution of India.
18. Clause (4) to Article 15 of the Indian Constitution.
19. N.M. Tripathi, *Minority and Law, Indian Law institute*, Delhi, 1972, p. 10.
20. Article 335, Constitution of India.
21. Rajni Kothari and Rushikesh Maru, 'Caste and Secularism in India', *in Journal of Asian Studies*, November, 1965, p. 33.
22. L.I. Rudolph and Susane Rudolph, 'The Political Role of India's Caste Association', *Pacific Affairs*, Vol. XXIII, Number 1, March 1960.
23. C P Bhambhri, 'Social Conflics and Politics in India', *in Indian Journal of political Science*, Vol. 40, No.4, December 1979, p. 571.
24. *Encyclopedia Britannica*, 1967, Vol. 15, p. 873.
25. Karl Marx, *Capital*, Vol II, P. 862.
26. Paul Mombert, '*Class*' in E.R.A. Seligman (ed), *Encyclopedia of the Social Sciences*, Macmillan, New York, 16th ptg. 1967, Vol. III, p. 532.
27. Marc Galanter, '*Law and Caste in Modern India*', *Asian Survey*, Vol. III No. 11, 1963, p. 547.
28. Leela Visaria, 'Harizan's Worsening Plight', in *Economic and Political Weekly*, Bombay, February 2, 1974.
29. The State of Education in India, *Competition Success Review*, Delhi, Vol. XXXV, No. 9, March 1999, p. 79-80.
30. M Hidayatullah, *Democracy in India and Judicial Process*, Asia Publishing House, 1966, p. 26.

31. *The Times of India*, December 31, 1979, p.6.
32. *National Herald*, February 27, 1974.
33. *Hindustan Standard*, March 4, 1974.
34. J D Sethi, 'Corruption, Crime and Confrontation', *in Indian Express*, November 25, 1983, p. 6.
35. Nani A Palkhivala, 'Squandered Legacy', *in Hindustan Times*, August 15, 1997.
36. Atul Kohli, *Democracy and Discontent*, Cambridge University Press, 1991, p. 3.
37. Vohra Committee Report, Ministry of Home Affairs, in *The Indian Journal of Public Administration*, Special Numer, July-September, 1995, p. 641.
38. *Ibid.*, p. 643.
39. L.S. Rathore, 'Political Culture of India's Ruling Class', Presidential Address - XII Rajasthan Political Science Conference, December 4-5, 1989, p. 9.
40. Kuldeep Nayar, 'The Vohra Report-Sparing the Culprits' *in Indian Express*, August 7, 1995.
41. *India Today*, Delhi, November 10, 1997, p. 34.
42. *The Hindustan Times*, Delhi, August 21, 1997.
43. 'Criminalisation of Politics', in *Competition Success Review*, Delhi November, 1998.
44. Hindustan Times, Delhi, September 2, 1997.
45. 'Crime Against Women' *Competition Success Review*, Delhi, December 1998, p. 117-18.
46. 'The Empowerment of Women', in *University News, A Weekly Journal of Higher Education*, Delhi, March 25, 1996, p. 17-20.
47. 'Baptism by Fire', in *The Hindustan Times*, Delhi, March 21, 1999.
48. 'Gender - based Follow', in *Hindustan Times*, Delhi, June 6, 1997.
49. 'Ladies Seat', in *India Today*, Delhi, July 20, 1998, p. 21.
50. V Mohini Giri, *Emancipation and Empowerment of Women*, Gyan Publishing House, Delhi, 1999.
51. 'Correcting Gender Bias', in *Hindustan Times*, Delhi, July 23, 1997.

6

WOMEN IN DECISION-MAKING POSITIONS IN POLITICAL SYSTEM

Sarojini Sharan

Women's participation in decision–making process is vital for the betterment of their human right conditions. If real democracy has to be sustained, the women, comperising about half of the world's population have to be incorporated at different levels and different processes of decision-making. This fact was realised at the UN convention on the political rights of women in 1952. All congresses worldwide emphasised the need for political participation of women. They discussed and planned strategies to achieve this objective. Significant deliberations on women's empowerment were made in: (a) World Plan of Action in 1975, in Mexico; (b) The Copenhagen Programme of Action 1980; (c) World Conference on the UN Decade of Women in Nairobi (1985); and, (d) the World Congress of Women in Beijing (1995). Women's involvement in decision-making processes at different levels was necessary for them to acquire confidence.

When analysing the woman factors in decision-making, the foremost consideration would be to find out whether women have taken key decisions or just helped in taking a decision. The next step would be to identify the internal and external situations in which she could take key political decisions, and third, the interaction processes followed by such decision makers. Moreover, the analysis should throw light on the formal as well as non-formal structures in decision-making system on central, state and local levels, wherein-women performed their roles as key or non-key decision-makers.

Thus, decision-making positions acquired by women would give a general idea of the vertical as well as horizontal mobility of women to power position. The study by its very nature generally becomes a study of elite women in decision-making positions. In this study, the key decision-makers are actors who could convert decisions into political action or one who possessed efficacy or who had impact upon the political system in some way or the other.

It is true that women in top power positions in politics were no indicators regarding the social, economic or political status of the women masses. But they indicated the span of mobility in recruitment process and gender toleration in a political system. This kind of study would help in understanding the elite structure in a society which in its turn would depend upon the political culture prevailing at that time.

Scope

The universe in this study is within the Indian context and limited to those women only, who were or are key or non-key political actors in the decision-making process, and whose efficacy could be assessed on the basis of the results of their performance.

Indira Gandhi

As Indira Gandhi was one of the strongest political leader in the world, this paper intends to start with her and then proceed to few other women who joined the political arena after her. These had been either chief ministers or held key party posts. Nevertheless, all of them have affected political scene in their respective states or at the national level. When this study was being completed, BJP led coalition had already taken over power at the Centre. The women's reservation bill could not be introduced in Parliament because some members in the opposition had scuttled it.

(a) Actor in Planetary System

Indira Gandhi's environmental interest revealed her as one of the first true planetary leaders. Maurice F Strong, executive coordinator, United Nations Office for Emergency Operation in Africa, wrote about her: "She was the first leader of any great nation to appreciate that the concerns for environment which has been so dramatically manifested in the late 1960s and early 1970s in industrialised societies had a profound relevance to developing countries. At that time, most of the developing world regarded the emergence of the environmental issue as a preoccupation of the rich, which threatened to divert attention and resources from the development needs of the poor, but Indira Gandhi saw the indispensable need to force an alliance between environmental and development concerns in meeting these needs."[1]

Maurice F Strong held that Indira Gandhi's ideas were the single key to the sources of Stockholm conference on environment in June 1972.

(b) As Key Actor in Indian Political System

Indira Gandhi's impact[2] on India's political system was such that it became unrecognisable and totally different from the Nehru period. Under Jawaharlal Nehru's style of politics, there was a system of checks and balances between conflicting regional interests and powerful party bosses. The dominant political leaders were accommodated by the federal structure of the Indian Constitution. This gave strength to India to weather the turbulent formative years. The Shastri government also followed the Nehruvian line.

The Indian political system was confronted with most serious internal crisis during the latter period of Indira Gandhi's regime. Well accepted peaceful procedures and peaceful means for resolving internal conflict were shattered. Fragmented political culture and battered accommodative attitude became the features of the Indian political system.

The systemic and structural failures became obvious. She had personalised and centralised Indian politics. Indira Gandhi was intolerant of political personalities who showed signs of entering into competition with her. She dismissed non-congress ministries in the different states and imposed her confidants as chief ministers in the Congress ruled states.

The structure of the Congress party changed qualitatively. There was enormous centralisation of power in the office of the Prime Minister's secretariat. The personalisation and centralisation of political authority made a dent in the capacity of the system to accommodate regional demands.

The political system was affected by Indira Gandhi's decisions in such a way that the system went on working under its inertia. Terrorism raised its head in Punjab and Kashmir. Democracy declined. The institutions of party parliament and judiciary were twisted to make her more secure in her decision-making position. The style became authoritarian and the Indian political culture broke off its moral moorings. In 1969, when the Congress was split, the political culture scenario changed basically. All political parties in India were affected by Indira Gandhi's decision to divide the historic Congress Party reducing it to a collection of subservient sycophants.

Indira Gandhi went on with her populist image, by propagating the concepts of a committed bureaucracy and a committed judiciary. She showed scant respect to the Constitution of India. Inspite of the fact that the Shah Commission report denied any threat to law and order in the country, Indira Gandhi declared Emergency in 1975. She claimed that Emergency was a necessity for preserving law and order in the nation. The probity of the civil service was impaired and press came under attack. The electronic media was misused and supersession of an army general was considered necessary.

There was no place for Nehru's style of consensus during Indira Gandhi's regime. She stressed on cohesion. The "syndicate" in Congress was delegitionised by her tirade against it. The breaking of consensus resulted into opposition agitational politics and the government had to become repressive.

Populism came to be established as an important element of politics. It meant direct appeal to the masses. Consequently, the intermediate structure and the elites were ignored. With the Sanjay Gandhi factor, musclemen and local mafia came to form the new infrastructure of politics.

Rajni Kothari had observed that "now, it is clear that almost the entire institutional order (not just the Congress system) has very nearly broken down. The system had under gone a series of changes."[3] The new model of politics had been as follows:-

(i) Displacement of a cabinet system of government.

(ii) The abrogation of parliamentary system by first permitting a brute use of party majority by the executive wing, and then under mining the simpler mechanics, let alone the spirit of election mandates by frequent recourse to defections and toppling of duly constituted governments.

(iii) The erosion of the federal framework by recourse to similar practices engineered from the very apex of the system.

(iv) The undermining of judicial independence and probity by executive manipulation of the concept of parliamentary supremacy.

(v) The uncalled for use of presidential powers.

Indira Gandhi had few equals in recent history in the art of power wielding. Her rapport with common people was extraordinary. After Mahatma Gandhi and Nehru, she had been the most charismatic leader in India. She could bypass all the stalwarts of her party as well as the most fiery leaders in the opposition. Even when she was out of power, the she enjoyed the same popularity among the masses. Her dynamism was unmatched and she was the only woman Prime Minister to be assassinated. The Congress syndicate was totally disillusioned with its scheme about her, that is, to use her as a sophisticated totem for the Congress.

Indira Gandhi was a bold key decision–maker and her decisions resulting into important actions, had great impact on the Indian political system, with its processes and its culture. As mentioned before, she personalised and centralised politics in India. By her decisions she eroded the federal system in India.

Indira Gandhi went on with her concept of 'committed judiciary'. It was during her regime that India witnessed Emergency for the first time. She displaced the cabinet system and abrogated the parliamentary system. During her regime, the constitutional system of India became Prime Ministerial system. Many important constitutional system of India became Prime Ministerial system. Many important constitutional amendments were passed by Parliament without any debates.

Some other Actors in Decision-making

After Indira Gandhi, some women leaders in states had made their strong impacts on state politics as well as on national politics. Keeping in mind the time frame for this chapter, after studying Indira Gandhi's role in decision-making process as key actor, I have taken current examples like Sonia Gandhi, Mamta Banerji, Jayalalitha, Mayawati and Rabri Devi. The former two were leaders of a national party. The others belong to regional parties and have adorned the chair of chief ministers in their respective states. Except Rabri Devi, all the other have been dynamic and active in politics. Their decisions and styles have left impacts on national parties, state politics and party politics.

The late, 1980s and 1990s have witnessed the emergence of women political leaders who have influenced political decision-making at the national and state level. Jayalalitha emerged as a powerful Chief Minister of Tamil Nadu after the death of M G Ramchandra. The, 1990s saw the emergence of Mamta Banerji is Bengal representing initially the Congress (I). She has steadily consolidated her position and could not be contained within the fold of the Congress

Party. In 1998, she broke away and founded the Triamul Congress. The year 1998 also witnessed the emergence of Sonia Gandhi as the prime decision-maker of the Congress party. She also exerted pressure on the government at the Centre. Mayawati made her presence felt in the politics of Uttar Pradesh with her Bahujan Samaj Party. Aggressive, and to some extent very articulated in her speeches and actions, she has emerged as a very strong leader of the Dalits.

The Sonia-Mamta-Jayalalitha trio is affecting the course of political events. They affected structure of their respective and influenced Parties them. The trio also challenged the Vajpayee government on several occasions. Mayawati, who was the Chief Minister of Uttar Pradesh twice, showed her persistence in the state politics and also as a leader of the Dalits. Rabri Devi is a puppet installed as Chief Minister of Bihar, the second-most populated state of India. Her installation developed certain serious constitutional and political trends in the politics of Bihar.

Sonia Gandhi

After a long silence, Sonia Gandhi decided to campaign for Congress (I). She started her first four campaign meetings in south India on January 16, 1998, and created an excitement among the Congress workers. She made a dramatic entry on the central stage at the Netaji Indoor Stadium, on August 9, 1998, where the Congress plenary session was being held. A virtual riot broke out as scrambled the members by to take a glimpse of her. She sat down on the floor, the place for All India Congress Committee (AICC) delegates. When Congress president Sitaram Keshri rose to speak, he was hooted down. He came down to Sonia, dropped his Gandhi cap at her feet and beseeched her to join the leaders on the dais. In 1993, P V Narasimha Rao, also had to face similar treatment and he had to invite her to the dais. At that time she had refused. The message was clear that the Nehru-Gandhi family and Sonia herself had greater appeal among the party workers. Ultimately, she displaced Sitaram Kesri from presidentship of the Congress.

Another occasion when the sycophancy regarding Nehru-Gandhi family had become more obvious was during the golden jubilee celebrations of Indian Independence on August 15, 1997. Sonia was given place of pride in the Central Hall, in the front row with Congress president Sitaram Kesri and the BJP president L K Advani. Other members of the Nehru-Gandhi family, Priyanka Gandhi and her husband Robert Vadhera were seated in the row just behind her. No other Congress leader has been able to pull as large a crowd as Sonia because of the Gandhi family factor..

Some old Congress men who joined other parties were of the opinion that Sonia Gandhi entered politics essentially to keep a hold on the Congress (I) as a political vehicle for her children.

The way the dynastic principle worked in Sonia's own estimation, could be assessed by her own prologue in *Rajiv* by Sonia Gandhi. She wrote: "We had both observed the world of politics from a distance. We had come to understand the critical line that distinguishes ambition from a sense of purpose." She remained non-political for a long time. But when Sanjay Gandhi met a violent death, Indira Gandhi turned to her elder son so that the dynastic principle could go on working. Sonia claimed that she "fought like a tigress" against this decision, but she respected her mother-in-law. "I understood Rajiv's duty to her. At the same time, I was angry and resentful towards a system which, as I saw it, demanded him as a sacrificial lamb. It would crush him and destroy him - of that I was absolutely certain." After Rajiv Gandhi was killed, she said at Sriperumbudur that she put aside her inclination to remain as a "private person," and stepped forward in the sanctified family tradition of duty before personal considerations.

Congress had been a party as well as a process because it was the principal carrie of India nationalism. More over "the dynamics of electoral competition at the local level created a broad convergence of political interest between particular sections. This under wrote the consolidation of an electorate between social classes, which dominated the realm of representative politics... The key to the Congress success was its ability to remain awake to local political situations...."[8] But the social factions deserted the party. One of the reason was dynastic political succession which ensures the survival of neither commitment nor vision. The Congress organisation, which was the key to its ability to recruit loyalties at the local level, is today in shambles. The decline began in Rajiv Gandhi's regime. Organisational elections were never conducted for about more than seven years. There was lack of local leader, who could create durable alliance. The electoral appeal of the Congress depended solely on the charms of the Nehru-Gandhi family. When Sonia became president of the Congress (I), she emphasised on reorganising it. On July 28, 1998, she led a Congress rally and marched to Rashtrapati Bhawan against "price rise and the all round failure of the BJP government." It seemed that she was taking pro-active steps to succeed in competitive politics. She marshalled support for the candidature of P M Sayeed for the post of deputy speaker of the Lok Sabha. These actions showed that after emphasising on strengthening organisational machinery, she appeared to have switched suddenly to a policy of bold initiatives. BJP deferred the decision on the election of deputy speaker and withdrew its candidate Rita Verma. BJP virtually admitted defeat. After playing this game, Sonia announced the prospect of assuming responsibilities of power. It was a dramatic change in the position of the Congress (I) president. Sonia earlier virtually rejected a call by Chandra Shekhar to bring down BJP. The reason behind the aggressive policy could be to retain her popularity among the party workers. Before scandal had tainted the name of her family, Sonia has been calling for transparency in the Bofors crisis so that the Nehru-Gandhi family's name was steer-cleared. But the CBI affidavit before the Delhi High Court candidly declared that "investigation had shown that the families of the then Prime Minister of India (Rajiv Gandhi) and Ottavio Quottrocchi were on very intimate terms with each other and they used to meet frequently. Quattrocchi and his family had free access to the Prime Minister's house." A E Services of Ottario Quottrocchi entered into negotiations to cheat "because the two parties to the agreement conspired to deceive the Government of India, and dishonestly induced it to part with money to the tune of US$ 7.34 million," says the CBI affidavit.

Sonia could not chart out a political strategy at Panchmarhi Congress (I) session to revive the party and even clarify its ideological positions on many questions.

There is no doubt that Sonia has rejuvenated the dying Congress party, to a certain extent. She is gaining popularity, and this became evident when the Central Election Committee (CEC) of Congress decided to complete the selection of candidates by January 11, 1998. There were disputes between various groups and for the final list all sought Sonia Gandhi's guidance in the matter. Sonia was not the president of the Congress at that time. She was waiting to take over the organisation, which she did later. Her entry into active politics helped the Congress (I) in its electoral battle against other political parties. But it exacerbated factional conflict within the Congress party itself.

Though belated, Sonia decided to come to the aid of a dispirited party, which was rapidly declining. She made difference to the outcome of the contest, and was able to produce another hung Parliament. The effect of her entry into electoral politics for the 12th Lok Sabha, lifted spirits within the Congress party, and attracted a noticeable degree of curious mass voters. BJP alone could not get majority and with "friends" it had to form another shaky coalition government at the Centre. Sonia controlled the drift away from Congress.

However, Sonia Gandhi has steadily consolidated her position not only as the head of the party, but also as a formidable player in the decision-making process at the national level. On January 12, 1999, at a function at the Ramkrishna Mission in Delhi she spoke strongly against conversion of Hindus, while just a week ago she visited Gujarat to express her solidarity with the Christians there.

The Congress party had been earlier in support of the reservation bill for women, and Sonia Gandhi had also announced her decision do implement 33 per cent reservation for women in her own party hierarchy. She had inducted four women — Mohsina Kidwai, Yanga Patai, Ambika Soni and Laxmi Devi — in the party working committee in as reported to have been effected in the last week of January in *The Hindustan Times* of January 29, 1999. Simultaneously, she also made a statement maintaining that the bill advocating for 33 per cent reservation would ensure only the entry of affluent women in the Lok Sabha and Rajya Sabha. On February 8, she lambasted the BJP government at the Centre for Misgovernance, while there was trouble brewing in the Congress led Orissa government, after the killing of an Australian Christian missionary along with his two young sons. After much discussion Sonia Gandhi took the decision that Chief Minister J B Patnaik be replaced. By taking this tough stand she sent out a loud message to the BJP government and Congress itself. She did what the BJP could not do in Gujarat. After her clear enunciation that the BJP and its front organisation have no monopoly over the Hindus or Hinduism. After visiting Tirupati, she chose Haridwar as her next venue to address partymen in Uttar Pradesh. By urging Congressmen to fight against communal and castist forces she has taken the battle not only to the territory of its principal enemy — the BJP but also to the other two strong parties in Uttar Pradesh the BSP and the Samajwadi Party.

After the massacre of Dalits in Narayanpur Bihar, on February 10, 1999, she expressed "deep shock and abhorrence." At another massacre of Dalits in Bihar within a fortnight while stating that "any government which is helpless in preenting such henous acts forfeits its moral authority to govern." She reenacted the visit of her mother-in-law in Belchi in 1978, by going to Narayanpur on February 13, 1999. It seemed to ring bells of warning for the Rabri government. However, the Congress party remained non-committal on President's rule in Bihar. Now Sonia Gandhi has very clearly stated that the Congress will oppose the ratification of President's rule motion in the Lok Sabha and Rajya Sabha. The Bihar Pradesh Congress Committee reacted sharply to the party high-commands decision, and requested Sonia Gandhi to reconsider her decision. Many senior leaders of the Bihar Congress Committee have resigned in protest.

The months of March and April of 1999 have been hectic for political turnovers. Sonia Gandhi has changed her attitude several times. The dismissal of navy admiral Vishnoo Bhagwat triggered off a controversy with the opposition parties rapping the government for reinstatement of the admiral. Personal insults were hurled at George Fernandes by all opposition parties, Congress and AIADMK leading the batllecry. Towards the middle and end of March 1999, Sonia Gandhi categorically rejected the Left offer on alternative government at a meeting in Calcutta. She maintained that the BJP led ruling coalition will collapse on its own. She promptly remarked to newsmen that the question of forming a government with the help of the Left parties does not arise. She also remarked that there was no need to talk to Mamta Banerji, but for Jayalalitta, she remarked, "why not, we can talk to her".

Sonia Gandhi still denies the plot to dislodge Atal government on April 10, 1999. Speaking at a huge meeting in Karimnagar, she maintained that the Vajpayee government was itself digging its grave. The Congress was ready to shoulder constitutional responsibility of forming government at the Centre if and when situation arises. She also rapped the government for its reluctance to set up a joint Parliamentary committee (JPC) to probe into the corruption charges against people in high government position. She recalled that the same party had earlier demanded setting up of a JPC to probe into the Bofors gun deal based on a report broadcast by a foreign radio station. Earlier on April 7 she denied that she was having talks with Jayalalitha.

The Vajpayee government fell on April 17, 1999, by the lowest margin of just one vote as the BSP leader Mayawati cast her vote while one day earlier she had given indications that BSP will abstain from voting in the Lok Sabha, Immediately efforts were made for the formation of an alternative government. The Congress being the second largest party claimed to form the government. Sonia Gandhi met President Narayanan on April 20. The spokesperson of Congress party Arjun Singh remarked, "we will have letters of support from all parties that voted against the Vajpayee government." He also maintained that the Congress will establish its majority and an alternate government will be formed by Sonia Gandhi. Sonia had meeting with other opposition party leaders including Jayalalitha, RJM leaders and Laloo Prasad Yadav. Mulayam Singh Yadav dealt a severe blow to the plans of Sonia Gandhi when he refused to support the government led by her. Despite hectic efforts Sonia Gandhi was unable to produce the list of 272 MP's. Sonia rejected the requests for sharing of power with other parties. Earlier, she had told the President that the Congress will form minority government with outside support. Samajwadi Party, RSP and Forward Block categorically opposed the plan for a Congress minority government. Sonia Gandhi was able to produce a list of only 239 MPs. As a result, the President had to dissolve the Lok Sabha. Fresh elections was declared by the Election Commissioner K P S Gill.

Sonia Gandhi after much speculation met Jayalalitha at a tea party, organised by Subramanium Swamy. The coming together of these two leaders was termed as a political earthquake.' Thereafter, they met several times. But ultimately the plans misfired and Jayalalitha finally packed her bags and left for Chennai on April 27, 1999.

Sonia Gandhi played the key role in toppling the Vajpayee government and the next general elections will be a testing ground for her acumen, charisma and manipulations. She has been able to rejuvenate the Congress party.

BJP has become vocal charging Sonia Gandhi as an alien. But, Advani speaking in Bhubaneshwar on May 12, 1999, did admit that Sonia is now an Indian citizen. Waves of resentment were also brewing within the Congress party. Sharad Pawar. Tarik Anwar and P A Sangma submitted a letter to the Party President on May 15 questioning the legitimacy of her candidature for Prime ministership. However, these three leaders were expelled from the party. Sonia Gandhi responded by giving in her resignation for the post of party president. Leaders like Pranab Mukherjee and Madhav Rao Scindia tried to perused her to take back her resignation, but Sonia was adamant. However, she presided over the AICC session held on May 25 and emerged stronger than before. Later, she took back her resignation and emerged as the undisputed leader of the Congress party. Sheela Dikshit played an important role in bringing together the party members. Speaking at the AICC session, Sonia Gandhi appealed to the 15,000 delegates to teach a lesson to those who had questioned her patriotism. In a typical Indira Gandhi style she did not compromise, and finally emerged as a very strong political decision-maker.

Mamta Banerji

Like Sonia Gandhi, Mamta Banerji was also instrumental in pulling down Sitaram Keshari from the presidentship. Mamta Banerji is a firebrand leader. She protested against alleged rigging in the election of delegates who were to elect the Congress president. election to the post of the Congress president was being held for the first time after 47 years. Mamta split vertically the Congress (I) in West Bengal on August 9, 1997. She declared the formation of a new state wing of the party and christened it the Trinamul (grassroots) Congress. Mamta boycotted the AICC plenary session held in Calcutta. She addressed a huge rally of the Trinamul Congress at the same time, and said that the new wing was needed "to save the party from fake leadership, and launch an uncompromising fight against the ruling CPI(M).

She claimed that she still belonged to the Congress. Her Trinamul Congress was the real Congress. She would use the same flag, the tricolour. She also claimed that it was she who represented the real Congress in West Bengal. She bitterly criticised the Congress president Sitaram Keshari, and alleged that he had reduced Congress (I) into a signboard organisation. She formalised the infrastructure of the Trinamul Congress, three days after the plenary session of the Congress (I) in Calcutta. Mamta announced the names of conveners of parallel district committee, heads of organisation and 116 — member steering committee. Mamta also formed 'Save Bengal Front'. She urged like-mined parties to be its constituents. She left her post as the West Bengal Congress president, for one of her loyalists. Many thought that Mamta would face disciplinary action for the formation of Trinamul Congress, holding a rally parallel to the Congress (I) plenary session by boycotting it. But nothing happened. Central leaders were unable to make her desist from holding the parallel rally. The party high command decided to ignore her and isolate her. Mamta set up a parallel party office and announced that her supporters would not be accountable to the AICC or the Pradesh Congress Committee. She said, "we looked towards Delhi for far too long. From now on we will fight our own battle".

The advent of the Trinamul Congress was seen to end the politics of polarisation between the Left Front and the Congress (I). One of the senior state Congress (I) leaders conceded that the presence of the Trinmul Congress had changed political equations. Congress (I) feared that Mamta's party would eat into its traditional support base in West Bengal. It received a jolt when former Union Minister Ajit Panja and Krishna Bose joined the Trinamul Congress.

Mamta did approve of the BJP candidate Rita Verma for deputy speakership. Though her Trinamul Congress gave its support to the BJP led collition, she joined the opposition on the opening day of the monsoon session of Parliament. She alongwith her partymen, accused the government of failure to control prices. She demanded that to check price rise, the government should ensure better deliver of essentials through the public distribution system to check prices. She also expressed disappointment with the government because it failed to introduce the bill for women's reservation in Parliament.

Mamta had entered the coordination committee of BJP and its allies with some reluctance. On the issue of rising prices of essential commodities, she resigned from the coordination committee. After much persuasion, she accepted Vajpayee's offer to join the Cabinet at the Centre, but she again put up a bargain – she wanted the railways portfolio for her party MP. Talks broke down on this issue. In a dramatic development after the visit of George Fernandes and Pramod Mahajan, a joint rally was held in Calcutta on February 10, 1999, where a mellowed Mamta did welcome and felicitate Fernandes and Mahajan after they had assured Mamta that most of the demands in the package for Bengal will he considered and fulfilled by the Centre.

Mamta was very critical of the communal killings and attacks on Christians in January and demanded the resignation of Home Minister LK Advani on January 28, 1999. She also trained her guns on Murli Manohar Joshi, another BJP hardliner. She reacted against the inclusion of Joshi in the three-member cabinet team on a fact-finding mission on the murder of an Australian missionary and his sons in Keonjhar, Orissa. Earlier Mamta had joined hands with the Congress demanding ban on Bajrang Dal. She had taken a mellow stand towards the Vajpayee government throughout the months of March and April 1999. She was impassioned in the Sabha during the no-trust motion against the government. She pledged her party's support to Atalji's government. But the Vajpayee government was edged out by just one vote. After hectic consultations between both the government and the opposition, Mamta agreed to a joint election, alliance in the new elections, but also reiterated that Trinamul Congress will have its own symbol and manifest.

Jayalalitha

The famous actor of Tamil cinema, the founder of AIADMK party and its symbol of two leaves was MG Ram chandran. He was also the Chief Minister of Tamil Nadu.

Jayalalitha was also the Chief Minister of Tamil Nadu. But she faced an electoral rout in 1996. A revolt broke out in her party, AIADMK. She was secretary of her party. Many top leaders left her faction. As a result, she was defeated. The deputy general secretary Thirunavukkarasu led a faction against her. Jayalalitha expelled him from the party and the latter expelled her from his faction.

Jayalalitha was a former film actress and a follower of M G Ramchandran. When she assumed chief ministership of Tamil Nadu, it was alleged that during that period three of her associates acquired assets worth more than Rs 66.65 crore, according to the chargesheet filed by officers of the Directorate of Vigilance and Anti-corruption (DNAC) in a case relating to Jayalalitha's wealth. It was alleged to be disproportionate to her known sources of wealth.

The chargesheet filed on June 4, 1997, before, the special court-III judge P Anbazhagan named Jayalalitha as the first accused. Other accused were her 'surrogate sister' Sasikala Natrajan and Sasikala's sister-in-law J I Thirunavukkarasu Lavarsi.. Jayalalitha had publicly renounced her relationship with Sasikala and with her foster son Sudhakan.

Besides the crisis created by corruption charges, Tamil magazine *Dine Manu* and a Tamil biweekly *Junior Vikatan* published a colour photograph of Jayalalitha with a group of people, which they claimed included 'Dhanu,' the human bomb, who assassinate Prime Minister' Rajiv Gandhi alongwith Sivarajan, the leader of the LTTE assassination squad. Since it was photograph of other persons totally unconnected with the murder of Rajiv Gandhi, the sensation flopped. It was a case of sheer media irresponsibility. But Jaylalitha had to go through humiliating experience.

Jaylalitha's party became the principal ally of the BJP led government in 1998. She kept on harping on her demand for the dismissal of the Karunanidhi government in Tamil Nadu on the grounds of failure of governance. On Cauvery issue, the AIADMK warned Prime Minister Vajpayee of "disastrous consequences" if his government did not notify immediately the scheme on Cauvery water in the official gazette and table it in parliament. According to her, there was no possibility of a compromise between Tamil Nadu and Karnataka.

The AIADMK chose to celebrate the 90th birth anniversary of Annadurai. She was isolated from other Tamil parties, and also from BJP in these celebrations. Her speech was carefully worded and was contered around three themes. First, was her justification for her repeated threats of reviewing support to the BJP led government. Second, was meant to be a warning to her allies at the Centre and in the state against treating AIADMK unfairly. And the third, was condemning the "anarchic DMK rule" in Tamil Nadu. She indicated to BJP that in a mixed vegetable dish, no single vegetable was important "The AIADMK was as important as the vessel in which the dish could be prepared." Jayalalitha tried to grab BJP attentions by alleging Karunanidhi's indifference towards maintenance of temples in the state, for which she had launched schemes when she was the Chief Minister in Tamil Nadu. Despite all these she was eager to retain her links with BJP.

Jayalalitha consciously put pressure on BJP led government at the Centre. Despite, all allegations of corruption, she is still a very popular political figure. Vajpayee had to tread carefully where Jaylalitha was concerned. No wonder, Jaswant Singh had to rush to Chennai quite often to pacify Jayalalitha and restore her good humour. At the meeting of the coordination committee of BJP and the allies, a common statement was released stating that the allies should not critirise the government in public, Jaylalitha had her reservations and refused to sign the statement. George Fernandes rushed to Chennai to appease Jayalalitha on February 2, 1999, but the 45 minutes talk could not bear any fruit. It has been evident that Jaylalitha had openly criticised the Vajpayee government on several occasions, and threatened to withdraw support of her party. She had maintained a belligerant stand towards the Vajpayee government. She pushed the government to the wall by demanding that George Fernandes be sacked from the Union government. She wanted to know why the defence minister was being shielded by the Prime Minister when serious charges had been made against him by a naval chief. As a prelude to putting out of the BJP led coalition, Jayalalitha withdrew her two ministers from the government after the Union Cabinet rejected outright all her three demands on the Vishnu

Bhagwat issue. She also held talks with other political leaders to explore the "formation of a government that delivers rather than promises and does not discreminate on grounds of religion, caste or region." The government on April 7, 1999, signalled that its ties with AIADMK have fallen apart and attacked Jayalalitha that she could enter into a deal with the Congress to dismiss the Karunanidhi ministry and seek withdrawal of corruption cases against her. Ultimately, on April 9, 1999, AIADMK withdrew from the coordination panel. By April 12. Jayalalitha was all set to withdraw support from the Vajpayee government. She declared that withdrawal of support to the Vajpayee government was inevitable as there was "no room for any rapprochement". She also admitted that it was a wrong decision to support the government, and that one year had been wasted. Later, she met Congress president Sonia Gandhi. To a query by a newsperson that wether she was a Prime Ministerial candidate, the AIADMK leader remarked, "I am not ruling out anything."

Earlier, in the last week of March Jayalalitha announced the reservation of 33 per cent party post's for women, and she promptly packed her party's hierarchy with 48 women joint district secretaries.

It was termed as a "political earthquake" when Jayalalitha and Sonia Gandhi met over a tea party arranged by Subramanian Swamy. They ultimately unseated the government. A very uncharitable comment became the headline of major newspapers, which was 'Two women send Atal packing'.

Mayawati

Mayawati is one of the m0ost dynamic Dalit leaders. She was earlier the general secretary of the Bahujan Samajwadi Party. She donned the chair of Chief Minister of Uttar Pradesh twice. First time she was the Chief Minister in 1995, with the outside support of BJP. Second time she became the Chief Minister in 1997, when BJP was a constituent of the her government.

Mayawati is shrewd and assertive. Ideologically, she

proclaims that she was against Manuwad. At a rally of the United Front government and its constituent partners in Lucknow against Mayawati, the erstwhile Prime Minister Deve Gawda supported the Samajwadi party's stand against Mayawati. They had alleged that the Schedule Castes and Schedule Tribes Act's were being misused. It had alleged oppression of Samjwadi Party workers. Mayawati issued counter waring to the U F at the centre, to hold back attempts to topple her government. Against the allegation of this act being misused, Mayawati justified her "casteist" action for enlarging her support base.

During her first Chief Ministership in 1995, Mayawati found that BJP was not unhappy with the government. It supported from outside and created no hurdles. She retorted to the remarks of Mulayam Singh that BSP was communal because it had formed alliance with BJP for her second Chief Ministership. She, however, ignored Samajwadi Party's remarks, accusing that Mulayam Singh or indulge in communalism only when it suited his purpose. When the daughter of a Dalit was helped by BJP to come to the position of Chief Minister Mulayam, finds communal forces behind. He had no aualms about joining BJP in 1989 to became Chief Minister himself.

Mayawati has been an opportunist like other politicians. Before forming the coalition with BJP, she had agreed to this "grand alliance" arrangement. But even then she had insisted to take up her chance first. Her condition for agreeing to remain in coalition with BJP was that they would have to agree to her being the Chief Minister first. The volatile Mayawati is perhaps the only woman Chief Minister, who confronted physical assault allegedly by "Samajwadi goons" at the state guest house in June, 1995.

As regards her style of functioning, one of the Samajwadi Party leaders, leaders, Beni Prasad Verma, in his speech addressed to a rally, compared Mayawati with Hitler. Soon after the elections in 1997, Bahujan Party had made it clear that it would join hands with any force that would make Mayawati, Chief Minister. BSP secured not only the Chief Ministership but also half the ministerial positions although it had only 66 MLAs compared to 173 MLAs of BJP. BSP was sure that power position would help it to grow. In the issue of the expansion of the ministry on March 27, 1997, Mayawati asserted that there was no need for it and left out many senior leaders of BJP. The allocation of portfolio also met with rough weather. Mayawati kept home, finance, health and planning. The CPM politbureau member Prakash Karat said that everybody knew Mayawati's style. Transfers and postings on a largescale started even before the government had begun functioning. He remarked that the real problems of the people would be neglected. Farmers would face difficulties, many public sector undertaking could be shut down, workers would be deprived of their jobs and growing crime would be the major problem in the state. However, BJP complained that it was not consulted in majority of transfers and postings. It also alleged that Mayawati had been misusing the Prevention of Atrocities against Scheduled Castes Act against the upper castes.

According to a report of Venkitesh Ram Krishna, Mayawati held that "the job of identifying and appointing loyal officers in key posts is of utmost importance for the government and it is being carried out smoothly.

Mayawati government's handling of law and order did not seem sound — there were communal, caste and sectional clashes. There were allegations and counter-allegations, too. The Samajwadi Party alleged that the government arrests their workers under the Scheduled Castes and Scheduled Tribes Atrocities Act and Goonda and Gangsters Act. These two acts had became the bone of contention among the coalition partners.

When the BJP government was formed under Kalyan Singh, it instituted a vigilance inquiry against bureaucrats considered close to Mayawati and reinstated officers suspended by Mayawati. Kalyan Singh transferred 184 senior bureaucrats in the first 15 days of his government.

BSP demanded a mechanism for regular consultation at the state level, like the one at the national level. Mayawati also complained that Kalyan Singh's measures were against

Scheduled Castes and Scheduled Tribes and an anti-Dalit mood was created in the state.

In the last week of May 1997, the Union Home Minister Indrajeet Gupta and Chief Minister Mayawati exchanged letters over law and order situation in Uttar Pradesh. Mayawati, however, denied any deterioration of law and order situation in the state. She personally directed administrative actions to be taken against senior officials, particularly in the police department. Senior bureaucrats described these actions as "self defeating frenzy". The Union home minister disapproved these so called "corrective" steps. It was alleged that the "punishment transfers" were made against those who had expressed views before the media against the state administration. According to Mayawati, these actions violated discipline of the police and brought disrepute to the administration.

One of the BSP ministers, whose women welfare department was taken away from him and was given the portfolio of culture and youth affairs, revolted and resigned. He also accused Mayawati of taking bribe during her regime.

Mayawati won the Lok Sabha elections of 1998. She is still very vocal and critical of the Vajpayee government. At the state level, she continusuely rapped at the BJP led Kalyan Singh government. She is undoubtedly a force to reckon with in the politics of Uttar Pradesh. She still is the undisputed leader of the Dalits and if strategies are planned with some care, and her harsh tongue is checked a little, she can form a strong political front of Dalits.

Mayawati did it again. After promising to abstain from voting in the Lok Sabha on no-confidence motion against the Vajpayee government, she cast her vote in favour of the motion and thus, her one vote toppled the government on April 26, 1999.

Rabri Devi

A great writer has said that some are born great, and upon some greatness is thrust. In a similar strain it could be said that (in Bihar) some are born leaders, and upon some leadership is thrust. It could be appropriately applied to Rabri Devi — the Chief Minister of Bihar. Her Chief Ministership is an example of family principle of succession". It was adopted for keeping Bihar under the freedom of the Rashtriya Janata Dal (RJD) supremo Laloo Prasad. The dynastic principle had been applied earlier also with Indira Gandhi and Rajiv Gandhi, and now on Sonia Gandhi by the sycophancy of the congressmen to maintain the influence of Nehru-Gandhi dynasty. Sonia came out of non-political "private life," and as suggested in her own writings, she jumped to national politics for family's sake. But she waited for the appropriate moment. Her intention seems to preserve her hold on the Congress party as a vehicle for her son and daughter. In Bihar, Rabri was suddenly made Chief Minister. In her case, it seemed to be Laloo's intention to keep RJD as a vehicle for his next generation. He did every thing hurriedly. He made a travesty of the principles of doctrine of responsibility in the cabinet system of the government, by appointing his wife Rabri Devi as the Bihar Chief Minister. He had resigned because he was facing corruption charges before a CBI-designated court. He surrendered on July 30, 1997. Laloo Prasad also violated the principle of probity and accountability in public life by appointing his wife as Chief Minister. As he was alleged to be a "trained" Chief Minister, the person who had to replace him should have been a person distant or independent of him, but this did not happen. The requirements of accountability and responsibility were put on the shelf.

In the appointment of Rabri Devi as Chief Minister, a high voltage drama in a very short period was played. Laloo Prasad, RJD legislators and Rajyapal Kidwai played the main roles in this drama. The people of Bihar were unable to believe the news that Rabri Devi was appointed the Chief Minister and sworn in within hours after the resignation of her husband from the post. On July 30, Laloo Prasad was remanded to judicial custody after he surrendered before the CBI designated court. He resigned as Chief Minister on July 25, 1997 after the court issued an arrest warrant against him. He proposed the name of his wife as his successor at a hurriedly-convened meeting of RJD legislative party.

The Rabri episode ensured proxy rule by Laloo who had said in jail, "being in jail does not mean I am a rotten egg. Several leaders had called on me and others will come." It was alleged that many Bihar officials met him regularly and received orders from When he came out of jail, he accompanied Rabri Devi every where and acted as an extra constitutional authority on behalf of her. It was alleged that Sitaram Kesri and I K Gujral had approved of Laloo's decision regarding installing his wife as Chief Minister.

Rabri Devi has no formal education and no interest or experience in active politics. When she became the Chief Minister of Bihar, she was neither a member of the Legislative Assembly nor the Legislative Council. She perhaps had never thought of such a windfall. Laloo had said that when his party legislators had unanimously elected her as a new leader, she was not ready to accept the new assignment. "It was only after a great deal of persuasion, that I prepared her for the changed situation."

The Governor of Bihar, Shree Sunder Singh Bhandari, gave Rabri Devi 15 days time to prove her majority in the Assembly. Before surrendering to the court, Laloo ensured and made his wife's position secured. He arranged for his wife to seek vote of confidence on July 28. She won the vote by a huge margin. She won confidence by winning 194 votes against 110.

To consolidate Rabri's position, Laloo made her appoint a jumbo ministry of 32 cabinet ministers and 44 minister of state. She became a target of controversy and butt of jokes by many. The CPI(M) leader Harkishan Singh Surjeet emphasised Laloo's decision as an insult to those who elected him. BJP and Samta Party were furious, but Kesri ordered his party's Bihar MLAs to ensure Rabri's accession to office. Rabri could not make speeches. The television focussed upon her everywhere, but barring very few occasions, no one could hear her voice. In the first week of October 1997. She had to face a tricky situation created by the non-gazzetted secretariat employees. Ministers and senior government servants were not permitted by the employees to attend their offices. It is said that she shut down the secretariat for four days and then the employees agreed to negotiate with her.

In month of September 1998, the Rabri regime was threatened by the Centre's recommendation to the President of India for the promulgation of Article 356 in Bihar for non-governance and detracting law and order. Every one knows that she is a puppet because she had not been trained in the art of politics. But gradually, she seemed to be maturing in carrying herself with confidence in public functions. The Rabri government was saved in 1998 as the President disagreed to promulgate Act 356. The Shankarbegha carnage at Narayanpur on the eve of Republic Day also threatened the Rabri government; it came under severe attack from all corners. The cabinet advised the President, to dismiss the Bihar government and promulgate Presidents rule. Ultimately, the Rabri government was dismissedon February 12, 1999, and President's rule was promulgated in Bihar for the seventh time. In a sudden development, the governor of Bihar, Shree Sunder Singh Bhandari was recalled to Delhi. Laloo Yadav continued attacking the BJP government. He received support from the Left parties. Sonia Gandhi did not comment on the justification or otherwise of President's Rule. Meanwhile, the pressures on BJP government mounted and the President's rule in Bihar was ended on March 8, 1999. The RJD government under Rabri came back to power again. A radiant Rabri Devi once again took oath as Chief Minister on March 9, 1999 and submitted a list of 164 members to the governor. Bhandari was sent to Gujarat as governor on March 13, 1999, and Chief Justice B M Lal was made the acting governor of Bihar on March 16. The RJD hailed his appointment, but very soon there started a rift between the governor and the Rabri government.

(c) Women as Legislative Actors

At the legislative levels of the Centre and the states, women have not been given much importance as political actors.

Though there has been a substantial increase in voting

participation by women, have not fared as contestants in national elections or state elections. They could never occupy more than 8 per cent seats in Parliament, and more than 10 per cent in state assemblies. In the Council of Ministers, the highest percentage of women had been 12.96 per cent in 1962.

With regard to the efficacy of women legislators in decision-making, there have been some studies in India as well as in Bihar. In R K Verma's study on rural political leadership, the writer held that women legislators had been contributing to the new models in 'developing national politics' of India. A Ph.D. thesis by Prabhawati, presented to the Magadh University in 1994 came to the conclusion that the representation of women in Lok Sabha was never substantial. In one of his studies, S M Sayeed was of the view that in near future because of social, cultural and practical reasons, female representation in legislatures would not increase.

The suggestions made in one of Dahelrup Drude's studies (1986) with regard to 'critical mass' theory becomes relevant here. In the context of study of women in the Scandinavian countries, she held that, when two factors combined in any political system women became 'critical mass' that is, politically strong. This happened (i) when women got at least 25 to 30 per cent seats in the legislatures; and, (ii) when support to women legislators from outside was given by strong women movement.

In the Indian political system, women in legislatures could not become a 'critical mass' because they were only 8 per cent in Lok Sabha and 10 per cent in state assemblies, and there were not sufficiently strong political women movements in India to support them.

In the legislative process, women legislators do not seem to have much impact. Recently, on the 81st constitution Amendment Bill, seeking reservations of one-third seats in Parliament and state legislatures for women, they could not be effective. Though women MPs had been united inspite of their diverse political allegience and ideologies, the bill could not be passed.

Though they differed ideologically, women fiom different parties had come together to support the bill. There were some prominent women among them like ratanmala, Savanoor an Uma Bharati, who had supported the stand takenby Sharad Yadav and the Muslimleague MPs that there should be sub-quota within the quota for the women of the backwarrrd castesand the minority communities.

The former Prime Minister I K Gujaral had inducted in his cabinet the most vocal women like Renuka Chowdhury, Jayanti Natrajan, and Kamla Sinha. Different impressions were created by this act of the Prime Minister. One view was that Prime Minister Gujral wished to correct the impression created by Sharad Yadav that Janata Dal did not intend to give space to women. The other view was that Gujral took this step to put a constraint upon them in raising a hue and cry over the women's reservation bill. Gita Mukherjee (CPI) refused any cabinet post because she wished to remain outside so that she could fight for the reservation bill for women. Thus, he had included five women in his cabinet; all of them were placed in the second rank.

There were some controversy from the very beginning among the women MPs on the formation of the committee on empowerment of women, to be chaired by Gita Mukherjee of CPI. It held its first meeting on the May 6, 1997. Margret Alva (Congress) was apprehensive that this committee would put hurdles in passing the 81st Constitution Amendment Bill 1996. According to Alva, there was no need for it because the joint committee had already discussed the bill in detail. The new empowerment of women committee would now review the bill and it would be scuttled.

The quota system became a goal in itself and created its own momentum. The original purpose was lost. Now sub-quota within quota would bring disaster upon the society. Quota for women in the *Panchayats* would, let us hope, gradually bring more and more women into the political field.

Madhu Kishwar in her two articles 'Not a gender war' and 'a Flawed measure' in *The Hindustan Times*, Patna, had discussed about the provisions of the reservation bill along with other related matters. She had pointed out that the lottery system of gender-based reservations proposed in the 81st amendment bill meant that fresh set of constituences would be earmarked for women at every elections. It would mean that the women would not be able to develop stable relationship with their constituences. That would be true for men also who would not like this scheme. Secondly, when once the bill was passed, the men would not like that women should be allowed to contest general constituencies. Third, in the Sheduled Castes and Scheduled Tribes constituencies, which were permanent, the male would not give space to women. Quota system would ensure that women would contest only women and never men. This would mean "a sure way to perpetually ghettoies women's politics". To add to all these harmful effects of the reservation bill, in another, it would be impossible for a woman to get elected twice to the legislatures in Centre or in states, because the same constituencies would not be likely to be reserved twice in succession.

The suggestion for multiseat constituencies should be considered seriously. These constituencies could be clustered together to make one. These would be represented by three people, one of whom must be a woman. The first two seats would go to the two candidates who polled the highest number of votes — man or woman. The third seat would to the woman who polled highest number of votes among the rest of the women candidates not elected on either of the two general seats in the constituencies.

After the fall of the Gujarat government and the installation of Vajpayee government in March 1998, preparations were on for introduction of women's reservation bill in the Lok Sabha. All major parties had included the issue of women's reservation in their election manifestoes. However, there was so much rumpus in the Lok Sabha that the bill could not even he placed on the table. Copies of the bill were destroyed by Laloo Yadav and Mulayam Singh Yadav, Sarad Yadav was also against the introduction of the bill. He maintained that the bill would be beneficial only to educated elite women.

The attitude adopted by most of the male MPs cutting across party lines was an expression of their fear and anxiety over the loss of more than 180 seats in the Lok Sabha, if 33 per cent seats were reserved for women.

At the grassroot level institutions, the 73rd Amendment to the Constitution did provide 33 per cent reservation for women in Panchayati Raj institutions (PRIs). It has produced very good results in Bengal, Maharashtra and Karnatak, but in Bihar, elections to PRIs have not been held even once in the last six years, since the passage of the amendment.

Some organisations like the People's Union for Civil liberties, Rashtriya Lok Samiti, Nav Bharat Jagriti Kendra and Jan Jagaran Kendra, Prayas, Catholic Centre and Xavier's Institute of Social Service came into existence for mobilising women, besides other programmes. Except Prayas, all these groups were part of wider national movement.

Apart from these organisations and action groups in which women are involved politically, socially, and economically, Bihar had witnessed the rise and growth of several woman organisation during the pre-Independence days. One such organisation was the Mahila Charkha Samiti, known as Mahila Charkha Class in its initial days. Several great personalities like Gandhiji, Rajendra Babu, Jay Prakash Narain and Prabhawati ji were associated with it and were involved in its activities.

Another important women's agency was the All India Women's Conference, already mentioned before, which in its earlier days was known as Women's India Association. At the Centre in Delhi, Margret E Cousins, the secretary of Women's India Association, made concerted efforts to establish the present All India Women's Conference. Its branches were gradually established in different states.

Another old and important women's organisation in Bihar had been the Bihar Council of Women. Working women had also organised themselves under the leadership of Lakshmi Menon. The Centre for Women Development Studies (CWDS) was started a few decades ago in Bihar by the encouragement and initiative of Veena Mazumdar. This organisation is quite active in the tribal belt with its social and economic programmes. There are some other NGOs like Aditi, which are also involved in women's field.

Political Parties's Role

Maciver defined political party as "an association organised in support of some principle or the policy, which by constitutional means endeavours to make the determinant of the government". This definition focussed attention on the associated and the organised aspects of a political party, while brining about the rational for its existence in terms of some guiding principle or policy and linking the same to political power as exercised by the government. Political parties are the closely connected with government, and thus, in decision-making position. The parties furnish the government with personnel.

In order to socialise the masses effectively, every political party must have competent leadership. Party workers or cadres must establish contacts with the people on a regular basis so as to aggregate and articulate their interests, educate them politically, and thereby, secure their support for the party. The party officers and workers aim at imbibing the ordinary members with the party spirit, imparting party ideologies and motivating them to be active in implementation of party programmes.

Since recruitment by political parties encourage circulation of elites, it infuse new blood to keep the party vikrant. Their neglect of women would not augur well either for the parties or the women, who formed half of the body politics.

Political parties in India have shown neglect of women in recruiting them for party posts like presidents, secretaries, treasures, spokesperson or whips at the Centre, state or local levels. The Congress party, as compared with any other party, has been most liberal towards women in their recruitment policies. But even then women members never exceeded 10 per cent limit, Even the Left parties did not find women very much fit for their tickets in elections or party posts. It was only BJP who found in Sushama Swaraj the party spokesperson. Though the number of women in party politics has increased, their appearance into the ranks of the politically active or key decision-makers or non-key decision-makers is still very low, if not nil.

There might be several reasons for acquiring less decision-making positions in a political party by women. Besides their socialisation or political culture in the society, one very important reason was that the party system in India itself is in shambles. They have no proper organisations or proper offices or definable ideologies or identifiable issues and long-term programmes. They seem to be interested only in seeking chairs for the sake of collecting benefits and privileges accruing from different positions. In such chaotic situation, even if women entered decision-making apparatuses of the party, they would have bleak future. They would affect very little - either the party system or the political system as a whole.

The role of, specially the mainstream political parties is very important. They have to be sensitise to provide space to women in their decision-making forum. Merely reservation of seats for women might not be much successful in creating a 'critical mass' in the legislature.

Women in politics have not been held in esteem and with respect by political parties as has been disclosed in a study *Bhog* by well known journalist Vikas Kumar Jha. The writer has narrated the sad story of many women party workers, who were lured into the organisation by politicians as "workers". He alleged that "women political workers" had been exploited by the male politicians for satisfying their lust. The writer of *Bhog* includes fake characters also in his study of Indian politics in order to establish his point. Vikas, in his earlier work, had thrown light on corruption in politics and a brief history of the country. In *Bhog*, Vikas has probed and made efforts to determine women's status in politics.

Political parties have gradually recognised the importance of including women's issue in their election manifestoes as witnessed during '91, '96 and '98 general elections. But neither in '96 nor in '98 the parties gave enough tickets to women. It has not gone beyond 10 per cent by any party. Women were given decision-making positions of the secondary level except Kanti Singh in Deve Gowda Ministry, some good vocal members in Gujaral Ministry like Renuka Chowdhury.

Conclusion

Indira Gandhi has been the lone example of a potent political decision-maker. At the planetary level, she was the first to strongly formulate a guideline for the prevention and presentation of environment. At the national level, she was a powerful and effective Prime Minister. She left her father Nehru way back in the game of real politic. She almost replaced the parliamentary form of government by a Prime Ministerial form of government. It is often remarked that she was the only 'male' is her Cabinet. She ruled her party and government as an autocrat, never witnessed before.

After Indira Gandhi, several other women politicians have emerged exerting considerable influence on the formulation of national and state level politics. Mamta Banerji exerted pressure on Congress party, even broke away from the party to formulate a new party which to her was the 'real' Congress party in West Bengal. She dictated terms to Vajpayee government regularly. The year 1998 saw the emergence of Sonia Gandhi as a leader with ample influence and political clout. To certain extent she has revived the Congress party. Then there is Jayalalitha, a very strong and popular leader of Tamil Nadu. Then there is Mayawati, the undisputed Dalit leader and an important decision-make in Uttar Pradesh politics.

The years 1998-99 witnessed the crucial role played by women leaders of the likes of Sonia Gandhi, Jayalalitha, Mamta Banerji and Mayawati. While Sonia Gandhi succeeded to a certain exact in pumping new blood in the otherwise anemic Congress party, Jayalalitha and Mamta Banerji put pressures on the Vajpayee government from its very inception. Jayalalitha continued threatening the government that she would withdraw. When the Vishnu Bhagwat issue flew up, Jayalalitha ultimately decided to withdraw the support of her 18 MPs on the issue of formation of JPC. The final act was performed by Mayawati when she voted against the government. These four women leaders brought down the Vajpayee government. Obviously in 1998 and early 1999, Indian political scenario has been virtually dominated by these women leaders. The coming years will be a testing ground for these women leaders.

References

1. *Front line* — April 18, 1997, June 27, 1997, August 22, 1997, September 5, 1977, February 6, 1998 & August 14/28, 1998.
2. Ganguly, Amulaya, 'Gender Based Folly', *The Hindustan Times*, Patna, Monday, June 9, 1992.
3. Gandhi, Sonia, Rajiv, *Viking, Penguin India*, 1992.
4. Karat, Brinda, 'The Multiple Struggles of Women'. *Frontline*, October 3, 1997.
5. Kisnwar, Madhu, 'Note a Gender War', *The Hindustan Times*, Patna, Tuesday, June 3, 1997, p. 7.

   'A flawed Measure', *The Hindustan Times*, Patna, Wednesday, June 4, 1997, p. 7.
6. Prabhawati, Ph.D. thesis (Magadh University), Published 1996, बिहार व्यवस्थापिका में महिला विधापिकाओं की भागीदारी (1952 से 1959 तक)

   Report of the Regional Round Table on Women's Participation in Policy and Decision making Process. October 10-11, 1991, Centre For Women Development Studies Bihar and Friedrich Ebert Germany.
7. Sayeed, G.M., राजनीतिक दल और महिला प्रतिनिधित्व लोकतन्त्र समीक्षाः जनवरी–दिसम्बर 1991.
8. Sharan, S., Women Prime Ministers in South Asia (1995). Common Wealth Publishers, 4378/4–B, Murari Lal Street, Ansari Road, Daryaganj, New Delhi-110002.
9. Stong, Maurice F., Indira Gandhi Commemorative Volume.

10. Verma, R.K., संसदीय व्यवस्था में शून्यकाल एक समीक्षा: लोकतन्त्र समीक्षा एनुअल ऑफ 1991.

11. Vijay, K. Tripathi, (Review) *The Hindustan Times*, Patna, June 8 of Bhog".

12. The Hindustan Times, Patna from September 1998 to May 1999.

7

WOMEN IN THE ELECTION PROCESS IN INDIA

Niroj Sinha

The process of election is the main wheel of a democratic system. With the prevalence of indirect democracy in almost all the democratic countries of the world, it assumes great importance as a mechanism for choosing representatives for elective offices by means of votes by the people. By voting, we constitute the government and choose our law-makers and law-executors. It is not only primarily a legitimising instrument for those in authority and for their governance, it is a positive right of the people, through which they decide the destiny of their political system.

The total population of any country does not constitute a homogeneous group. Similarly, our society is plural and consists of various well-organised groups and communities with different interests and needs competing for a share in political power through the mechanism of elections. Not each group has equal access to power in a democratic polity despite the popular myth of equality for all. There are minorities identified on the basis of religion, race and ethnicity all over the globe. Women do not constitute a minority in numbers as they constitute nearly 50 per cent of the total population of any country, but practically have a minor position and only a marginal access to polity due to gender bias.

Feminists have thrown up gender as the most potent, significant and enormously useful analytical concept. The feminist scholarship places gender, the sociocultural manifestation of being a man or woman as the focus of study in research. Gender is defined as the social construction of relations between women and men and among various groups of women or men. Sex is defined as the biological similarities and differences between and among men and women.[1]

Gender and patriarchy combine together to push women to the periphery of politics. Politics is regarded strictly as a male preserve. Rationality, self-discipline, competition, aggression, orderliness, universality to mention a few, are the priced qualities in political parlance. On the contrary, irrationality, indiscipline, particularity, submissiveness impulsiveness are some of the qualities associated with feminine nature. The result is the distancing of women from everything political.[2] Women are perceived as part of the social structure and not as part of the "power" phenomenon, which Seinon De Behaviour calls as "being rather than doing".[3] This sociocultural perspective in addition to mass-scale illiteracy and poverty of Indian women prevents them from a meaningful involvement in the political process.

Women's right to vote and to stand for elections has only been a legal reality for about 100 years globally. Although men's vote was not extended initially to all classes and races, generally their universal enfranchisement preceeded women. It was first adopted by the European countries, the Americas and Australia.[4] The end of World War II in 1945 brought former colonial countries in Asia and Africa to grant women's suffrage, and the trend has continued worldwide, with South Africa enfranchising black women and men as late as 1994.[5]

Although the right to stand for elections, to be a candidate and to be elected follows in theory from the right to vote. Earlier several countries had granted suffrage only.

Women's right to vote was restricted to male candidates only. Canada granted women the unrestricted right to vote in 1950, but not until 10 years later did they gain the right to be candidates. Conversely, some countries put women's right to be elected as their first political right. USA, Norway, the Netherlands, and Guyana, for example, allowed women to run for office and to be elected by an all male electorate. Kuwait disallows women both voting and candidate's rights while extending them to men, and four others, Saudi Arabia, Qatar, Oman and Somalia — deny them to both genders. Since Finland adopted both these fundamental democratic rights in 1906, over 95 per cent of the countries of the world have followed suit by the end of the 20th century.[6]

India

The Constitution of India 1950, guarantees equal opportunity for participation in politics to both men and women. Women were given this right equally with men in recognition and as a 'token' of appreciation by the national leaders for the massive role played by them in the freedom struggle. The Preamble to the Constitution of India resolves to secure to all its citizens. Justice, social and economic and political; Liberty of thought, expression, belief, faith and worship; Equality of status and opportunity; and to promote among them all, fraternity, assuming the dignity of all individuals and the unity of the nation. Article 14 of the Constitution ensures "equality before law" and Article 15 "prohibits discrimination" interalia of sex among other things.

The gradual transfer of power from the British to Indian hands gave women experience in participation in democratic process. The Government of India Act of 1935 extended the franchise to more than 6 million women, a great improvement on the earlier figure of 3,15,000 under the act of 1919. But for this franchise right, women did have to wage a grim battle. Lord Lothian, the head of the franchise committee after meeting the women's delegation led by Sarojini Naidu, remarked that "they were very firm in their demand for equality as a basis of the new Indian Constitution". As early as 1930, a meeting of the representatives of women's organisations had demanded immediate acceptance of adult franchise without sex discrimination. Though rejected by the British government, the Karachi session of the Indian National Congress in 1931 accepted these demands and committed itself to women's political equality regardless of their status and qualifications.

In 1937 elections, eight women were elected from general constituencies and 42 from reserved constituencies. The Constituent Assembly set up for the drafting of the Constitution of free India in October 1946, had among its members, Sarojini Naidu, Durgabi Deshmukh, Renuka and Hansa Mehta among other notables.

Women as Voters in India

India has experienced 12 general elections to date. It has not been possible for election analysts to decide which particular way the women have voted, but their votes have undoubtedly been included in this "on course" corrective voting for giving a fresh lease of power to the elected parliamentary form of government.

With the rising number of electorate, the percentage of women voters has also registered a steady rise constantly from 37.1 per cent in 1952 to 69.70 per cent in 1971. However, in 1977 the difference was 9.7 per cent to increase further to 10.77 per cent in 1977 and 10.94 per cent in 1980. In 1984, women had polled a higher percentage of votes to fall again steadily in 1989. Since then, however, there has been a discernable fall from 69.70 per cent to 55.85 per cent in 1977 and 51.22 per cent in 1980. The year 1984 was a 'watershed' when the percentage of women voters went upto 68.17 per cent to fall again in 1989 to 43.90 per cent and 47.42 per cent in 1991. In the 1996 Lok Sabha, elections the total number of women voters in the country was 28,03,69,086, while that of male voters was 30,98,15,776.[7] There was a slight improvement in 1998 elections (see Table I).

As compared to the total voter turnout, the figures for female voters have always been less by approximately 6 per cent. Looking at the trends in female voting, similar fluctuations as in total voting are evident. In 1967, the percentage of female votes was 55.48 per cent marking a decrease of 6.33 per cent. This decrease is somewhat equal to the fall in total voting percentage, which shows that in comparative terms, women's voting did not depict a discouraging trend.

A better comparative assessment can be had by looking at the difference in the percentage of male and female voters. This difference has always been unfavourable to women.[8] (See Table-I). In, 1991, the percentage difference was 27 per cent but in 1996 it narrowed down to 5.14 per cent (see Table I).

The general inferences of Table I are that women have shown a gradual increase in the exercise of their franchise, and this increase has been proportionate to the increase in total voter turnout. In 1971 elections, there was decrease in the percentage of voters in general. The difference between male and female voters was 11.85 per cent. The low turnout was due to various factors operating at that time. The split within the Congress Party; election being held one year earlier due to the dissolution of Lok Sabha, etc. Both these factors proved detrimental to the mobilisation of voters in the 1971 election. However, the fact that the difference between male and female voting did not widen with the total fall in mobilisation shows that the female voters were more mobilised than their male counterparts while the total voter turnout increased only by 0.50 per cent (54.76 per cent to 55.35 per cent), the increase in female voter turn out was 2.52 per cent (46.64 per cent to 49.15 per cent)[9]. In 1974 and 1980, there was no improvement, rather a decreasing trend was visible with tremendous increase in 1984, when women's vote percentage was 68.17 per cent nearly 5 per cent higher than the percentage of male votes. It fell drastically is 1989, 1991, 1996 and 1998 (see Table I).

Another interesting feature is that states have been more or less steadily maintaining a consistent record of either maximum or minimum mobilisation of women as voters. While the states of Kerala and Tamil Nadu have maintained their position as maximum mobilisers of women, Orissa and Madhya Pradesh have been equally persistent in leading the list of minimum mobilisers of women. The difference between the maximum and minimum mobilisation of women has always remained high. The states of Kerala, Tamil Nadu, Maharashtra, Andhra Pradesh and Gujarat in the southern and western regions have shown a relatively higher degree of electoral participation by women. The states in the northern region with exception of Punjab and Haryana in the west and West Bengal in the east have shown a persistent trend of low mobilisation. Orissa, Madhya Pradesh, Bihar, Uttar Pradesh Rajasthan, Assam, Himachal Pradesh, Jammu and Kashmir present a dismal picture of persistently low mobilisation in absolute terms, and particularly in relation to men with percentage difference actually increasing in Madhya Pradesh. Except for Bihar and Uttar Pradesh the states with low mobilisation have been those which were late in participating in the Independence struggle. Socially extensive and severe restrictions on women's activities outside the family have been prevalent in these states. Economically they are poor with comparatively less urbanisation and industrialisation. Female literacy also has been lowest in these states. These are some of the factors that account for low political consciousness and less enthusiasm for the exercise of franchise rights among women.[10]

Table II shows those states and Union territories where the turnout of female voters has been highest upto four places; among these only Kerala and Tamil Nadu figure in the Table. Both have shown fluctuations, but the decline has been much too steep in the case of Kerala. It was a decline of 3.6 per cent as against an increase of 4.4 per cent in Tamil Nadu if one takes the figures of 1967-1971 (Table II).[11]

Regarding Union territories, the highest figure for mobilisation of women since 1962 has never gone below 71.71 per cent. In 1967, it was as high as 86.10 per cent.[12] In '71, '77, '80, '84, '89, '91, '96, and '98 the Union territories have maintained this trend.

The states and Union territories showing greater mobilisation of women socially and politically, are not backward and economically they are not deficient. Most of them being coastal areas they were the first to be exposed to the Western culture of the Dutch, Portuguese and the British colonisers. Places such as Delhi and Chandigarh, though not falling into the above category, have a cosmopolitan cultural outlook, an industrial base and urban character. The social structures of these states and Union territories are not very rigid and male dominated. On the contrary, a state like Kerala has a maternal society, which ensures a relatively dominant place to women.[13]

Inspite of regional imbalances, the mobilisation of women voters is not depressing. But it is also not a factor which should lull us into satisfaction as regards women's political participation. Way back in the 1970s the committee on the Status of Women in India in its report had commented, "women's participation in the political process has increased both in elections and in their readiness to express their views on issues directly concerning their day-to-day life, their ability to produce an impact on the political process has been negligible."[14] It still holds true even after the passage of two decades.

The increase in the turnout of women voters, particularly of the lower castes and classes may be attributed to a high degree to mobilisation, rather than their own political consciousness. The Scheduled Castes and other poor and backward communities are aware of the importance of their vote, but this awareness about the issues affecting them needs tremendous mobilisation in order to be translated into a political exercise like voting Moreso with regard to women who have many disincentives such as poverty, daily work, violence, health and patriarchal family norms.

The parties have recognised the significance of women voters, and have been exerting themselves to devise various methods. Mostly adhoc promises are made to women during election campaigns. Moreover, there was any correlation between the camping promises and voting support. It also reflected on the low impact that the women's movement had helped in educating the women as well as in making a dent on the patriarchal politicians (92).[15] In 1984, much of the victory of the Congress could be attributed to a sympathy vote by womenfolk against the slaying of Prime Minister Indira Gandhi on a women-to-women basis ('92).[16]

Women as Contestants

The number of women candidates contesting for the Lok Sabha has been extremely discouraging. It has not been much above 5 per cent of the total number of male candidates. Table III gives a picture of the women contestants for Lok Sabha from 1952-1998. The number of women contestants, however, has increased since 1952 with the exception of 1957 when it came down to 45 from 51. There has been a steady increase in the number in 1991-1996 to fall again in 1998.

The fall in the number of women candidates is not surprising since in this election the total number of candidates was much smaller than in 1996, may be due to the changes made by the Election Commission, and also the unexpectedness of the general elections (see Table III).

The difference between male and female contestants of the Lok Sabha seats has also shown a declining trend from 1977 onwards—94. 17 per cent in 1977 to 93.82 per cent in 1980 and 90.23 per cent in 1984. The differences had increased slightly in 1991 and 1996.

The actual number of seats contested by women has been less than the number of women contestants since some of the seats were contested by more than one women.

The number of seats in the first to five general elections were 6, 5, 5, 5, 9, respectively. The number and percentage of the successful women candidates increased in 1957 from 19 to 25 and from 37 per cent to 62 per cent. Since then there has been a steady decline. In 1971 only 21 were successful out of a total of 86 (See Table III). In 1971, a sudden spurt in the number of independent women candidates from 10 in 1967 to 31 in 1971— added to the total number. At the same time independent candidates fared very poorly—only one succeeded, and thus the overall percentage fell from 42.4 to 25.9, an all time low. The number of contestants rose steadily from 1980 onwards from 142 in 1980 to 599 in 1996 to fall again in 1998 (See Table III). In the 11th Lok Sabha elections about 2/3 of the total 599 female candidates were independents. Experience has shown that women have rarely been successful as independents. Party build up and support is necessary for women to win elections. In the 1991 elections, a relatively novice candidate Rita Verma from Dhanbad in Bihar won due to the massive support of BJP. Not exactly similar, but such experiences have been often repeated. The election of Alka Nath (1976) from Chindwara in Madhya Pradesh is another such example.

Statewise: The number of women contesting for Lok Sabha in the states and Union territories has roughly been in accordance with, though not in proportion, to the total number allocated to them. The maximum number of women have entered the race in Uttar Pradesh except in 1951 and 1971 when Bihar, the next biggest state in terms of Lok Sabha seats, took the lead by one number. In the elections of 1996, Uttar Pradesh has returned 10 women to the Lok Sabha, the largest contingent from one state. Some of the Union territories such as Delhi, Goa, Daman and Due and Madhya Pradesh have put up greater percentage. Madhya Pradesh needs special mention, since it has shown a poor turnout of voters.[18] (See Table II).

The number of women candidates in various states and Union Territories shows wide fluctuations from one election to another. It has fluctuated in Uttar Pradesh, but in Bihar and Madhya Pradesh, the number has gradually gone up. In Kerala, it remained constant at one for the first three elections, then marked a slight increase to three in 1967 and four in 1971. In Orissa, no woman contested in the first three elections, but in 1967 one and in 1971. Two women contested. In the Union Territories along with Jammu & Kashmir, Haryana and Mysore may be clubbed into one category, as the number of women contestants in them for all five general elections was either nil or just one.[19]

The number of successful candidates has naturally been

greater in Uttar Pradesh, Bihar, Madhya Pradesh and Andhra Pradesh, where the number of contestants has also been greater. Orissa, Haryana, Goa, Daman and Due and Manipur are the states and Union territories where women contested but were not returned to Lok Sabha in the first five general elections. In 1996, Haryana returned one, but Manipur, Assam, Arunachal Pradesh, Mizoram, Nagaland, Sikkim, Tamil Nadu, Jammu and Kashmir, Kerala, Maharashtra, Meghalaya, Himachal Pradesh did not return a single contestant to Lok Sabha.

The number of contesting or elected women candidates for Lok Sabha in a particular, state or Union territory does not appear to be decisively related with the literacy among women in that area. Laxmi N Menon, while analysing the first general elections, inferred that the number of women candidates was in inverse proportion to the percentage of literacy among them.[20] The electoral history of different states over the years does not project a consistent pattern of correlation between female literacy and their candidature. Literacy is not a single variable in this respect, and it influences the number of contestants, but only in combination with other factors. The social ethos and taboos prevailing in the state or in a particular constituency vis-a-vis women's role in politics did influence the success or otherwise of its female contestants, but only in a small way. What mattered most were the personality of the contestants, including their family background and involvement in politics, local conditions, campaign strategy and the political party to which the candidate belong.[21]

Political Parties and Female Contestants

The maximum number of female candidates have been fielded by the Congress Party from 25 in 1957 to 49 in 1996. However, it has remained much below its stipulated target of 15 per cent of the total candidates. CPI and erstwhile Praja Socialist Party have been fielding female candidates from the very beginning, but the number has been small. In the 1996 elections, CPI(M) put up five female candidates and CPI fielded four. Smaller, unrecognised parties have shown continuous fluctuations.

As in number, the Congress has also covered the maximum area. Congress women candidates have appeared in most of the states during Lok Sabha elections except in 1971 when they were confined to states and one Union territory. Madhya Pradesh has always secured maximum tickets for women except in 1971. The largest number of independent candidates has come from Uttar Pradesh Bihar and Rajasthan. The rest of the parties have put up women candidates largely in their strongholds - BJP in Uttar Pradesh CPM in Kerala and West Bengal and erstwhile SSP in Bihar and Uttar Pradesh. Madhya Pradesh has also been favoured by most of these parties in terms of putting up a women candidate. The average of women contestants to Lok Sabha per seat is 0.30 per cent. Average share among contestants is 3.2 per cent and the success ratio is 28.5 per cent Table IV.

Notwithstanding a few exceptions, the women contestants have been found poorly, in articulate, in overall perspective and the issues pertaining to the particular contests. They have heavily depended upon either the party machine or the hands of loyal men workers in conducting their respective election campaigns, and after taken recourse to emotional and sentimental appeals to establish rapport with the voters. In 1989, 29 women were elected to Lok Sabha while in 1991 the number was 33 and in 1996 it was 38. In 1998, it increased to 40 (see Table III).

Women elected to Lok Sabha

From 1952 to 1967, the percentage of women who contested and won was much higher than the men — 45.09, 65.05, 52.30; and for males it was 25.50, 39.54 and 25.95. In 1971, there was a sharp fall to 24.41 per cent from 46.96, rose slightly to 27 per cent in 77 to fall again to 19.71 per cent in 1980. It improved slightly to 25.6 per cent in 1984. Since there has been a steady decline in the percentage, successful women candidates in relation to the number of female contestants—13.6 per cent in 1989, 12.00 per cent in 1991 and 6.88 per cent in 1996. In 1998 it was 72 per cent (see Table III).

The percentage of women in the Lok Sabha in relation

to the total number of seats has been very low, from 4.4 per cent in 1952 it increased slightly in 1957 (5.4 per cent) in 1962 (6.7 per cent), 1967 (5.9 per cent) to fall again to 4.2 per cent in 1971, 3.4 per cent (the lowest) in 1977 to increase slightly to 8.1 per cent in 1984 to fall again to 5.2 per cent in 1989. There has been a slight improvement in 1991, 1996 and 1998 (see Table III).

It is ironical that although the success rate of female contestant has invariably been higher in relation to males, they are still a very small percentage of the total number of contestants and so their presence in the Lok Sabha is small, not even 9 per cent. The difference between male and female contestants is very high, hence, the gap is very wide. Therefore, although the number of female contestants has increased over the years, it is still a very small percentage of the total, and thus, despite their high success rate their presence in the Lok Sabha is negligible (see Table IV). *Women is Rajya Sabha*: The presence of women in the Rajya Sabha is much better. Till 1996, while women were only 6 per cent is Lok Sabha, on an average the percentage of women MPs in the Rajya Sabha has been 10.3 per cent. However, it has to be noted that women also of through nominations to the Rajya Sabha. Many of them have not fought electoral battles (see Table V).

Many factors are responsible for this state of affairs the ideology of the Gandhi-Nehru era has totally disappeared. Elections have become very costly and expensive and most of the female aspirants cannot muster enough funds for fighting elections. Added to these are the extreme criminalisation of politics, excessive use of muscle and money power. Politics is a dirty game and many women do not wish to enter it. The support of political parties could do wonders, but all major political parties are reluctant to put up female candidates despite the high rate of their success in elections. For example in the 1998 elections in Bihar, BJP had put up two female candidates and both won.

It is true that women suffer from economic dependency, illiteracy and, a particular image of the self nurtured through the socialisation process, and these factor, also influence their entry into the election process. The gender bias of the political parties adds to it. With the backing of a strong party, a woman candidate can also win elections—Rita Verma has won thrice since 1991 on BJP ticket from Bihar. Same was the case of Alka Nath from Madhya Pradesh.

The fact remains that unless in Dehlerup's word, they become a 'critical mass', that is, by having 30 per cent to 40 per cent seats in the House, things are not going to change.

Women is Legislative Assemblies

In the period from 1952-57, the percentage of women in states, Legislative Assemblies has certainly not impressive. Delhi as an average of 5-9 per cent women representatives. Next comes Madhya Pradesh with an average of 5.1 per cent. The lowest average is found in Nagaland with 0.5 per cent (see Table VI).

Table gives a picture of the women contestants in Vidhan Sabhas. The average of women Contestants per seat is 0.19 per cent. The 6 per cent of share among contestants is 2.8. The average success ratio of women contestants is 21.0 per cent. The statewise percentage of women contestants is given in (see Table VII).

Impact of Women on Electoral Politics

Inspite of mafia politics, money and muscle power, Indian women have come on the political agenda of the country through the technique of collective action cousciousness — raising programmes, petitioning and lobbying. Many struggles in Karnataka did result in the implementation of a 30 per cent reservation for women at the local and state level in early and mid-80s. Thus, all is not lost. Glimmering of hope can be seen in the determined efforts made by women of progressive social organisations and movement to challenge vested interests (caste, class and gender) and make a determined bid for power.[22]

Women issues and demands have found a place in election manifestoes of almost all the parties in the 1990s. The demand for 33 per cent reservation for women was taken account of in the 1991 election manifestoes, but not complied with in 1996 elections. The bill for 33 per cent reservation for women in the Lok Sabha and the state legislature was placed before the Lok Sabha as the 86th Amendment to the Constitution in September 1996, but could not be passed. Male members cutting across party lines joined hands in ridiculing the bill, despite intense lobbying by women MPs of all parties and their threat to boycott the Lok Sabha session until. The bill is passed, the Bill has yet to see the light of the day. In the 1998 elections, all Parties—from Congress to BJP to RJD pledged the implementation of 33 per cent reservation to women. There is a strong demand both from inside Lok Sabha and outside by women activists to implement the demand by passing the women's reservation bill immediately. As Pramila Dandvate had remarked in one of her interviews to the *Hindustan Times* in December 1996 that the male MPs are afraid of losing 1/3 sats in the Lok Sabha, and what it would do to their patriarchal authority and control over the Lok Sabha proceeding. The bill could not be even placed on the table in 1998 under the Vajpayee government. The RJD and the Samajwadi Party chief Mulayam Singh and Laloo Prasad Yadav displayed utter disregard for parliamentary decorum document was torn into shred this is how women are made to remain in the margin of politics. Due to their scarce representation in Lok Sabha, their voice can hardly he hard. They are often pushed to the wall and gradually become a silent minority.

Women's movement had till recently taken an indifferent interest in election process, but with the debate on reservation of seats for women in the legislative bodies, some interest has been created which is reflected in the mobilisation of women's group during election campaign, etc. Some groups in Pune made a united front that is the Stree Mukti Andolan Sampark Samiti. The Krantikari Mahila Sangathan (KMS) of Pune has been actively involved in electoral politics. It has put up candidates independently or jointly with political parties like the Republican Party of India, Janata Dal or with social action groups[23] as in Mumbai. This organisation, which came into existence in the early 1980s, has grown considerably and has branches in other cities outside Pune. It is involved at two levels — contesting elections at grassroot level, and participating in election campaign for raising consciousness.[24]

There are many women's groups in Ahmedabad, Pune and Bangalore, which have prepared women's manifestoes. They conduct exposure programmes on 'Know the Candidate' and leaflets concerning women's issues such as exposing a candidate who has a criminal involvement in murder, rape or molestation cases.

In Bangalore, Vemochana, a women's group campaign against such candidates, who have committed violence against women, by organising street corner meetings, writing in newspapers and issuing leaflets as a result of its campaign, many a candidate lost elections. The campaign against the gangrape of a Kasthakari Sangathana activist by CPI (M) Cadres resulted in the CPI(M) candidate losing his Lok Sabha election.[25]

The Nari Samata Manch, another feminist group in Pune, though small in size, has also tried to address itself to the issue of electoral politics. Putting up candidates for elections is beyond their capacity, but they considered it important to mobilise and educate women voters.[26]

Nevertheless, the issue is of grave concern for democratic politics all over the world. Worldwide the representation of women in single or lower national assemblies in 1997— including authoritarian and long-standing democratic countries — was 11.6 per cent. The range was from 0 per cent in Comoras, Djbouti, Kiribati, Micronesia, Palan, Papua New Guinea and Tonga to 40.4 per cent in Sweden in 1997.

At the United Nations Fourth World Conference on women, a commitment to achieve women's equal representation in parliaments and other governmental bodies was made by unanimous vote on September 15, 1995. One hundred and eighty eight nations participated in the conference held at Beijing in China. The delegates not only pledged to seek equality in governmental decision-making for women, but also specified in their plan of action how nations might achieve it. These included governmental review of electoral systems and adjustment or reforms of them, and positive-affirmative action by political parties to nominate and elect women. Following up on the United Nation's Universal Declaration of Human Rights, which specifies that every citizen has the right to participate in the government, the Beijing Conference adopted this statement—'Women's rights are human rights.'[27] Therefore, women are entitled as a matter of simple justice and democracy, the delegates stated, to all political rights now afforded to men.

At the Beijing Conference stress was laid on two factors—electoral reforms and positive/affirmative action by political parties.

Proportional Representation and Women's Elections

In long-standing democracies, proportional representation has been repeatedly documented as the most significant factor among contextual variables, explaining women's election to Parliament (Rule 1981, 1987, 1994 Norris 1985, 1997).[34] Wilma Rule through her studies has derived the correlation between proportional representation (PR) and women's election to Parliament. Her study revealed that the party list proportional representation countries were generally higher regarding women's recruitment to legislatures of single member plurality/majority countries. She maintains of a 10 candidate constituency gives a women a greater chance for party nomination than does a lower magnitude of three or more. It allow the electorate to choose on an open party list. The preference vote has been used successfully in Finland and Denmark.

Rule gives her observations on updated percentage of women's parliamentary representation in long-standing democracies in 1993 and 1997, and remarks that there has been an upward swing. The three major explanations are: (i) Political party quotas or goals to nominate an increased percentage of women to Parliament in PR countries; (ii) Laws requiring that a proportion (quota) of women be placed on party list in PR countries; and, (iii) Electoral system change from single member plurality to proportional representation. The first measure was adopted just by Denmark, Finland, Norway and Sweden with great success in the 1980s. The same happened in Spain in 1996 elections and Great Britain in 1997 elections. The second strategy was adopted in Italy after the 1992 elections. A new election law provided that ¼ of Italian Parliament was to be elected from party list and the remainder from single member districts. In 1994 elections the success of women on party list was 33 per cent but it was only 9 per cent in the case of single member constituency election. The third approach resulted in New Zealands rank as the sixth highest nation in women's parliamentary representation among long-standing democracies by 1997.[35]

There is an urgent need of electoral reforms in India. The abovementioned strategies, which yielded very good results in long-standing democracies, could be tested in this country too.

The proportional representation facilitates quicker change than a single member majority/plurality system.[28] It is easier for a political party to add women to its list for 10 constituencies averaging ten contestants. Then it is to change 100 single member majority or plurality constituencies from male to female representatives.

The laws requiring a quota of women to be nominated on party list provide that women's name be positioned so that they could be elected if their party won sufficient votes in the election.

Election laws may be changed to provide for proportional representation in place of single member constituency.

Positive action in the form of laws to ensure proper representation of women in Parliaments have been proposed by nine developing countries, which have a majority/ plurality system. A bill for providing 33 per cent reservation to women in the Lok Sabha and state Legislative Assemblies in India was introduced in the Lok Sabha in September

1996 and 1998, but despite much publicity, debates and discussions, it has still to see the light of the day.

Dehlerup Drude (1986) has suggested several measures which when adopted could assists in augmenting women's place in political life. This included changing electoral laws (for instance, proportional election system tended to be more favourable to women than election system with single member constituencies) women's political parties (*successful use in Iceland in 1983*), and public campaigns to bring more women into politics.[29] Political parties should evolve a system of 'revolving funds' to finance women contestants.

The most important is to sensitise political parties towards gender issues. Laws should be made to make it obligatory for political parties to nominate a percentage of women in their list of contestants. If the 1996 and 1998 elections are any pointer, political parties in India have failed miserably on this score, despite their commitments as reflected in their party manifestoes in 1991, 1996 and 1998 elections. The opposition directed towards the 33 per cent reservation bill for women by almost all major political parties reflects the male antagonism towards the entry of women in politics.

It becomes imperative for liberal democratic governments on the one hand to go ahead with electoral reforms and seriously provide for their implementation, and on the other hand, it becomes a responsibility of women's organisations and movement to exert pressure for the same, especially in the wake of the Beijing Conference of 1995. According to Bernis Lot "power generates power and powerlessness generates powerlessness. Because the society is patriarchal where men hold power, more power will always be given to men, and women will be made powerless, incapable, on the margin. This is a reminder to the fact that women's under representation in legislative bodies all over the globe with the possible exception of Nordic and Scandenevian countries is a matter of grave concern for the future of democracy. Also, the status of women's rights. The right to political participation is a human right.

Table-I

General Elections in India 1952-58

Years	Electors			Voters			% of Votes		Per cent of difference in votes polled by male and female
	M	F	T	M	F	T	M	F	
1952	96267500	77946135	173213635	50975932	29733270	80709202	55.0	37.18	17.9
1957	102205638	91446431	193652069	5992441	35405424	91329685	56.0	39.6	16.4
1962	113944234	102427981	216372215	70703050	47764170	118467220	62.1	46.6	15.5
1967	130423737	120173708	250597445	86460463	66264048	152724511	65.7	55.5	11.2
1971	143474831	130619662	274094493	87382907	64153895	151536802	69.7	66.0	9.7
1977	167019151	15415576	32174327	109609940	84653975	194263955	65.62	55.09	10.77
1980	185270315	170380385	355590700	115133649	87271764	202405413	62.16	51.22	10.94
1984	196730499	182810109	379540608	134122962	107123935	241246887	63.61	68.17	4.56
1989	262045142	236861287	498906429	173291744	135758755	309050509	70.90	43.90	2.7
1991	261832499	236531302	498363801	161254832	121479655	282725847	52.56	47.42	5.14
1996	309815776	282756512	592572288	192279727	151028308	343308035	62.06	53.41	5.65
1998	316692628	289191475	605884103	208117527	167336507	37454034	65.71	57.86	7.8

Source: Statistical Profile of Women in India-1997.

For 1998: Report of Election Commission 1998.

Table-II

Minimum and Maximum Mobilisation of Women Voters

Sl. No.	Minimum	Percent-age	Maximum	Percent-age
		1962		
1.	Orissa	13.25	Kerala	67.08
2.	Himachal Pradesh	22.04	Tamil Nadu	64.55
3.	Madhya Pradesh	28.90	Andhra Pradesh	60.31
4.	Bihar	32.96	Punjab	58.15
5.	Assam	37.23	Maharashtra	54.29
		1967		
1.	Orissa	33.05	Kerala	74.20
2.	Bihar	40.74	Tamil Nadu	73.94
3.	Madhya Pradesh	42.48	Haryana	69.19
4.	Himachal Pradesh	44.05	Punjab	68.43
5.	Uttar Pradesh	48.96	Andhra Pradesh	65.29
		1971		
1.	Himachal Pradesh	33.38	Tamil Nadu	69.17
2.	Orissa	33.74	Kerala	63.30
3.	Bihar	37.01	Haryana	60.48
4.	Madhya Pradesh	37.59	West Bengal	58.74
5.	Uttar Pradesh	38.84	Maharashtra	56.12
		1977		
1.	Orissa	36.67	Kerala	79.61
2.	Madhya Pradesh	45.13	Haryana	70.39
3.	Jammu & Kashmir	47.69	Punjab	69.25
4.	Assam	47.80	Tamil Nadu	65.43
5.	Uttar Pradesh	49.02	Andhra Pradesh	58.57
		1980		
1.	Orissa	38.78	West Bengal	68.18
2.	Madhya Pradesh	41.50	Tamil Nadu	63.34
3.	Uttar Pradesh	43.22	Kerala	60.77
4.	Bihar	43.91	Punjab	60.21
5.	Assam	44.67	Haryana	59.61

Sl. No.	*Minimum*	*Percent-age*	*Maximum*	*Percent-age*
		1984		
1.	Orissa	48.60	Manipur	90.00
2.	Madhya Pradesh	48.63	Lakshadweep	89.30
3.	Rajasthan	49.13	Andaman & Nicobar	78.32
4.	Bihar	49.18	Kerala	77.92
5.	Uttar Pradesh	50.48	Dadra & N. Haveli	75.16
		1989		
1.	Jammu & Kashmir	21.18	Lakshadweep	89.43
2.	Madhya Pradesh	46.73	Tripura	81.87
3.	Gujarat	49.01	Kerala	79.68
4.	Meghalaya	49.70	West Bengal	76.92
5.	Rajasthan	49.83	Nagaland	75.70
		1991		
1.	Madhya Pradesh	35.31	Lakshadweep	85.38
2.	Gujarat	37.05	Nagaland	78.17
3.	Goa	38.94	West Bengal	74.88
4.	Rajasthan	39.35	Sikkim	74.63
5.	Maharashtra	43.10	Assam	73.26
		1996		
1.	Gujarat	29.64	Lakshadweep	91.35
2.	Rajasthan	36.71	Nagaland	85.47
3.	Jammu & Kashmir	39.09	West Bengal	80.86
4.	Uttar Pradesh	41.03	Dadra & N Haveli	79.00
5.	Madhya Pradesh	46.97	Goa	77.50
		1998		
1.	Jammu & Kashmir	39.23	Lakshadweep	87.70
2.	Nagaland	43.07	Dadra & N Haveli	79.50
3.	Delhi	48.52	West Bengal	77.50
4.	Uttar Pradesh	50.33	Daman & Diu	75.34
5.	Chandigarh	52.93	Meghalaya	74.92

Sources: Report of the Election Commission

Table-III

Lok Sabha Elections-1952-1998 (The Gender luers)

Year	Total Seats	Total No. Contes-tants	Male		Women		% of elected		Difference of % M.F.	Per cent of women in Lok Sabha
			Total No.	Elected	Total No.	Elected	Male	Female		
1952	489	1874	1831	475	57	23	—	—	94.55	4.4
1957	494	1518	1415	467	45	27	31.7	60.0	94.60	5.4
1962	494	1935	2915	459	70	35	24.0	50.0	93.45	6.7
1967	520	2369	2302	490	67	30	21.3	44.8	94.34	5.9
1971	520	2784	2698	499	86	21	18.5	24.4	—	—
1977	542	2439	2369	523	70	19	22.1	27.1	93.82	3.4
1980	542	4620	4478	514	142	28	11.5	19.7	93.82	5.1
1984	542	5574	5406	500	164	42	9.2	25.6	90.23	8.1
1989	529	6160	5692	502	198	27	8.5	13.6	94.17	5.2
1991	521	8699	8374	492	325	39	5.9	12.0	93.82	7.16
1996	543	13952	13353	504	599	39	3.77	6.68	90.23	7.18
1998	543	4693	4438	503	255	40	11.3	15.6	79.5	7.2

Table-IV

Women Contestants in Lok Sabha Elections 1952-1996

Year	*Contestants per seat*	*Share among contestants (%)*	*Sucess ratio (%)*
1952	0.10	2.7	43.1
1957	0.14	4.4	38.6
1962	0.14	3.4	50.0
1967	0.13	2.8	47.0
1977	0.13	2.9	27.1
1978	0.17	3.1	25.6
1980	0.26	3.1	19.1
1984	0.29	2.9	27.7
1989	0.37	3.1	14.3
1991	0.60	3.7	12.0
1996	0.90	3.4	7.9
Average	0.30	3.2	28.5

Note for Table 3, 4, 5: Contestants per seat=number of women contestants/total number of seats.

Share among candidates=number of women contestants/number of all contestants ×100.

Table-V

Women's Representation in Parliament 1952-1996

Years	Lok Sabha			Rajya Sabha*		
	Seats	Womens MPs	Percentage of Women MPs	Seats	Womens MPs	Percentage of Women MPs
1952	499	22	4.4	219	16	7.3
1957	500	27	5.4	237	18	7.5
1962	503	34	6.8	238	18	7.6
1967	523	31	5.9	240	20	8.3
1977	544	19	3.4	244	25	10.2
1978	521	22	4.2	243	17	7.0
1980	544	28	7.9	244	24	9.8
1984	544	44	8.1	244	28	11.4
1989	517	27	5.3	245	24	9.7
1991	544	39	7.2	245	38	15.5
1996	543	39	7.2	223	20	9.0
Average	526	30	6.0	238	23	10.3

* The composition of Rajya Sabha change every two years. We have picked up only those years which allow comparison with Lok Sabha. The average for Rajya Sabha is based on these years only.

Table-VI

Women's Representation in State Legislature 1952-1997 (Percentage of Women MLAs)

States	*1952***	*1957*	*1960-65*	*1967-69*	*1970-75*	*1977-78*	*1979-83*	*1984-88*	*1989-92*	*1993-97*	*State Avg.*
Andhra Pradesh	2.9	3.7	3.3	3.8	9.1	3.4	4.1	3.4	3.7	2.7	4.0
Arunachal Pradesh	—	—	—	—	—	0.0	3.3	6.7	3.3	3.3	3.3
Assam	0.5	4.6	3.8	4.0	7.0	0.8	0.8	4.0	4.0	4.8	3.2
Bihar	3.6	9.4	7.9	2.2*	3.8	4.0	3.7	4.6	2.8	3.4	4.3
Goa	—	—	—	6.7	3.3	3.3	0.0	0.0	5.0	10.0	4.3
Gujarat	—	—	8.4	4.8	3.2	NE	2.7	8.8	2.2	1.1	4.2
Haryana	—	—	—	7.4*	6.2	4.4	7.8	5.6	6.7	4.4	6.2
Himachal Pradesh	0.0	—	—	0.0	5.9	1.5	4.4	4.4	5.9	4.4	3.6
Jammu & Kashmir	—	NE	0.0	0.0	5.3	1.3	0.0	1.3	NE	2.3	1.5
Karnataka	2.0	8.7	8.7	3.2	5.1	4.0	0.9	3.6	4.5	3.1	4.5
Kerala	0.0	4.8	3.9*	0.8	1.5	0.7	3.2	5.7	5.7	9.3	3.6
Madhya Pradesh	2.1	10.8	4.9	3.4	5.4	3.1	5.6	9.7	3.4	3.8	5.1
Maharashtra	1.9	6.3	4.9	3.3	9.3	2.8	6.6	5.6	2.1	3.8	4.7
Manipur	—	NE	NE	0.0	0.0*	NE	0.0	0.0	1.7	0.0	0.3
Meghalaya	—	—	—	—	1.7	1.7	0.0	3.3	NE	1.7	1.7

Mizoram	—	—	—	—	0.0	3.3	3.3	2.5	0.0	0.0	1.4
Nagaland	—	—	0.0	0.0	NE	0.0	0.0	1.7	0.0	0.0	0.5
Orissa	9.6	3.6	1.4	3.6	1.4*	4.8	3.4	6.1	4.8	5.4	4.0
Punjab	2.2	5.8	5.2	1.0*	5.8	2.6	5.1	3.4	5.1	6.0	4.0
Rajasthan	0.0	5.1	4.5	3.3	7.1	4.0	5.0	8.0	5.5	4.5	4.8
Sikkim	—	—	—	—	—	—	0.0	0.0	6.3	3.1	2.3
Tamil Nadu	0.3	5.9	3.9	1.7	2.1	0.9	2.1	3.4	9.0	3.8	3.6
Tripura	—	NE	NE	0.0	3.3	1.7	6.7	3.3	NE	1.7	3.0
Uttar Pradesh	1.2	5.8	4.4	2.8*	5.9	2.6	5.6	7.3	3.3*	4.0*	4.1
West Bengal	0.8	3.6	4.8	2.9	1.6*	1.4	2.4	4.4	7.1	6.8	3.4
Delhi	4.2	—	NE	NE	7.1	7.1	7.1	NE	NE	4.3	5.9
Pondicherry	—	—	6.7	3.3	0.0	0.0	3.3	3.3	1.7	3.3	2.6
Period Average	1.8	6.3	4.9	2.9	4.4	2.8	3.8	5.3	4.5	4.0	4.0

Notes: Table entry stands for % of women MLAs elected to state legislatures in the relevant elections.

States did not exist;

NE: No elections held in that year/period;

* : Two elections held during this period. The figure given here is an average of the two;

* : In 1952 the Election Commission did not recognise women as a separate category. The figures given here are based on name recognition and hence liable to under-reporting of women representatives.

Table-VII

Women Contestants in State Assembly Elections 1952-1996

Years	*Contestants per seat*	*Share among contestants (%)*	*Success ratio (%)*
1952	0.10	2.7	43.1
1952	0.06	1.2	31.4
1957	0.11	3.1	58.0
1965	0.10	2.4	48.8
1967-69	0.08	1.6	35.3
1970-75	0.12	2.5	36.1
1977-78	0.15	2.4	18.5
1979-83	0.16	2.5	23.6
1984-88	0.26	3.1	20.3
1989-92	0.38	3.2	11.8
1993-97	0.47	3.8	8.7
Average	0.19	2.8	21.0

Table-VIII

Women Contestants in State Assembly Elections: State-wise Averages 1952-1996

States	*Contestants per seat*	*Share among contestants (%)*	*Sucess ratio (%)*
Andhra Pradesh	0.18	3.5	22.0
Arunachal Pradesh	0.07	2.4	46.7
Assam	0.14	2.3	22.4
Bihar	0.20	2.4	16.7
Goa	0.19	3.0	22.7
Gujarat	0.18	2.7	20.9
Haryana	0.36	2.8	17.3
Himachal Pradesh	0.17	3.1	21.7
Jammu & Kashmir	0.09	1.8	16.3
Karnataka	0.23	3.9	19.7
Kerala	0.13	2.7	27.5
Madhya Pradesh	0.20	3.0	25.2
Maharashtra	0.20	3.3	18.3
Manipur	0.08	1.4	2.9
Meghalaya	0.11	2.5	14.7
Mizoram	0.09	1.8	16.7
Nagaland	0.03	0.5	14.3
Orissa	0.16	2.8	25.9
Punjab	0.16	2.9	25.2
Rajasthan	0.20	2.7	24.6
Sikkim	0.28	4.8	8.3
Tamil Nadu	0.19	2.6	18.9
Tripura	0.13	3.0	22.7
Uttar Pradesh	0.28	2.6	14:8
West Bengal	0.12	2.6	27.8
Delhi	0.35	4.1	17.2
Pondicherry	0.18	3.7	14.3

Note : The figures stand for average of the relevant indicator for all elections held in that state from 1952 to 1997.

Table-IX (a)

Partywise Position of Women in the Vth Lok Sabha Election

Name of the Party	*Total No. of seats*	*Total No. of candidates who constested election*			*Total No. of elected persons*		
		Male	*Female*	*Total*	*Male*	*Female*	*Total*
Indian National Congress	519	420 95.24%	21 4.76%	441	337 80.23%	15 17.42%	352
Bharatiya Jansangh	—	157 98.12%	3 1.87%	160	20 12.73%	02 66.66%	22
Communist Party of India	—	84 96.56%	3 3.44%	87	22 26.19%	1 33.33%	23
Communist Party of India (Marxist)	—	83 97.65%	2 2.35%	85	24 28.91%	1 50%	25
Swantra Party	—	51 91.07%	5 8.92%	56	7 13.72%	1 20%	8
PSP	—	62 9.24%	1 1.58%	63	2 3.22%	—	2
SSP	—	90 96.77%	3 3.23%	93	3 3.33%	—	3
Independent	—	1.104 97.36%	30 2.64%	1,134	13 1.17%	1 0.90%	14
Congress O & Others	—	220 92.44%	18 7.56%	238	16 7.27%	—	16

Table-IX (b)

Partywise Position of Women in the VIth Lok Sabha Elections

Name of the party	*Total No. of seats*	*Total No. of candidates who contested election*			*Total No. of elected persons*		
		Male	*Female*	*Total*	*Male*	*Female*	*Total*
Indian National Congress	542	470 95.52%	22 4.47%	492	147 31.21%	7 31.81%	154
Lok Dal/Janata	—	382 94.32%	13 3.20%	405	286 74.86%	9 69.23%	295
Communist Party of India	—	88 6.70%	3 3.29%	91	6 6.81%	1 16.66%	7
Independent	—	1200 98.03%	25 2.04%	1225	9 0.75%	—	9
Communist Party	—	51 96.22%	2 3.77%	53	20 39.21%	2 100%	22
Congress (O)	—	19 100%	—	19	3 15.78%	—	3

Table-IX (c)

Partywise Position of Women in the VIIth Lok Sabha Elections

Name of the party	*Total No. of seats*	*Total No. of Candidates who contested election*			*Total No. of elected persons*		
		Male	*Female*	*Total*	*Male*	*Female*	*Total*
Congress (I)	542	360 91.83%	32 8.16%	392	334 92.77%	19 59.37%	353
Congress (U)	—	202 95.28%	10 4.72%	212	13 6.43%	—	13
Janata Party	—	412 5.37%	20 4.62%	432	29 7.05%	2 10%	31
Janata Party Secular	—	184 6.58%	10 3.42%	294	39 13.78%	2 20%	41
Communist Party	—	46 95.83%	2 4.17%	48	10 21.73%	1 50%	11
Communist Party of India (Marxist)	—	60 95.23%	3 4.77%	63	34 56.66%	2 66.66%	36
Independents	—	2161 7.29%	60 2.71%	2221	8 0.32%	1 1.66%	9
Others	—	255 98.07%	5 1.93%	260	34 13.33%	1 0.39%	35

Source: Election Commission Reports.

Table-IX (d)

Partywise Position of Women in the VIIth Lok Sabha Elections

Name of the party	Total No. of seats	Total No. of Candidates who constested elections			Total No. of elected candidates		
		Male	Female	Total	Male	Female	Total
Congress (I)	509	446 86.31%	39 13.69%	485	363	37 94.87%	401
Janata Party	—	202 98.05%	04 1.95%	206	10 4.95%	—	10
Bhartiya Janata Party	—	214 95.96%	09 4.04%	223	02 0.93%	—	02
Communist Party of India (Marxist)	—	58 96.66%	02 3.34%	60	09 8.62%	01 50%	06
Communist Party of India (Marxist)	—	57 95%	03 5%	60 (36.84%)	21 36.84%	01 33.33%	22
D.M.K.P./L.K.D.	—	164 96.47%	06 3.53%	170	03 1.82%	—	03
Independents and Others	—	4112 97.76%	94 2.24%	4206	58 1.41%	03 3.19%	61

Source: Mirchandani, C.G. & Murthi, K.S. 1984 Lok Sabha Elections: Massive Mandate for Rajiv Gandhi; UNI-DCM Computerbased study, New Delhi-1985.

Table-IX (c)

Partywise Position of Women in the IXth Lok Sabha Elections 1989

Name of the party	*Total No. of seats*	*Total No. of candidates who constested election*			*Total No. of elected persons*		
		Male	*Female*	*Total*	*Male*	*Female*	*Total*
National Parties	529						
Congress (INC)	—	456	54	510	183	14	197
Janata Dal	—	239	5	244	141	2	143
Bharatiya Janata Party (BJP)	—	216	10	226	80	5	85
Communist Party of India (CPI)	—	47	2	49	11	1	12
Communist Party Marxist (CPM)	—	60	4	64	31	2	33
ICS (SCS)	—	14	0	14	1	0	1
JNP (JP)	—	152	4	156	0	0	0
Lok Dal (B)	—	113	4	117	0	0	0
National parties Total	—	1298	90	1380	447	24	471
State parties Total	—	140	3	143	270	27	
Registered parties Total	—	896	29	925	16	3	19
Independents Total	—	3630	82	3712	12	0	12
Grand Total:		5963	197	6160	502	27	529

Total No. of female candidates — 197;

Total No. of elected candidates — 27

Report of the Election Commission 1989.

Table-IX (f)

Partywise Position of Women in the Xth Lok Sabha Elections 1991

Name of the party	*Total No. of seats*	*Total No. of candidates who contested election*			*Total No. of elected persons*		
		Male	*Female*	*Total*	*Male*	*Female*	*Total*
National Parties	521						
Indian National Congress (INC)	—	421	47	468	212	20	232
Bharatiya Janata Party (BJP)	—	464	28	492	110	10	120
CPM	—	57	3	60	33	2	35
CPI	—	39	3	42	13	1	14
ICS (SCS)	—	26	2	28	1	0	1
Janata Dal (JD)	—	295	12	307	57	2	59
Janata Dal (S)	—	10	0	10	0	0	0
Janata Party (JP)	—	326	19	345	5	0	5
Lok Dal (LKD)	—	74	4	78	0	0	0
National parties	—	1712	118	1830	431	35	466
State parties	—	465	24	489	48	2	50
Registered parties	—	814	29	843	4	0	4
Independents	—	5383	154	5537	1	0	1
Total		8374	325	8699	484	37	521

Total No. of female candidates — 325;

Total No. of elected candidates — 37

Source: Report of the Election Commission, 1991.

Table-IX (g)

Partywise Position of women in the XIth Lok Sabha Elections 1996

Name of the Party	*Total No. of seats*	*Total No. of Candidates who contested election*			*Total No. of Elected persons*		
		Male	*Female*	*Total*	*Male*	*Female*	*Total*
INC	543	480	49	529	124	16	140
BJP	471	441	27	471	147	16	161
AIIC (T)	321	299	22	321	4	0	4
CPI	43	40	3	43	11	1	12
CPM	75	70	5	75	31	1	32
JD	196	185	11	196	42	4	46
JP	102	98	4	102	0	0	0
SAP	81	77	4	81	8	0	8
National parties	1818	1693	125	1818	367	36	403
State parties	451	433	18	451	123	4	127
Registered parties	1048	1016	32	1048	4	0	4
Independents	10635	10211	424	10635	9	0	9
Total	24952	22353	599	24952	503	40	543

Total No. of female candidates — 599

Total No. of electes candidates — 43

Source: Report of the Election Commission, 1996.

Table-IX (h)

Partywise Position of women in the XIIth Lok Sabha Elections 1998

Name of the Party	*Total No. of seats*	*Total No. of candidates who contested election*			*Total No. of elected persons*		
		Male	*Female*	*Total*	*Male*	*Female*	*Total*
Congress (I)	543	435	38	477	141	10	151
Janta Dal	—	181	10	191	6	0	6
B J P	—	356	32	388	182	15	197
C P I	—	52	6	58	9	2	11
C P M	—	63	8	71	32	3	35
B S P	—	241	10	251	4	1	5
S A P	—	54	3	57	12	0	12
National Parties		1386	107	1493	356	31	387
State Parties		445	26	473	95	6	101
Registered Parties		807	64	871	44	5	49
Independents		1838	77	1898	5	1	6
Total		4476	274	4750	500	43	543

Total No. of Female Candidateed — 274

Total No. of Elected — 43

Source: Report of the Election Commission, 1998.

References

1. Nelson, Barbara, *Women and Knowledge* in *Political Science-Texts*, Histories and Epistemologies, *Women and Politics* 9 (Spring 1989) pp. 1-25.
2. Coolie, M Diana, *Women in Political Theory from Ancient Misogyny to Contemporary Feminism* (Introduction) Wheatsheaf, Sussex 1988.
3. This has been the running theme of the work by Simon De Behaviour *The Second Sex* English translation by Parsel M.M., Penguin, 1987.
4. Dahl, Rober A., *Democracy and its Critics*, New Haven, Yale University Press, 1987.
5. *Democracy Still in the Making* (Geneva Inter-Parliamentary Union, 1997) p. 28.
6. *Ibid.*, p. 102-105.
7. *Nai Duniya* (Daily newspaper) Indore, April 1996, p. 8.
8. Muni, S.D., Women in Electoral Process in Vina Majumdar (ed) *Symbols* of *Power*, Allied Publishers Pvt. Ltd. 1979, p. 26.
9. *Ibid* p. 28.
10. *Ibid* p. 28.
11. *Ibid* p. 31.
12. *Ibid* p. 31.
13. *Ibid* p. 32.
14. *Towards Equality*, Report of the Committee on the Status of Women in India, Government of India 1974, pp. 95-101.
15. Kaushik, Susheela, 'Women and Political Participation' in *Women in Politics: Forms and Processes*, published by Friedrich Ebert Stiftung New Delhi, 1992.
16. *Ibid.*
17. *Op. cit.* Muni, p. 33.
18. *Ibid.*, p. 33.
19. *Ibid.*, p. 34.
20. Menon, Laxmi N., Political Rights of Women in India, UNESCO Seminar N-4
21. *Op cit.*, Muni pp. 34-35.

22. Kumari Ranjana in *Women in Politics: Forms and Processes* (Introduction), Published by F.E.S., New Delhi, 1992 pp. 6-7.
23. Pore Kumud, Women's Participation in Policy-making; in *A Note in Women in Politics: Forms and Processes.* F.E.S. pp 100-101.
24. *Ibid* p. 101-102.
25. *Op. cit.*, Ranjana Kumari, p. 7.
26. *Op. cit.*, Pore, p. 100.
27. Rule Wilma, Political Rights and Electoral Systems and the Legislative Representation of Women in 73 Democracies: A preliminary Analysis, Paper presented at IPSA World Congress, Seoul, 1997.
28. Norris, Pippa, 'Chasing Electoral Systems: Proportional, Majoritarian and Mixed System, International Political' in *Science Review*, 18, p. 310.
29. *Op. cit.*, Dahlerup.

8

PATTERNS OF WOMEN'S PARTICIPATION IN POLITICS: THE CASE OF HARYANA

Sharda Jain

The state of Haryana was carved out of the erstwhile composite Punjab on November 1, 1966 under Punjab Reorganisation Bill passed by Parliament on September 10, 1966.[1] At present, it comprises 17 districts[2] divided into 10 Parliamentary and 90 state Legislative Assembly constituencies. Though many oral traditional interpretations are given to define the word 'Haryana', the most logical one seems to be that the term stands for *Haryalee*, that is, greenery. The state has geographical boundaries marked by Shivaliks in the north and river Yamuna in the east. Chandigarh, which lies to its northwestern part, is the common capital of both Punjab and Haryana. Thus, surrounded by Punjab in the northwest, Himachal Pradesh in the north, Uttar Pradesh in the east, Rajasthan in the southwest and also being very close to Delhi, Haryana is sure to have cultural, social and linguistic influences of the neighbouring states, which can be clearly witnessed in the mode of living as well as social, cultural and linguistic patterns of its people.

Though Haryana was carved out of the much backward regions of Punjab, its agricultural and industrial progress has been phenomenal. Today, it is reckoned among the major progressive states of India, like Punjab, Gujarat and Maharashtra. Its net per capita gross domestic product (GDP) in 1990-91 was Rs 7,516, which was next only to that of Maharashtra and Punjab. Due to development efforts like 100 per cent electrification, improved irrigation network, better roads and enterprising farmers, Haryana has earned the status of being a frontline state of India. The state is not only surplus in foodgrains, it also makes available large quantities of food to the central pool to serve the needs of deficit states. Haryana is an important manufacturer of some major industrial goods too as its districts of Gurgoan and Faridabad are home to some major domestic and multinational industries.

The other socioeconomic developmental indices in Haryana show a positive trend though much remains to be done, particularly in the field of women's development. According to 1991 census, the total population of Haryana was 16,463,648 out of which 12,408,904 comprises of rural and 4,054,744 of urban population. The following Table shows the population profile of Haryana according to 1991 census.[3]

	Total Population	*Male*	*Female*
Total	16,463,648	8,827,474	7,636,174
Rural	12,408,904	6,657,334	5,751,570
Urban	4,054,744	2,170,140	1,884,604

The above Table shows that about 78.12 per cent of the population of Haryana resides in rural areas. Though there is a marginal increase in the female population of Haryana resides in rural areas. Though there is a marginal increase in the female population of the state over last decade, yet the sex ratio remains adverse due to neglect of women during childhood as well as in the later stages when they become child bearers, mothers of daughters or widows. Sex determination and abortion of female foetus is also responsible for high female infant mortality rate. Moreover, desire to have more than one male child also counts for increasingly adverse sex ratio in Haryana. Thus, male domination in this state, as is the case almost everywhere else, establishes the fact that the status of women has improved only marginally despite concerted efforts at all levels.

There is certainly an improvement in women's literacy level in India since Independence. Yet, female literacy rate in Haryana in 1991 was 40.47 per cent as against male literacy rate of 69.10 per cent. Out of a total of 148,582 enrolments from Haryana in Indian universities in 1995-96, 57,375, constituting 38.6 per cent, were those of women.[4] The school dropout rate of girls is alarmingly higher due to certain factors like non-availability of schools in villages, shortage of 'only for girls' schools, forcing girls to take care of siblings when mothers go out to work in fields, early marriages, and above all, society's attitude towards girl's education. These facts prove that girls are at a disadvantageous position vis-a-vis boys as far as education in Haryana is concerned.

Further, the economic position of women anywhere is an important determinant of their status in society, which in turn, determines their political status too. Haryana is basically an agricultural state where the women's contribution in terms of field workforce is remarkable with around 70 per cent of them working as cultivators and labourers. But, due to their invisibility in work, they are left of various developmental programmes.

Such a disadvantageous social and economic position of women in India as a whole as also in Haryana is largely responsible for their political segregation and alienation. Yet, despite a hostile environment of discrimination, inequity, attitudes and ideologies that has become more and more deep-rooted with every passing year of patriachal mind-sets, women all over India, including Haryana, are experiencing a change for better since 1947. Though the struggle for women's equality and rights has been long, during our national movement it was envisaged that women's participation as voters and their presence in decision-making bodies would contribute to social reforms and nation building. Although there was no struggle comparable to

British and American women's movements, Indian women pursued the issue of their political status with support of nationalist leadership, a factor that mattered so much with colonial masters. Hence, with the growing demands of nationalists for participation in local and national governing bodies, the question of women's political status also became urgent on national agenda.

While framing the fundamental laws of the land, the founding fathers of our Constitution gave due consideration to these long-standing demands of women for improving their all round condition. Women all over India, without any social or economic bias, were accorded equality of right and status as has been enshrined in Article 14, 15 and 16 of our Constitution in addition with the safeguards prescribed under the Directive Principles of State Policy. Numerous laws have been enacted and policies formulated thereafter to mainstream the marginalised women so as to give them a fair share in decision-making processes.

Yet, in reality, women's participation in decision-making in all social, economic and political organisations still remain highly fragile despite all constitutional and institutional safeguards. No political party has done much to give a justified share to women in decision-making despite the promises of 33 per cent reservation for women at party level. Only very few women are the members of various political parties. The fate of the much published women's reservation bill became victim of the rigid stand taken by some male chauvinists, who stood in the way of women getting what was long overdue to them. Though India had one of the most powerful woman Prime Ministers for nearly 17 long years and also has many women as Chief Ministers, it has yet to usher into a phase of mass political participation of women in decision-making bodies.

The Case of Haryana

The socioeconomic profile of the women in an orthodox and tradition-bound Haryana, as described earlier in previous pages, is a clear indication of their weak political status in decision-making bodies. However, their participation in political process can be categorised as voters, members of Legislative Assembly (MLAs), members of Parliament (MPs) and, since the adoption of the 73rd Amendment to the Constitution of India, as participants in local-self-government in rural areas (called Panchayati Raj system).

Like women all over India, the Haryana women have also enjoyed equal voting rights under a system of universal adult suffrage since Independence (as residents of Punjab state before 1966). However, it is doubtful that they exercise their voting rights independent of the direction, influence or pressure of their male family members who dominate almost every economic and political decision. Women being socially backward and economically dependent are not in a position to exercise their rights on their own choice. Moreover, illiteracy is also a big drawback and a hurdle in having a grasp over the nature of problems and other political issues. These problems apart, the Haryana women have participated in large numbers as listed electors and actual voters in Lok Sabha, state legislature and local bodies elections and have a say, direct or indirect, in decision-making progress.

As far as the Haryana women's representation in both houses of Parliament and in Haryana Legislative Assembly is concerned, the picture is as dismal as is that of women's representation on all-India level. The following statistical Tables would reveal the political participation of women of Haryana in various capacities at different levels of decision-making bodies.

Sex-wise Classification of Electors, Voters, Contestants and Elected Members to Lok Sabha from Haryana*, 1984, 1989, 1991, 1996

Year	*Electors** Male/Female*	*Voters*** Male/Female*	*Contested Male/Female*	*Elected Male/Female*
1984	4,142,218/ 3,583,368	2,918,080/ 2,215,719	190/10	10/0
1989	5,197,963/ 4,438,725	3,578,181/ 2,628,944	321/03	10/0

(Continued on next page)

(table Continued)

Year	Electors** Male/Female	Voters*** Male/Female	Contested Male/Female	Elected Male/Female
1991	5,242,284/ 4,483,613	3,608,869/ 2,974,927	192/06	09/01
1996	6,005,913/ 5,146,943	4,321,738/ 3,539,125	285/09	09/01

Source: Election Commission of India

* There are 10 seats in Lok Sabha from Haryana.

** Electors are persons registered for casting vote.

*** Voters are persons who actually cast their vote.

Sex-wise Classification of Rajya Sabha Members from Haryana 1994, 1996*

Year	Total	Male	Female
1994	05	03	02
1996	05	05	00

Women MLAs in Haryana 1987-88, 1991-92*

Year	Total Male/Female	Contested Male/Female	Elected
1987-88	90	1,287/35	85/05
1991-92	90	1,844/41	84/06

Source: Election Commission of India.

These Tables show how limited is women's representation in various representative organs from Haryana. Only one woman from Haryana out of 10 seats in Lok Sabha and that too 25 years after the formation of the state is quite a disturbing phenomenon though such is the trend everywhere in India. Rajya Sabha seems to be better represented by women. Gender discrimination rules the scene even in state legislature, where women constitute a very small percentage vis-a-vis men. Even the elected women are not always very articulate and their interventions are generally confined to the issues related with women and their welfare though these issues are certainly of great importance. Their participation in elections depends on the mobilisation of political parties, general awareness among the community about voting and the prevalent political culture in a particular area. Unfortunately, no serious effort has as yet been made to mobilise women as a political constituency by any political party. The reluctance of political parties to field women candidates as well as the high cost of elections are two big deterrents to women candidates.

Haryana being, by and large, a rural and agricultural state looks down upon women as uninformed about and disinterested in matters that are political. Moreover, since they are yet to emerge as a well-organised pressure or interest group, they are not taken seriously as a political force except as voters at the time of elections when they and their votes are highly maneuvered by their male family members. Nevertheless, this fact cannot be generalised in case of those women whose social and economic status is above the normal level.

The reality of the highly low political participation of women and their absence from decision-making bodies has always remained an important issue on national agenda. Media and various women organisations of national and international level have always kept the issue of a fair share for them in social, economic and political life of the state alive. These efforts have started bearing fruits and the result is the adoption of the measures promising a better deal for women. One such measure in India was the adoption, by Parliament, of the 73rd Constitutional Amendment Act in 1993, which ushered into an era of realisation of the long-standing dream of grassroot level democracy. The three-tier system of local governance, called Panchayati Raj system, enables the common people, including women, to hold the reigns of power at the lowest level down from village to district level.

The Panchayati Raj system gave a much needed succor to women everywhere in India, including Haryana, as it proposes to reserve one-third of the total number of seats in *panchayats* for women and also one-third of the chairpersons at all levels have to be women. In those states where the *panchayat* elections have been held, the results are very encouraging and the reserved quotas for women have been filled. The unprecedented and overwhelming response marks a turning point in the political profile of women as they have acquired the reigns of the grassroot level leadership, which is very crucial in bringing a change in society from within.

The following figures from Haryana *panchayats*, where elections were held in 1994, reveal the status of women participation as leaders and decision-makers.

Women in Haryana Panchayati Raj System, 1994

Gram Panchayats (GP)			*Panchayat Samitis (PS)*			*Zilla Parishad (ZP)*		
No. of GPs	*Total Members*	*Women*	*No. of PS*	*Total Members*	*Women*	*No. of Members*	*Total*	*Women*
5,958	54,159	17,828 (33.10%)	110	2,418	807 (33.37%)	16	303	101 (33.33%)

Source: Institute of Social Sciences, PRIs Data Centre, New Delhi.

The above Table clearly shows a positive trend in meeting the target of 33 per cent reservation for women in decision-making bodies at the grassroots. However, skepticism exists regarding the role of this newly emerged class of women leaders who, by and large, are illiterate, socially backward and politically weak. It is feared that the deep-rooted caste hierarchy, patriarchy and disadvantaged position of women would surely make them nothing more than the proxies and rubber stamps of men.[5] It is also feared that these untrained, unsocialised women would be unfit to perform those duties that would be attached with the post of various position holders, particularly in the context of policy-making and implementation in the 29 developmental field that are mentioned in the amendment.[6]

There might be some truth in these apprehensions, but the elected women at all the three tiers of Panchyati Raj system in Haryana have been performing their new-found duties well despite their limitations and stress under which they are working. There is an improvement in their awareness level despite the constraint of illiteracy and too many duties at home front. They generally intervene actively on various local issues like prohibition, education, unemployment, women's issues, roads, drinking water and construction of school buildings, etc. They have displayed an ability to mobilise women more easily on women-related issues. However, when it comes to financial issues, they are found to be at a discount. The steady growth and regularity in attendance of women members and gradual disappearance of shyness in sitting along with men is a sign of their political maturity and awareness of their worth.

These developments have long-term implication on a decentralisation of power, which is very essential for effective mainstreaming of women in development.

The participation of the women of Haryana in decision-making and leadership roles at grassroots and at regional and national level is a significant change, though at the latter two levels, the participation figures are not very encouraging. But, with the strong on-going demand of various women activities and groups for 33 per cent reservation in Parliament for women, the pattern of women's participation in decision-making is sure to become realistic once this demand is translated into practice. What is required is that while the women should be included in decision-making processes to enable to exercise power, they need to be equipped with suitable means to shoulder these responsibilities. Education of both men and women is equally important for gradually diluting the patriarchal mind-set of society as well as to instill self-confidence in women. Otherwise, their representation would end up as mere tokenism.[7]

References

1. Singh, K S (ed.), *People of India*, Haryana, Vol. XXIII, Manohar, Anthropological Survey, of India, 1994.
2. The 17 districts of Haryana are: Ambala, Bhiwani, Faridabad, Gurgaon, Hissar, Jind, Kaithal, Karnal, Kurukshetra, Mahendragarh, Panchkula, Panipat, Rewari, Rohtak, Sirsa, Sonepat and Yamunanagar. See: Bhatt, S C (ed.) *The Encyclopaedic District Gazetteers of India*, (Vol. 3), Delhi, Gyan Publishing House, 1998, pp. 61-62.

3. *Ibid.*, p. 63.
4. *Selected Educational Statistics 1995-96*, Planning, Monitoring and Statistical Division, Deptt. of Education, Ministry of Human Resource Development (HRD), Govt. of India.
5. Kaushik, Sushila, *Women Panches in Position: A study of Panchayat Raj in Haryana*, Delhi: Centre for Development Studies Action, 1997.
6. *Ibid.*
7. *Country Report*, Fourth World Conference on Women, Beijing 1995, HRD, Govt. of India.

9

EMPOWERMENT OF WOMEN THROUGH POLITICAL PARTICIPATION: WITH SPECIAL REFERENCE TO MADHYA PRADESH

Rashmi Srivastava

Political Participation

Social scientists broadly define political participation as being the process through which an individual plays a role in the political life of his society, has the opportunity to take part in deciding what the common goals of that society are, and the best ways of achieving these goals.[1] Political participation refers to actual participation in these voluntary activities by which members of a society share in the selection of rulers and directly or indirectly in the formation of public polity.

L Mibrath feels, "Every person participates at least passively in the political system in which he lives...there is no such thing as not behaving".[2] As traditional liberal democratic theory is viewed, literature often shows concern that there is widespread political participation by large majority of citizens. The rationale of this is simple: that to have a government of the people there must surely be a great many people politically involved.[3]

The previous survey researches consistently show that most people are just not politically oriented. These studies show that only small percentages, probably lesser than 10 per cent in all democratic countries, belong to a political class. R. A. Dhal comments, "... in most political systems those who display great political interests concern, information and activity are not a large majority of the adults: generally, no doubt, they are a minority".[4] S. M. Lipset even comments, "the belief that a very high level of participation is always good for democracy is not valid."[5]

The object of this author is to critically examine the participation of Indian women in the politics of the country. The new emerging women power and the ground realities have been examined in general and in particular in Madhya Pradesh.

Women in Indian Politics

While we must acknowledge the contribution of modern historians in discovering information regarding the position of women in the early periods of our history, it has to be emphasised that all information relates to the elite sections of society, viz., the high caste and upper strata. Very little material is available on the lives and conditions of the large majority of women, who were not members of the elite group. From 500 BC to the medieval period, women of these classes not only lost their position and freedom, but sank into a state of subservience. During the early medieval period upto 1200 AD, some women of the upper strata received considerable education, some of them distinguishing themselves in the field of scholarships. But this tradition diminished gradually and the lifestyle of women in general deteriorated considerably.

At the time of the advent of the British rule in India, literacy among ordinary women was almost nonexistent. Even women of respectable families felt uneasy about being educated. The major impetus in changing the attitude towards women, however, came from the national movement for Independence. Indian women at the turn of the century were brought out of their homes to participate in India's struggle for freedom from British supremacy by some of the nationalist leaders of the time, specially, Mahatma Gandhi.[6] In order to build a mass movement, the message had to be extended to all classes and the participation of women in the national movement was a necessary part of the programme. They were brought into active participation and political leadership.

The greatest advantage of women's participation in national life was that it brought them to the forefront. Indian women after Independence received rights that had been won after a long struggle by women in the West. The Constitution of India grants equal rights to women in all respects, and in political field the right has brought capable women into the ruling apparatus, both at the Centre and at the state level. There has been considerable change in the status of women. Vijaya Lakshmi Pandit was the first women to rise to the high office of the president of the General Assembly of the United Nations. Indira Gandhi was the first Prime Minister in the history of a sizable and significant country. There have been women governors of states, women ambassadors and delegates to international bodies, and there are women legislators and members of the Central and state cabinets presently shaping the history of India.

As women have become more and more conscious about their identity, their very 'self' has persuaded them to show their mettle in a male-dominated society. Women domain in India has become larger and their roles have expanded and, in some ways, become more complicated. Not only in politics, but also in other fields like medicine, science, journalism, sports, beauty contest of Miss Universe and Miss World, superintendent of Tihar jail, activists for agitation or protest movement, the new emerging Indian women have made a mark of their own. The emerging woman power is also exhibited by the fact that, one by one, male bastions are falling before the onslaught of talented women of the 20th century. The Indian military establishment has opened up half of its door for women.

The 'woman power' is significant in police services, and the '*mahila*' battalion of the CRPF was the first women's paramilitary force in Asia. The first 'all women police station' was started in 1973 in Calcutta. All women *panchayat* was started in Madhya Pradesh.[7] At present a woman has been successfully presiding the Rajya Sabha. In Parliament, women Congress MPs have always been more than the women MPs of other parties. There has been representation of women from different religions and castes of the country. Though the representation of women has been from all parts of the country in Parliament and the government, the number of women from northern side of country has always been more.[8]

It is evident from the data that women in India have proved to be good voters. The common women use their franchise like men. But the representation of women in all the 12 Lok Sabhas was found between 3.4 to 7.9 per cent (see Table 1).

Table 1. Women in Lok Sabha

Lok Sabha	*Seats*	*Women Candidates*	*Elected*
1952 I	444	51 (2.7%)	22 (4.9%)
1957 II	500	70 (4.4%)	27 (5.4%)
1962 III	503	68 (3.4%)	34 (6.7%)
1967 IV	523	66 (2.8%)	31 (5.9%)
1971 V	521	86 (3.1%)	22 (4.2%)
1977 VI	544	70 (2.9%)	19 (3.4%)
1980 VII	544	142 (3.1%)	28 (5.0%)
1984 VIII	544	159 (2.9%)	44 (7.7%)
1989 IX	525	189 (3.1%)	27 (5.3%)
1991 X	534	195 (3.7%)	39 (6.7%)
1996 XI	540	191 (3.4%)	39 (7.1%)
1998 XII	543	167 (3.0%)	43 (7.9)

Source : Shoma A Chatterji - *The Indian Women in Perspective* - Ajanta Publications, Delhi, 1993, p. 137 & *India Today*, 16 Feb. 1998.

On an average the number of women in Lok Sabha has nearly been same as the number of women in the Rajya Sabha. The number of women candidates for these elections have been 51 to 267 including independent candidates. It is also notable that mostly these women candidates belong to some political personalities as wife or daughter. Very few of them belong to political party worker class.[9] In the 11th Lok Sabha, there were only 39 women members, three up from last time's 36. In the 12th Lok Sabha, the number had risen too. The year 1998 saw the emergence of Sonia Gandhi reviving the Congress Party, and Jayalalitha as a strewed politician putting pressure on the BJP government, and finally withdrawing the support of her 18 MPs. She paved the way for the downfall of the BJP government in April 1999. Mayawati did the rest. These women leaders emerged as significant political decision-makers. In keeping with the general trend in the 12th Lok Sabha, at least half of them are first timers. Also, many of the women parliamentarians belong to the backward classes. Some of the women MPs in the 12th Lok Sabha were Sushma Swaraj, Uma Bharati and Vasundhara Raje Scindia of BJP; Mamta Banerji of the Trinmul Congress and Mayawati of BSP.[10]

However, the position of women in the Indian political scene remains, by and large, low-profiled and unrecognised except for those women who are from elite families, who are related closely to political leaders through blood or through marriage, and women who are high-profiled in other professions and their glamour is considered to be a plus point with their entry into the increasing glitter of politics.

It is a well known fact that the main political parties of India do not regard women candidates as much capable and efficient winning candidates as the men candidates. For political parties, women are good voters but not good candidates. In the present political situation, this may be true because manipulation, criminalisation, use of black money, use of muscles power, immorality, character assassination, false propaganda have become the measures to win the election. Naturally, most of the women are becoming alienated from politics. They think that politics is not worth for them. Their family responsibilities, socially backwardness, illiteracy, conservatism, powerlessness, lack of confidence have increased their political apathy. Very few women get family support, encouragement and help for their political life. If we analyse the reasons, we can say that women in general don't feel politics is women's domain. In most cases while statistics and reports say women are influenced by their husbands, the more important reason is because they feel they do not know anything of politics and are often too shy to ask the difference between Janata Dal and BJP. These inhibitory factors have held many educated but self-conscious women away from being an active part of the politics.[11]

The obstacles in the way of women remain more or less the same as they were many years ago. There is the problem of fitting politics into the running of a home and the raising of a family, both of which are full-time jobs in a patriarchal society. Women representation in higher posts is very low in India (that is, 2.3 per cent of the total posts). There are on an average 27.4 per cent of women administrators in industrialised nations and 10 per cent in developing countries. Some of our neighbours fare even better. The percentage of women administrators and managers has been given in Table 2.[12]

Table 2. Women Administrators and Managers (as percentage of total)

Canda	42.4
USA.	42
Singapore	34.3
Thailand	21.8
Srilanka	16.9
Malaysia	11.9
China	11.6
Bangladesh	5.1
Pakistan	3.4
India	2.3
Industrialised Nations	27.4
Devloping Nations	10.0

Source : UNDP Report 1997.

The current political culture in the country makes women's participation in politics difficult. One woman politician has expressed that women are never taken seriously in politics. They have to prove themselves at every point. They have to work harder than their male colleagues and yet their bonafides are suspected and often they get no credit. People wonder and ask which leader has done her a favour and why? In India, with few women in public life, men find it difficult to look upon them with respect, obsessed as they are with their traditional image of the household women. Sonia Gandhi, Jayalalitha, Lakshmi Paravathi and Mamta Banerji do not represent the ordinary Indian women.[13] If you ask people whether women should take part in politics, everyone including the men will say yes. But when it comes to their actual participation, there are still a number of invisible barriers that block their entry. While a change has begun to take effect, the political voice of Indian women is still muted.

A recent study[14] conducted by UNESCO in seven South-East Asian countries indicates that in terms of awareness, party membership, contesting elections, voting or deliberate abstention from voting and decision-making, women's participation has not been impressive. They remain in the periphery of power and influence, says the study.

Are more women taking part in election than before? Answer to this question tend to focus on two facts: either everyone talks about how many women get elected, or they focus on the proportion of women that turns out to vote. None of the two fully reflect the changing pattern of women's participation. The percentage of women who turned out to vote in various elections increased in the first two decades. After that it has fluctuated without any systematic trend. But one thing has not changed—there has always been a gap of 8 per cent to 17 per cent between men's and women's turnout (see Table 3).

Table 3. Gender Gap in Turnout (in percentage)

Election	*Men*	*Women*
1952	55	38
1957	56	39
1962	62	47
1967	67	56
1971	61	49
1977	66	55
1980	62	51
1984	68	59
1989	66	57
1991	61	51
1996	62	53
1998	60	52

Source : CSDS Data Unit 1998.

As one might expect, the states which record the lowest turnout of women are Bihar, Uttar Pradesh and Rajasthan. These are also the states which record low female literacy and high female infant mortality.[15]

Women's representation in the 11th and 12th Lok Sabha has been also negligible. According to a press statement issued by a consortium of 18 centres for women's studies and improvement, the number of women candidates was barely 3 per cent. "We have lost faith," said Mohini Giri, chairperson of the National Commission for Women (NCW), whose political core meeting on April 11, 1996 took stock of the situation.[16] There are only 43 women in the 12th Lok Sabha, occupying 7.94 per cent of the seats. It is better than the first Lok Sabha, which had only 4.9 per cent women members. But the progress is insignificant if viewed in relation to a population that has 91 women for every 100 men.[17] There has been a downslide in women's participation in mainstream politics. It indicates that women's representation is generally determined by the leadership's attitude, more than anything else. Mostly the leaders are interested in "winning candidates." While more women are entering politics and winning elections, their representation in the Union government continues to be abysmal. Only four women found berths in the 43-member BJP-led government in 1998. The number of women ministers in Centre and states has been given in Table 4.

Table 4. Women Ministers in Centre and States

Year	*Ministers in Centre*	*Ministers in States*
1952	3	5
1957	3	12
1962	5	21
1967	5	10
1971	3	18
1977	2	22
1980	8	5
1984	5	10
1989	1	12
1991	5	15
1996	5	18
1998	4	18

Also, the percentage of women in the governments of different countries can be seen in Table 5.[18]

Table 5. Women in Government (in percentage)

Sweden	47
Norway	41
Finland	35
USA	21
Canada	19
India	9
Japan	7
Bangladesh	5
Pakistan	4
World average	7
Developed Countries	12
Developing Countries	6

Source : UNDP Report 1997.

The NCW has worked on the bill to ensure 33 per cent representation of women in future elections. It has also commissioned six groups to study poll issues of women candidates. Meanwhile, Women's Political Watch (WPW), a group committed to ensuring women's role in public policy and political leadership, has come out with a manifesto. WPW manifesto's highlights include a full-fledged ministry for women's development and constitutional amendment to ensure 33 per cent representation in party echelons and public offices.

The 81st Amendment Bill was introduced in the Lok Sabha and on 13 September, 1996. It was referred to a select committee which gave its report in the winter session of the house. The bill provides 33 per cent seats in the Lok Sabha and state assemblies, one-third of these to be reserved for Schedule Caste/Schedule Tribe women, applicable after the dissolution of the house or the assembly in existent at the time it is passed, the 181 Lok Sabha seats to be rotated by a draw of lots, and the bill not to apply to states/Union territories where seats reserved for Schedule Caste/Schedule Tribe is less than three. Thus, it will not be applicable in 10 states/Union territories.[19] The bill has not been passed as yet. Women's representation in the Lok Sabha and state assemblies on the basis of reservations has been hijacked by the messiahs of caste-based and religion-based politics, who have used every opportunity to weaken democratic forces in society by promoting the worst kind of casteist and communal tendencies in India. Women's representation in politics is a first step for women empowerment, but categorising women on the basis of caste and religion is a step towards their further segregation in society.[20]

We also get a happier picture of women's participation in political activities. The two comprehensive national election surveys conducted by CSDS in 1971 and 1996 reveal a significant rise in the proportion of women among the politically active class of citizens of those who now take an active interest in the campaign, more than one-third comprise women. Their level of identification with parties has gone up. Their share has more than doubled among those who attended election meetings and those who are members of political parties (see Table 6).

Table 6. Women More Politically Active (Percentage Share of Women Among those who Said Yes)

Political activities	*1971*	*1996*
Interest in politics	27	35
Membership of parties	9	23
Attendance at election meeting	7	19
Feel close to party	25	36

Source: National election surveys conducted by CSDS in 1971 and 1996.

A silent revolution is taking place in the arena of electoral politics. New patterns are being woven in the social fabric. Gender divide has begun to make a difference. Mobilisation of women in politics could change the face of Indian politics. To be sure, their level of participation is still very low as compared to men. Women are still less than one-fifth of the party members. Politics and elections are still considered to be a men's domain.[21]

One social issue pushed by women that has found resonance with mainstream political parties is prohibition. During the last Andhra Pradesh assembly elections, the Telugu Desam Party romped home victorious, aided greatly by its women power. The promise for prohibition of liquor in rural areas, if voted to power by Bhajan Lal and Bansi Lal in Haryana and A K Anthony in Kerala has definitely enhanced their clean image and popularised them among the women. At a recent meeting of women's organisations from 12 states against alcohol, held in New Delhi, decision was taken to push for prohibition at local levels. Significantly, in Chhattisgarh (Madhya Pradesh) and Uttarakhand (Uttar Pradesh) regions, women campaigning against alcohol are a force to reckon with. In Madhya Pradesh, the new women's policy that awaits legislation, has provision for closure of liquor vends if more than 50 per cent of the local women oppose it.

Regarding natural resources, tribal women in Madhya Pradesh, Orissa and Uttar Pradesh have been continuing their struggle for rights over wild grass and trees which are their source of livelihood. They have demanded protection of their interests. The tribal women in Madhya Pradesh are also very active in 'Narmada Bachao Andolan' (Save Narmada Movement) under the leadership of Medha Patkar. She has proved to be a very strong woman leader with strong arguments against mega dams, specially the Sardar Sarovar Project on river Narmada. She argues that there are already other hydropower projects in Madhya Pradesh, which are lying incomplete for want of money. When it comes to considering the Sardar Sarovar Project, Madhya Pradesh has to weigh the costs and benefits. As against 57 per cent of power that it will get, it has to weigh submergence of prime agricultural land, displacement of not less then 33,000 families and loss of forest land.[22]

Case Study of Madhya Pradesh

There are 4,46,13,317 voters in Madhya Pradesh. About half of them, that is, 2,15,45, 800 voters are women.[23] In Madhya Pradesh six Lok Sabha constituencies have more women voters than men. All these six seats are reserved seats: Bastar and Kanker for Schedule Tribes, and Sarang Garh, Mahasamund, Rajnand Gaon and Balaghat for Schedule Castes. In the remaining 34 constituencies, women voters are lesser in number than men. In the last five years, it is noted that in the country, the number of women voters is increasing rapidly in proportion to the men voters. The percentage of this increase for women is 15, while for men it is 13.49. But in three states, this proportion is just opposite. Madhya Pradesh is one of these states.[24]

Madhya Pradesh has played a significant role at the Centre. Najma Heptulla, Deputy chairperson of the Rajya Sabha, has been successfully presiding the house. Out of the 40 Lok Sabha seats from Madhya Pradesh, women representation is 11 per cent. Women representation from Madhya Pradesh in Lok Sabha has been as follows: The early Lok Sabha of 1957, 1962, 1967 had three, five, four women members respectively, and they were from Congress party. From 1971 to 1984 in four Lok Sabhas, there were two women from Madhya Pradesh, one from Congress and one from the then Jansangh. In 1989, all the three women from Madhya Pradesh were from BJP. Now the trend has changed and it is found that BJP has more women MPs in comparison to Congress. In 1991 and 1996, in each Lok Sabha out of five women, two were from-congress and three from BJP. In the Lok Sabha elections of 1998, from Madhya Pradesh, one women was from Congress and three were from BJP (see Table 7).

Table 7. Party-wise Women Representation from Madhya Pradesh in Lok Sabha (Total Seats from Madhya Pradesh are 40)

Years	*Congress*	*BJP*	*Total*
1957	3	-	3
1962	5	-	5
1967	4	-	4
1971	1	1	2
1977	1	1	2
1980	1	1	2
1984	1	1	2
1989	-	3	3
1991	2	3	5
1996	2	3	5
1998	1	3	4

Vijayaraje Scindia has represented Madhya Pradesh seat in Lok Sabha eight times, that is, two times from Congress, one time as independent and five times from BJP. Uma Bharti and Sumitra Mahajan, both from BJP and Mini Mata from Congress represented four times.[25] Chhabilit Netam and Alka Nath were elected from Congress in 1996, when their husbands Arvind Netam and Kamal Nath had been elected from their constituencies for the fourth time, but were forced to vacate their seats due to political reasons. At present, Vijayaraje Scindia and Uma Bharti, well known BJP leaders are from Madhya Pradesh. For the 12th Lok Sabha elections, from Madhya Pradesh, there were 26 women candidates, which was significantly lesser than the number of women candidates (75) who contested the 11th Lok Sabha elections (see Table 8).

Table 8. Party-wise Women Representation from Madhya Pradesh in 11th & 12th Lok Sabha Elections

Party	Women candidates	
	11th	*12th*
Congress	5	2
BJP	4	4
Indira Congress (T)	2	0
BSP	2	1
Janata Dal	0	1
Janata party	0	0
Socialist party	0	1
MP Vikas Congress	1	0
Shiv Sena	0	1
Samta Party	1	0
Independent	56	8
Others	3	8
Total	75	26

Though the main political parties are in favour of 33 per cent reservation for women in Lok Sabha, yet nominations of women candidates was much less. Though the Congress (I) contested all the 40 seats, yet it had only two women candidates. Similarly, BJP contested 39 seats with only four women candidates. The other political parties who have contested on lesser seats, did not give tickets to women candidates or just nominated one or two women candidates. As there is heavy manipulations in distribution of tickets by major political parties, women politicians contest for a small number of seats in comparison to men. The political parties have been giving preference to men for contesting elections.

In state Legislative Assembly, Madhya Pradesh has prominent women legislators from Congress (I) and BJP. Some of them participate very actively in assembly meetings. Women ministers in Madhya Pradesh have proved that they are capable to shoulder this responsibility also.

In Madhya Pradesh politics, Vijayaraje Scindia has

played a significant role in the 1960s, when she withdrew herself from Congress and gave a challenge to the leadership of D P Mishra, the then State Chief Minister of Madhya Pradesh. The result was in the form of the defeat of the Congress for the first time in 1967 assembly elections.[26] She also formed a new party, and had a collaboration with the Jansangh Party. As her party was not recognised by the Election Commission, its candidates contested the fourth Vidhan Sabha elections on the Jansangh symbol. It was a golden chance for Jansangh to extend its jurisdiction in Madhya Bharat area. In Chambal region, Congress was unable to get even a single seat, but Jansangh got all the 15 Vidhan Sabha seats and four seats of Lok Sabha. Scindia became the leader of the non-Congress MLAs of Sanyukta Vidhayak Dal (SVD) government in 1969, and contested the 1972 assembly elections as the candidate of Jansangh. Scindia also formed a syndicate of princely families at the time of abolishment of privy purses by Indira Gandhi. The old Congress royal families supported Scindia and contested the Vidhan Sabha elections against Congress on this issue. Rani Padmawati of Khairagarh and Gayatri Devi of Saraipali were among them.

The analysis of Vidhan Sabha elections of Madhya Pradesh is as follows: Except in 1990, the women legislators mostly belonged to the Congress Party in 1957, there were 29 women MLAs, 27 were from Congress and two were independent. In 1962, out of 15, 13 were from the Congress and one from RRP and one from the Ramrajya Party. In 1967, eight were from Congress, one from Jansangh and one was independent. In 1972, 15 were from Congress, one from Jansangh and two were independent. The minimum number of women legislators in Madhya Pradesh was in 1977. Out of six women, three were from Congress, two from Janata Party and one was an independent. In 1980, all 14 and in 1985 also, all the 27 were from Congress. Only in 1990, out of 12 women MLAs, five were from Congress and seven from BJP. In 1993 10 were from Congress, five from BJP, one from BSP and one was independent.[27] The present Vidhan Sabha has 25 women, in which 18 are from Congress, six from BJP and one from BSP (see Table 9).

Table 9. Party-wise Women Representation in Madhya Pradesh Vidhan Sabha

Year	*Congress*	*BJP*	*Janta Party*	*BSP*	*Others*	*Indepedent*	*Total*
1957	27	-	-	-	-	2	29
1962	13	-	-	-	1 RPR 1 Ramrajya	-	15
1967	8	1	-	-	-	1	10
1972	15	1	-	-	-	2	18
1977	3	-	2	-	-	1	6
1980	14	-	-	-	-	-	14
1985	27	-	-	-	-	-	27
1990	5	7	-	-	-	-	12
1993	10	5	-	1	-	1	17
1998	18	6	-	1	-	-	25

The list of elected women candidates for Madhya Pradesh Vidhan Sabha 1998, is given in Table 10.

Table 10. Elected Women - Madhya Pradesh Vidhan Sabha Elections 1998

Sl. No.	*Name*	*Party*	*Constituency no.*	*Category*	*Constituency Name*	*Margin of win*
1.	Yashodhara Raje	BJP	026	G	Shivpuri	7,300
2.	Sudha Jain	BJP	039	G	Sagar	3,847
3.	Kusum Mehdele	BJP	056	G	Panna	8,250
4.	Vidyavati Patel	BSP	067	G	Gurh	5,503
5.	Shakuntala Pradhan	Congress	081	ST	Naurozabad	3,718
6.	Ratanmala Singh	BJP	125	SC	Chandrapur	11,006
7.	Phulodevi Netam	Congress	148	ST	Keshkal	343

(Contd. on next page)

(Table contd.)

Sl. No.	*Name*	*Party*	*Constitu ency no.*	*Cate-gory*	*Constitue-ncy Name*	*Margin of win*
8.	Pratibha Shah	Cong-ress	153	ST	Chitrakoot	3,801
9.	Pratibha Chandrakar	Cong-ress	166	G	Khairatha	158
10.	Geeta Singh	Cong-ress	171	G	Dongargaon	878
11.	Ganga Bai Ureti	Cong-ress	190	ST	Shahpura	4,544
12.	Urmila Singh	Cong-ress	210	ST	Ghansour	18,088
13.	Kaushalya Gohiya	Cong-ress	193	ST	Panagar	1,388
14.	Sadhana Sthapak	Cong-ress	205	G	Gagarwada	3,983
15.	Savita Dewan Sharma	Cong-ress	223	G	Hoshangabad	15
16.	Sushila Singh	BJP	248	G	Vidisha	544
17.	Sanyogita Deshmukh	Cong-ress	286	G	Shahpur	383
18.	Vijaylaxmi Sadho	Cong-ress	290	SC	Maheshwar	277
19.	Jamuna Devi	Cong-ress	303	ST	Kukshi	28,381
20.	Kalpana Parulekar	Cong-ress	362	G	Mahidpur	13,485
21.	Preeti Bhargav	ress	Cong-	267	GUjjain South	2,477
22.	Sulochana Ravat	Cong-	305 ress	ST	Jobat	12,938
23.	Swarup Bai	Cong-ress	306	ST	Jhabua	15,534
24.	Nirmala Bhuriya	BJP	307	ST	Petlavad	8,392
25.	Pushpa Bharti	Cong-ress	316	SC	Suwasara	4,098

In 1998 Vidhan Sabha elections, there were 61 women

candidates for 320 seats. BJP nominated 26 and Congress nominated 25 women candidates; BSP contested 130 seats and its women candidates were eight; Janata Dal contested 31 seats with two women candidates (see Table 11).

Table 11. Women Candidates from Different Political Parties for Vidhan Sabha Elections, 1998

Political Party	*Total seats Contested*	*Women Candidates*	*Winner Women*
BJP	320	26	6
Congress	320	25	18
BSP	130	8	1
JD	31	2	0
Total	801	60	25

For the 1998 Vidhan Sabha there was not a single woman candidate from either party in nine Lok Sabha constituencies (each Lok Sabha constituency has seven-eight Vidhan Sabha seats).

For five times one or two women have won Vidhan Sabha seats as independents candidates. Since last two elections (1996 and 1998), though less in number, that is, only one, BSP women legislator's presence has been found in Vidhan Sabha.

Maximum women candidates contested from Sarangarh Lok Sabha constituency, which is reserved for Scheduled Castes. For eight seats, there were five women candidates, that is, two from BJP, one from Congress and two from BSP. The Jhabua Lok Sabha constituency is also reserved for Scheduled Tribes. Among its eight seats, four women candidates contested—two from BJP and two from Congress.

Inspite of about 50 per cent women voters and the claim from different parties for giving more chance to women candidature, the women representation in the Vidhan Sabha has been insignificant in Madhya Pradesh. There has been neither a women speaker nor a women Chief Minister in this state, though 24 Chief Ministers and 12 speakers had been there.[28] From 1967 to 1972, Vijayaraje

Scindia was the leader of the Vidhan Sabha, but Govind Narayan Singh became the Chief Minister. Even the office of deputy speaker or leader of opposition has not been given to any women. The candidature of women in all Vidhan Sabha elections, has not exceeded from 4.5 per cent.[29] (see Table 12).

Table 12. Women Candidature in Madhya Pradesh Vidhan Sabha Elections (from 1977 to 1998)

Years	*Total Candidates*	*Women Candidates*	*Percentage*
1977	1,994	43	2.15
1980	2,000	50	2.50
1985	2,450	76	3.80
1990	4,216	150	3.55
1993	3,729	169	4.53
1998	1,418	61	4.30

In Madhya Pradesh ministry, out of about 40 ministers, 10 per cent are women. After the 1998 Vidhan Sabha elections, Chief Minister Digvijay Singh had nominated four women ministers.[30] As in previous years, this time also important departments have not been given to them. They have been made ministers for the Department of Women and Child Development, Tribal Welfare, Narmada Valley Development etc, which are non-significant departments.

The most striking participation of women in the politics of Madhya Pradesh is found at the grassroots level. Through 73 and 74 Constitution amendments, women were given one-third reservation at grassroots level. Madhya Pradesh was the first state where the Panchayat Raj Adhiniyam was set up and enacted in 1994.[31] According to provisions of this act, atleast one-third of the offices of *sarpanch* in each division shall be reserved for women. Madhya Pradesh is a backward state, but women have been certainly empowered through this legislation. In the beginning it was thought that rural women are illiterate, backward, conservative, follow *pardah* system and are just shadows of their male counterparts. That their husbands will look after the functions of the *panchayat* on behalf of them. These *mahila panchayats* were initially known to be headed by their husband and not by the actual elected women *sarpanch*. But very soon, after the *panchayats* were formed, these *mahila sarpanchs* were found to understand all proceedings of *panchayat* and their power. Now they don't need to take advice from their husbands any more. They are also supervising with more efficiency and honesty, the works done by the *panchayats* for better development of the village.

Reservation for women in local bodies in Madhya Pradesh has provided ample opportunities for women to enter into politics at local level and ultimately at the state and national levels. Prior to the 73rd and 74th amendments to the Constitution of India, women had few occasions and opportunities in entering into local bodies because of male dominance. The situation was highly disappointing for women, specially in rural areas. Now due to these constitutional amendments and due to their implementation by the Madhya Pradesh government, women have been able to get power at each of the three levels of the *panchayat* system, that is, at the village level, block level and district level. The elections for Panchayats held in 1994 had 30,922 villages, 459 blocks and 45 districts. The number of seats were 4,43,429 for village *panchayats*, 9,097 for *janpad panchayats* and 946 for *zilla panchayats*. At each of these levels, reservation was provided for Scheduled Caste, Scheduled Tribes and other backward classes in proportion to their number in village population. In each of these categories, horizontal reservation was provided for women. A particular constituency which is to be reserved is selected by drawing lots. The total number of seats reserved for women came out to be 1,64,040. Out of these, 24,339 were for women belonging to Scheduled Castes, 48,993 to those belonging to Scheduled Tribes and 61,993 to other backward classes.

In the urban areas, Madhya Pradesh has achieved success in keeping the one-third seats reserved in municipal bodies. Certain wards were reserved for women in city areas.

There are 404 municipal bodies in Madhya Pradesh in the form of city *panchayat*, municipality and municipal corporation depending upon population of the city. In all these, seats have been reserved for women. In these local bodies, constituencies are smaller, number of voters is less, voters are easily approachable, door to door campaigning is possible, and hence, women candidates have been participating with greater efficiency.

According to the rules of reservation in these local bodies, wards are reserved for Scheduled Castes and Scheduled Tribes in proportion to their percentage of the population of the city. If the percentage of Scheduled Castes and Scheduled Tribes of a city population is such that the quota of 50 per cent wards is not fulfilled for their categories, then the remaining percentage of wards will be reserved for other backward classes, subject to a maximum of 25 per cent. One-third of wards in each category will again be reserved for women candidates. The selection of wards for reservation is done by draw of lots. Due to this reservation policy for women, urban people have noticed a definite change in the system, with women contesting elections in each category—general, Scheduled Castes, Scheduled Tribes and other backward classes. Women have been holding the posts of mayors in municipal bodies and it has been a pleasant experience for the people to watch them doing their duties with devotion. Women representatives attend meetings of the municipal bodies actively and are working as the members of various committees. Women mayors have been facing disturbing elements prevalent in local politics. Through this empowerment, women have proved themselves courageous, brave, patient and capable to deal with all sorts of political deeds.

References

1. Eakin, TC, *Students and Politics : A Comparative Study*, Popular Prakashan, Mumbai, 1972, p. 96.
2. Mibrath, L, *Political Participation*, Rand Mc Nally & Co., Chicago, 1965, p. 26.
3. Mayo, HB, *An Introduction to Democratic Theory*, Oxford University press, New York, 1960. p. 20.

4. Dahl, RA, *Modern Political Analysis*, Prentice Hall, Englewood Cliffs, N.J. 1963, p. 58.
5. Lipset S M, *Political Man, Doubleday*, Garden City, 1960, p. 181.
6. Shoma A Chatterji, *The Indian Women in Perspective* - Ajanta Publications, Delhi, 1993, p. 116.
7. 'The New Emerging Women Power : The Ground Realities?", in *Competition Success Review*, New Delhi, Vol. XXXIII, No. 2, August 1996, p. 37.
8. Rashmi Srivastava, The Role of Women in Indian Politics', in *Political Science Review*, Jaipur, Vol. 21, No. 4, Oct-Dec. 1982, p. 358.
9. *Dainik Bhaskar* (Newspaper), Indore, 11 April 1996.
10. 'Women - Vocal Minority'; in *India Today*, Living Media Ltd., New Delhi, Vol. XXI, No. 13, July 1-15, 1996, p. 47.
11. 'Why women should vote', in the *Hindustan Times*, Delhi, Saturday 3, 27 April 1996.
12. 'Women Administrators and Managers', in *India Today*, Living Media Ltd., New Delhi, Vol. XXIII, Number 5, January 27 - February 2, 1998, p. 16.
13. 'Spirit of Mandate 1996', in *Down to Earth*, Science and Environment, New Delhi, Vol. 4, No. 24, May 15, 1996, p. 14.
14. 'A New Political Landscape', in *India Today*, Living Media India Ltd., New Delhi, Vol. XXIII, Number 7, February 10-16, 1998, p. 40.
15. 'A New Political Landscape', *Ibid.*
16. 'Spirit of Mandate 1996', *opcit.*
17. 'Women's Bill-Ladies Seat', in *India Today*, Living Media India Ltd., New Delhi, Vol. XXIII, Number 29, July 14-20, 1996, p. 21.
18. 'Women in Government', in *India Today*, Living Media Ltd., New Delhi, Vol. XXIII, Number 14, March 31-April 6, 1998, p. 16.
19. 'An Agenda for Empowerment', in *India Today*, Living Media India Ltd., New Delhi, Vol. XXI, No. 19, October 1-15, 1996, p. 75.
20. 'Woes of Gender Politics', C P Bhambhri on Women's Bill, in *The Hindustan Times*, New Delhi, August 5, 1998, p. 13.

21. 'A New Political Landscape', *op. cit.*, p. 41.
22. 'All Legitimacy Stands Destroyed', in *Frontline*, May 7, 1993, p. 127.
23. Data based on the 1.1.1998 census for the Assembly Elections 1998, *Rojgar and Nirman*, Bhopal, 29 October, 1998, p.1, 9, 10.
24. *Nai Dunia* (Daily Newspaper), Indore, 18 April, 1996, p. 8.
25. Girija Shankar, *Election Politics in Madhya Pradesh*, Anamika, Bhopal, 1998, p. 126-143 (Part-2).
26. *Ibid.*, p. 26 (Part 1).
27. *Nai Dunia* (Daily newspaper), Indore, 9 November, 1998 and 30 November 1998, p. 9-12.
28. *Avantika* (Daily Newspaper), Ujjain, 23 October 1998, p. 2.
29. *Nai Dunia* (Daily Newspaper), Indore, 23 October 1998, p. 3.
30. 'Ministers Portfolio at a Glance', in *Janmat*, Madhya Pradesh Journal, Bhopal, Year 2, No. 2, November 1998, p. 11.
31. Madhya Pradesh Gazette (Extraordinary), 1994.

10

POLITICAL PARTIES AND WOMEN: ASPECTS OF THE ISSUE WITH REFERENCE TO THE SITUATION IN ASSAM

Anuradha Dutta

Nearly five decades after the Constitution of India guaranteed adult suffrage to all citizens irrespective of sex, the stark reality is that women continue to be deprived of their legitimate share in elected bodies due mainly to male bias reflected in the choice of candidates by political parties. The issue of women's participation as candidates cannot be viewed in isolation from the general position of women in society. The proportion of women parliamentarians worldwide even dropped from 12.5 per cent in 1975 to 10 per cent in 1993. The Human Development Report 1995, for the purpose of human development index ranking calculation, introduced the gender empowerment measure (GEM). It concentrates on participation, measuring gender inequality in key areas of economic and political participation and decision-making. As the Human Development Report 1996, it differs from the gender-related development index, and indicator of gender inequality in basic capabilities. This report also shows that women representation in national parliaments has not changed a whit ever since 1993, the global average is still 10 per cent. The percentage is less than that in India, and in the states of the Union, it is a very dismal picture. It is also disturbing to know that nearly 100 countries have practically no women representation in parliaments.

Ever since 1937 when limited franchise was granted, women have been participating in the political process both as voters and candidates on a token basis, as it were in provincial and national elections. The past history of women's political participation shows that no serious attempt was ever made by political parties to mobilise women as political pressure groups in their own right. In the years after the enforcement of the Constitution, the number of women contestants in any election has not increased in any significant manner. The Report of the Committee on the Status of Women in India (TOWARDS EQUALITY, 1974), making a critical analysis of the problem covering three general elections (1962, 1967 and 1971), made the inference that literacy was not one of the facts that determined the number of women contestants or their success. It said, "the backing of the party which sponsors them, the personality of the contestants, including their family background role in determining the success or failure of women candidates". One or the other factor did operate in the 1998 Lok Sabha elections also.

Political parties seem to be uniformly reluctant to field women candidates. The high cost of electioneering is another deterrent to most women candidates. The empowerment of women could be brought about only if it is based on granting them basic economic right, educational rights and political rights. It is an imperative necessity to provide opportunities to women in the decision-making processes at all levels to make empowerment of women a meaningful reality.

The evolution of women's role from a private to public life was influenced principally by westernisation as also by their massive participation in the freedom movement. The twin processes generated an awareness among women. Through most of the last century and the early part of this century it was men who provided leadership to the movement to improve the status of women in the family and society. During the nationalist movement the initiative to enlist women as active political participants came chiefly from Mahatma Gandhi. Women as a group were manipulated by him for reasons of politics, although he was also genuinely concerned with their welfare and status in Indian society. In Assam as well, there were a number of women freedom fighters. The nationalist movement mobilised women as Congress supporters, also characterised by some as 'Gandhian women', and their activities received support and encouragement from the male members of the family. In a man-dominated society, men proved to be more active in politics and their views and opinions influenced their wives, sisters and daughters. Women's participation in the national movement was at three levels: (i) women as a part of the general mass of the people who joined the *satyagarh* programmes; (ii) women as a small group who took up social issues like *khadi* or the problem of Harijans: (iii) a limited number of women, an elite group, who had a total commitment to the freedom movement. The presence of elite women in politics did not create any significant change in the lives of the majority of women. Women politicians, however, proved that besides being a wife and mother, a women could add new dimensions to her sphere of activities in the society. Politicians and social reformers expected that the example of elite women adopting a new role should spread far and wide embracing larger sections in their fold. These elite women were directly or indirectly moulded by politicians and social reformers to exercise leadership role among women in general. But circumscribed as they were by social and religious taboos and diverse conventions limiting their public role in given circumstances, plus lack of rigorous training, their participation in active politics stood at a somewhat restrained level. In Assam, a very small group of elite women came out for open political activities due mainly to their close relations with political leaders. Their participation was, however, limited to constructive programmes which gave them greater freedom to innovate activities aimed at social reform at the local level. The political career of a majority of women of this genre began with direct or near direct contact with Gandhi.

To Gandhi women's participation in politics was something in the nature of a *dharma*. Gandhi enabled women to project a new and revolutionary image of women as equal comrades in Congress meetings and processions. Thus, participation of women in Gandhian politics had camouflaged for a time the difference of sex role and attitude. Acceptance of women in Gandhian politics remained an exception to the rule of continuous and active participation at all times and circumstances. Which is why in independent Indian, women continue to be barred from the decision-making process in this traditional, albeit 'modernised' society.

Alike in other provinces of British India, Assamese women were very active in the programmes of the freedom movement. The struggle attracted women, but the leadership failed to sustain their interest and continuity due to an evident lack of a definite policy of associating women on a regular basis, as part of a system. At times during the freedom movement, Congress arranged for training programmes for women. Kamala Devi Chattopadhyaya viewed the issue as one of social and political concern least they should drift apart from their home and usual routine.

The Congress accepted the goal of complete equality for women and men only as a matter of formality, not as a programme of action. Real equality was disapproved of by men for reasons of a deeply engrained notion of custom and tradition. Women delegates to Congress sessions did not increase substantially. Women were restricted to their exclusive group with little access to positions worth their name in the organisational hierarchy.

The situation in Assam was no different There were a number of eminent freedom fighters from the province covering all districts. But the hangover from the past is all too clear, if we go through various election reports. Women members of the Assam Legislative Assembly have been few. Some instances could be cited in support of our contention. This relates to higher legislative bodies also. Pattern of political behaviour from different regions show different factors that influence political participation—they are social status of women, economic position, cultural norms and above all regional outlook towards women's participation in wider society. But Kerala, which has a record of rapid growth of women's political mobilisation and women's literacy, also has a record of electing very few women members to the legislature. On the other hand, Uttar Pradesh with low profile of women's participation has elected a large number of women to the legislature. It is also important to know about the state, the Constitution, the state policy and its impact on all conditions of women's status. After Independence, the state has been considered as the most active agency endeavouring to bring about total change. But today the state is unable to satisfy the social, educational, cultural and health facilities to vast masses of people whose only power is their own labour. The role of the state in India in shaping the gender role have affected the other Sphere of life too. The role of the political party towards women is reflected in the role of the state in particular and society in general.

The government of India Act of 1935 provided representation of women by reservation in the Assam Legislative Assembly because there was greater number of women in Shillong than in any other state. The Act permitted women to contest in general elections also. In 1937, two women candidates contested the reserved seats as independent candidates. For the first time in political history of Assam, one woman became a member of the Legislative Assembly. The number of women who contested the general election, in 1946 was five. Only one candidate was nominated by the Congress. Four candidates contested the reserved seats for women in Shillong. Padma Kumari Gohain, who was the first Assamese to contest elections, was a municipal comissioner prior to her candidature contesting the elections as an independent candidate. But she lost her security deposit as she polled only 839 votes.

In 1952 general elections, six women filed their nominations. Two were from hill district of Khasi and Jaiantia. In the plains, three women Congress candidates contested. Out of them, two won and the third lost by a margin of 213 votes. Padma Kumari, who contested for the second time, lost as an independent candidate. Similarly, in the second general elections there were 11 women contestants, three of them withdrew, out of the remaining eight, five Congress supported candidates were successful. Two of them were sitting members. Bonli Khongmin, who was the only Congress candidate was defeated because her rival was leading a movement which demanded separation of the hill district from Assam. Khongmen was a member from 1946 to 1952. Another independent candidate from Mikir hills was Sahani Rajang, who was defeated. Thus, without party support no women candidate could win elections. But Chandra Prava Saikiani was defeated in 1952 elections inspite of Congress nomination and being an excellent social worker. In the second general elections the number of women candidates were more but neither political parties nor independent women candidates took any interest. In the third general elections, there were only four women contestants, and all of them were supported by Congress. Similarly in the fourth general elections, nine women contestants were fighting, and seven of them were supported by the Congress. Two other independent candidates lost their security deposits. One was a tribal women and the second an independent women candidate, who was put up by her husband because he was refused a Congress ticket. Thus, women are simply instruments either in the hands of husbands or political parties. Similarly, at times the number of women candidates increased, but it was not at the initiative of political parties. Though majority of women candidates sponsored by the Congress Party were either wife or other relatives of the Congress leaders, there were also a group of women in rural area capable of progressive thinking and have the potential for viable social participation. But conscious efforts to secure their involvement specially by political party were not there. Thus, Srimati Bonily Khongman was the first woman to represent Assam in the Lok Sabha in 1952. In 1957, two women, namely, Shrimati Rani Manjula Devi and Begum Mafida Ahmed represented Assam in the Lok Sabha. Thereafter, Shrimati Jyotsna Chanda and Renuka Devi Barkataki were elected to the house in 1977. Since 1952, only three women were elected to the Rajya Sabha, namely,

Shrimati Pushpalata Das (Congress), Shrimati Bijoa Chakravorty of Asom Gana Parishad (AGP) and Shrimati Basanti Sharma of Congress (I). Obviously, political parties have been interested only in tokenism, thereby, contributing to low participation of women as candidates. Most women MPs and MLAs belonged to educated families.

In the 1991 elections, out of 166 candidates contesting 14 Lok Sabha seats from Assam, only five were women. Three of them were independents, only two were nominees of political parties, one each from Janata Dal and the Asom Jayiyatabadi Dal. The Congress (I) and AGP did not nominate any women as a candidate. This speaks eloquently about the 'he-man deviation' due to which all parties suffered. The irony of the situation is that women formed a colossus, as it were from the point of mass participation in the six- year old Assam movement over foreigners' issue. Women are considered capable as flag bearers, but they are not considered capable of fighting elections.

The major parties, Congress (I) and AGP never took any worthwhile measure to induct women into the decision-making process. In the 1996 elections, only a few women were nominated as candidates. If an euphemism was to be used, all political parties have been found to be singularly unfortunate in all their relations with women insofar as nominating in all their relations with women insofar as nominating them as candidates at elections is concerned. This was least expected after an example was set, although under constitutional compulsions, for one-third representation by women in the PRIs. It appears that political parties, both all- India and regional, failed to move beyond the district level. This made short shrift of women political participation. A leading women leader of AGP of the district level applied for an Assembly seat in the last elections. This was denied to her although her claims were legitimate. She was apparently asked to remain satisfied with mayorship of the Guwahati Municipal Corporation.

It deserves to be reiterated that women's participation in the Assam movement (1979-85) took place in an environment when there was no competition between men and women for leadership. Women's leadership qualities as also heroism were the subject of public adulation during the euphoric days. But once the halcyon days of a popular movement were over, the party elite, male-dominated as is the case with every other political party, chose to ignore the leadership qualities of women who mattered. The agenda for women's activities came to be confined as usual to adhoc functions like campaigns, mass rallies, protest demonstrations and the like.

In pre-election, women's conventions as also meetings of political parties, assurances and declarations in response to demands, had been galore about nominating about 15-20 per cent women as candidates in the ensuing elections. But in actual practice, political parties could never rise above paper declarations and oral pronouncements. The result is that after the last election to the Assam Assembly and the Lok Sabha, there is no women MP in the Lok Sabha while in the State Assembly of 126 members, there are only six Women MLAs — three from AGP, two from Congress (I) and one from People's Democratic Front (PDF) a Bodo group.

The role of women in politics has been a matter of serious debate for the last three decades or so. The women's movement has been at the head of demands for increased participation of women in the decision-making process. Almost every all-India party or state/regional party invariably floats women's wings with a view to mobilising women for campaigns and for supplementing their programmes of action. But prior to the compelling realities of the situation forced by the 73rd and 74th Constitution Amendment Acts, which provided for, among others, one-third seat reservation for women (including Schedule Castes and Tribes women in proportion to their population in an area) in the *panchayats* and *nagarpalikas* (that is, PRIs), an assigned role for women in elective bodies was never taken up seriously. Even the hesitant recommendations of the 'Towards Equality' report were not considered seriously by political parties. The report recommended to the political parties to adopt "a definite policy regarding the percentage of women candidates to be sponsored by them for elections to Parliament and state assemblies. While they may initially start with 15 per cent, this should be gradually increased so that in time to come the representation of women in legislative bodies has some relationship to their position in the total population of the country with regard to the state." Stony silence marked the official positions of the political parties that mattered. But as a direct consequence of the constitutional amendments providing for reservation of seats for women at the third tier of democracy, it lay in the logic of events that similar reservation, at least to begin with, be made for the other two tiers, that is, the state and national levels. And when the last elections came, the matter floated to the top of the agenda when women-related issues came up. Therefore, it is instructive to make some reference to the election manifestoes of the parties, both all-India and state/regional to see how they view the women's problems, and their participation in the decision-making processes.

The Congress (I) manifesto, even while taking credit for launching of measures for the welfare of women and providing for reservations for women in PRIs, pledged to provide for reservations for women in state legislatures and Parliament, although the exact percentage was not stated.

BSP has devoted a total of three pages in its 80 page election Manifesto providing for a 29 point near complete agenda for women aimed at their 'total empowerment'. It pledged 33 per cent reserved seats for women in all elected bodies, including state assemblies and Parliament. It is surprising that despite fine declarations, some of its MPs were found to be engaged in scuttling the measures when the 33 per cent quota bill came up in Parliament. BJP was one of the few parties to have pledged one-third reservation of seats for women. But reservations of a good number of MPs from other parties and BJP's own vocal women MPs regarding the reservation bill has succeeded so far in putting the issue in the cold storage, at least for the time being.

CPI's Assam state committee's election manifest recognises the rights to equality for women in all spheres and reservation (quota not stated) of seats for women in matters of political participation. Welfare programmes have been suggested and, as for an important right, it demand inclusion of women's names in relevant title deeds relating to land ownership.

Incidentally, all left and regional parties condemned atrocities on women and called for remedial measures.

CPI(M) Assam state committee manifesto called for 30 per cent reservation of seats for women for the legislative assembly and Lok Sabha, Like CPI, it also called for inclusion of women's name in the land title deeds.

BJP's state committee manifest only called for "effective steps for social justice for women".

AGP, which now heads the five - party (AGP, CPI, CPI(M), Autonomous State Demand Committee and United People's Party of Assam) electrical alliance state government in Assam, viewed the problem of women from the point of welfare measure. CPI(M) and Autonomous State Demand Committee (ASDC), although alliance partners, are not in the government but support it from outside. Autonomous State Demand Committee (ASDC) in its separate election manifesto called for 30 per cent seat reservation for women in the Lok Sabha, state assemblies, the autonomous councils and other such elective bodies to ensure greater political say of the women.

The eight-party Left Democratic Alliance (LDA) consisting of SUCI, Congress (S), Revolutionary Communist Party of India (RCPI), Revolutionary Socialist Party (RSP), CPI, Marxist Lennenist (ML) United Reservation Movement Council of Assam (URMCA), United Minorities Front Assam (UMFA) and PLP (S), an electoral outfit which could return two UMF MLAs only, issued a 18-point programme of action : its 15th point related to elimination of crimes against women, punishment of those guilty of crimes, and prohibition of indecent display of women in electronic and other media. All parties pledged its loyalty to socialism, secularism and democracy. The combination or the separate manifestoes of some of the constituents did not specifically call for seat reservation for women, although in election campaigns they are known to have called for equality of status for women in all matters.

Finally, the Samajvadi Party (S) Assam state unit in its 1996 election mainfesto pledged that effective steps would be taken in defence of women's dignity and to eliminate all sources of oppression inflicted on women. It was stated that special steps need to be taken to ensure legimitate status for women in the fields of employment, different social activities and political representation.

It appears a good number of political parties—it is they who nominate candidates—are to come out of the narrow grooves of treating women's problems as merely the usual welfare—related measures. Society has to be increasingly sensitised to the well-grounded position that women's fundamental human needs ought to be adequately articulated by their representatives in state and national elective bodies. It was a matter of right and not one of seeking charity or doling out favours. It was a matter of extending democratic rights and processes to women. The dichotomy between increased political participation of women as voters and fewer participants as candidates at election ought to be put an end to and hence, as a first step, the 33 per cent quota bill needs to be cleared sooner than expected. Around 1 million women are being inducted into the decision-making process at PRI-level. Reservation of seats for women would be conducive to making our democracy more meaningful. The world could become a better place to live in if both the female and male halves are given equal importance. It has been well said that democracy is functional only when citizens, both women and men, are political equals. Political empowerment of women is the crying need of the hour to bring in some balance in the male-female divide. Gone are the days when emphasis was wholly laid on the value of supportive duties traditionally known as 'women's work'.

Much depends on the behaviour pattern of political parties to ensure realisation of the goal of women's political empowerment. The women's movement has a significant role to play in all this, combined with a combination of academic and activist programmes of the women's study research centres, having regard to ground realities in different areas.

Political parties behave as they do because they seem to believe in and practise adhocism in dealing with women's problems. Their attitude is greatly influenced by tokenism. They display an overdose of conservatism in that women are not generally considered as winning candidates. In fact, more often than not, winning possibilities led political parties to choose candidates on casteist and communal considerations. As for women candidates, without much prodding, they seem to seize upon the 'deceased leader's wife syndrome' to nominate women candidates regardless of their assessment of candidates in the usual run of things. There may not be anything wrong in this when the sympathy factor is taken into consideration. Be then at it might be, the strategy worked in three assembly constituencies in Assam in the 1999 elections — Teok, Nazira and Dergaon constituencies. Similarly, Srimati Basanti Sharma was twice elected to Rajya Sabha from Assam acting on the sympathy factor. What is sought to be conveyed is that while these considerations may still be there at the discretion of nominating political parties, a reservation quota will go a long way in doing away with adhocism on the part of political parties in nominating women candidates.

Secondly, if entry of women into politics is difficult because of male domination in the society, their acceptance in the structure of the party's organisation is even more difficult. The references to a number of election manifestoes showed how parties continue to view women's problems basically as welfare-related problems. It appears to be the prevailing psyche in political parties as also mass organisations that very few women come up to the level of leadership. As for mass organisation, trade unions and peasant organisations with lakhs of membership also justify our contention. In Assam, the All Assam Students' Union (AASU) is a very powerful students' organisation and, yet, fewer are the women at the leadership level. Even as elected members, women would not be free from the discipline of patriarchy's politburos. Which is why the need arises to democratise the party structure in such a why as to institutionalise women's inclusion in the party bodies to enable them to have a share in decision-making even at the party level. Women's wings of parties as also mass organisations could hopefully play a useful role in generating a climate of opinion in favour activising political parties with a fair share of women functionaries. A case exists for some sort of social audit in political parties, albeit on a voluntary basis.

Thirdly, access to significant decision-making positions in political parties continue to elude women because of a variety of factors, domestic, public and political. A lot depends on women's own efforts to enhance their awareness to deal effectively with problems arising out of women being considered as a liability and a so-called peripheral element. Women may owe allegiance to different political formations. But they have got to increase their own awareness as a distinctive constituency as women. If the women — half of the society's population — become assertive, it is bound to have a decided impact on the political culture of the society, its political parties and all concerned.

Fourthly, one of the greatest hurdles in contesting elections is the prohibitive cost of running a campaign. The limits set by the Election Commission are indeed still skyhigh for capable but economically disabled women, and even men. A majority of the voters are poor and nearly half of the population live below the poverty line. Election expenses will continue to be a problem even after the 33 per cent reservation becomes a reality. In the interest of free and fair election, electoral reform on a very comprehensive basis is the need of the hour. It must be a systemic overhaul, not merely the removal of particular ills discussed generally. While the power of money and black money culture, is to be eradicated, fundamental reforms in the electoral system should ensure the quality of democracy and governance, accounability in all matters being a never-failing requirement.

Fifthly, women in general are also to be aware of their legal rights—a large number of them in the series of women-specific and women-related legislations in the era of

Independence. A good many legislations are there aimed at giving due recognition of their status, protection of the dignity of women and prevention of violence against them as also their exploitation. It is an important task of the women's movement and all bodies connected with women's and society's development to promote awareness about the constitutional and other rights through what is called legal literacy. As the mass of women become conscious of their rights, they could utilise their new knowledge in furthering the cause of empowerment.

Last but not least, it is a fact that they themselves find an active political career difficult to combine with home-making. Women's participation in politics was not the result of any well thought out decision of any organisation. It originated slowly and in most cases unconsciously when they were simply drawn into political activity of other members of the family, principally during the freedom movement. It was idealism that moved both men and women. It is idealism again in the changed context combined with consciousness about rights as citizens that could make the difference even today. Voting is a basic activity from which no citizen could keep aloof. Participation as voters could as well lead to participation as candidates, given the political will of the society. Some traditional factors like religion, customs and traditions could at times militate against women's participation in an active way in the decision-making processes of the locality, state and the country. But at this distance of time, women have become more mature to take time by the forelock to register their presence actively in the decision-making elective bodies at a level for meaningful development in all areas of national endeavour.

Thus, women constitute only one to two per cent of the contestants till today. Those who belong to well known parties like Congress, always have better chances as we have seen in various elections in Assam. In the State, women who have contests come from urban middle class educated, elite background. Like any other part in Assam too after the growth of insurgency and terrorism election has become a complex matter. Common citizen either man or woman, therefore, hesitate to contest election. Parties inspite of the long history of women candidate contesting in Assam election pay no attention. Though there are women's wings in each political party, but they have no positive role to play. Very few women participate or witness political activities like meetings, rallies or campaigning. One of the greatest hurdle in contesting election is the exorbitant expenditure. As women have limited independent resource, it completely eliminates women in the poverty sector from entering the area. Thus, upper caste, upper classes urban women alone can join the political sphere as party does not help an unknown women candidate. The politician and social reference expected that the example of elite women would filter down and will be accepted by women of other caste and classes. Like any other part of the country, the social and religious convention and lack of training and discipline among women have limited their participation in Assam politics.

References

1. Report of Inter-Parliamentary Union: The Action Plan. 1994.
2. Paniel L Fowlkes & Jerry Perkens: "*Gender Soles and Party Soles* as it Appocared in *The American Political Science Review* Vol. 13 1979, p. 772.
3. Louis Maisel, 'Party Reform and Pohitical Participation: The Democrats is Maine' in Meisel and Paul M. Saclls (ed) *The Future of Political Parties*. Beverly Itills, Calif, Sage Publishers, 1975 pp. 202-8.
4. Edmond Constantini & KH Creck, 'Women as Politicians: the Social Background Personality and Political Career of Femaly Party Leader': *Journal of Social Issues*, Vol. 28, 1972, pp. 217-236.
5. Rajani Kothari: *Politics in India*, Orient Longman, New Delhi, 1970.
6. Manor James, 'Parties and Party System in India, in Atul Kohli's *Indian Democracy*, 'Parties and Party System in India', in Atul Kohli's *Indian Democracy*, Princeton University Press 1988.

7. Weiner Myron, *The Indian Paradox* (ed.) Ashutosh Varshney Sage Publication. New Delhi, 1989.
8. Weiner Myron, *India at Polls 1980*, American Enterprise Institute, Washington DC 1983.
9. JK Chopra, *Women in Indian Parliament* Mittal Publication, 1993.
10. Snehalata, Pande Women and Public Activity, Ajanta Publication Delhi 1100071990.
11. HK Barpujari SK Barpujari & AC Bhuyan (Ed) *Political History of Assam*, Govt. of Assam.

11

RESERVATION AS A STRATEGY FOR POLITICAL EMPOWERMENT–THE ONGOING DEBATE

Rachna Suchinmayee

Introduction

Women throughout the world have a low socioeconomic and political status. Even though democracy made great gains in 1989-1991, women members average only 11 per cent of world's legislatures.[1] The presence of woman in formal democratic process is woefully inadequate at all levels, centre, state and local/grassroot level. They are on margin in political decision-making processes. This fact has evoked concern in recent years about the political status of women. It has been increasingly realised that unless empowered politically, the socioeconomic status of women cannot be improved. Thus, the movement for the political empowerment by women has steadily gained momentum today.

International Concern

A brief outline in international arena regarding the voices raised for political empowerment of women, becomes essential. Preparations were made by the United Nations Organization (UNO) for a convention, way back in 1952, about women's political rights. Again in 1967, there was a Declaration on Elimination of Discrimination against women by the UN General Assembly. 1975 witnessed an international conference in Mexico, where a world plan of action was drafted. It emphasised that political participation comprised of women having voting power, their acting as pressure groups, their being elected as representatives and as governmental employees. Again in 1980, there was a conference in Copenhagen, which was named as 'Participation in the Political and other Decision-making Processes and participation in Efforts to Promote International Coperation and Strengthen Peace.[2] The year 1985 witnessed a conference at Nairobi, where forward looking strategies for the advancement of women and the international blue print for action until year 2000 was planned.

In this context, the 1995 Beijing conference was a landmark, where the focus was on political empowerment of women, and consequently, on the issue of women's reservation. This received an international recognition. The Inter-parliamentary union meeting held in New Delhi on 1997 February 14-18, attended by about 240 representatives from 78 countries, focused on the theme: 'Towards Partnership between Men and Women in Politics.[3] The final consensus was that establishment of quota for women's political participation was legitimate and practical. It was also felt that women need to be established in the political system as well in the membership and hierarchies of political parties, and with respect to candidates chosen by them to contest election.

Experiences have proved that despite the constitutional arrangements, women all over the world have not been given actual power. It was realised that democratic norms cannot be realised if marginalised sections, which include women, are not in the mainstream of political process. There will be no change in the political milieu of the country, particularly since most women both as voters and vote-seekers are within the patriarchal structure. Not only a change within the existing political structure is required, but also within women's own perception of sensitive issues that directly concern their lives.[4] Why we need the strategy for affirmative action, or positive discrimination in favour of women is because the age-old traditions have kept women the periphery of political power. This calls for a debate, devising methods through law for their access to political power. This again brings us to the debate on quota system/ reservation for women as a strategy for their political empowerment.

With this backdrop, an attempt has been made to understand the extent and magnitude of women's political participation in free India.

India

True to the spirit of freedom struggle, and in recognition of the important role played by women in freedom struggle, and also the promises made by the leaders of the nation, the Constitution of India pledges itself to full equality among men and women. The Preamble to the Constitution of India resolved to secure to all its citizens: Justice, social, economic and political; liberty of thought, expression, belief, faith and worship; Equality of status and opportunity; and to promote among them all fraternity assuming the dignity of all individuals and the unity of the nation.

To action these national objectives, the Constitution guarantees certain fundamental rights and freedom such as freedom of speech, protection of life and personal liberty. While these may be termed as positive rights, the negative rights are the prohibition of discrimination on the basis of race, caste, religion, sex or denial of equal protection on such grounds.[5] Indian women are the beneficiaries of these rights in the same manner as men. Article 14 ensures "equality before law and Article 15 prohibits any discrimination" interalia of sex. All these provisions ensure equal opportunity of political participation by women along with men, and that they needed to be represented within the system and the status quo. This false sense of complacency that women have been granted political right along with men on an equal footing by the Constitution, remained for quite some time. Thus, in the 1950s and the '60s there was no such open expression. However, with the

'70s studies undertaken by the Committee on the Status of Women in India (CSWI), revealed shocking data (as per 1971 census). This was a watershed year which raised concern among lawyers, thinkers, planners, regarding the servitude position of women in India. Since then, the demand for improvement and the political empowerment of women started at the global level.

Why Reservation?

Before coming to the issue of the strategies, debates and resultants of the problem of women reservation, it becomes necessary to debate on the need for reservation. A very pertinent question arises as to why reservation is the only alternative for the victims of age-old oppression and exploitation? The remedy, if rationally thought upon, can only be either 'equal opportunity' or 'reservation'. For some time, equal opportunity will not work because of the top-dog/ under-dog attitude that dies hard. Can there be equality immediately in an unequal society? Reservation is a means of protecting the weaker sections of society, who have for centuries been socially, historically and politically exploited, giving them a chance to come on a par with the stronger sections and be prepared to take advantage of 'equal opportunity'. Women are in this category a historically victimised group. Women are nowhere in the planning process after five decades of democratic politics. Economic independence cannot alone suffice. Power at political level would only change the status quo, Parliament is a sad spectacle. Reservation, thus, aims at giving not only *panchayati* women, but all women participation in public life.

Beginning of Serious Concern

The Committee on the Status of Women in India (CSWI) though agreeing to the problems especially of rural women's life, only recommended the establishment of statutory women's *panchayats*. In case of state assemblies and Parliament, the committee failed to address the problem of under-representation caused by institutionalised inequalities, which 25 years of democracy had failed to dislodge.[6] But with an increase in grassroots organisation, the new groups of poor women demonstrated for greater dynamism and challenge. The issue of reservation was periodically raised by political activists as well as serving women legislators in various government-sponsored conferences.

The Rajiv Gandhi government in 1985, took the issue of women as a priority issue. Subsequently, women's division within social welfare became a Department for Women and Child Development within the Ministry of Human Resource Development. But this did not make much impact, as in 1988, the first draft of the National Perspective Plan (NPP) for women to the year 2000, which recommended 30 per cent reservation for women in all elective bodies — from *Panchayats* to Parliament, put in a proviso that in the initial years, this quota may be filled by nomination co-option. The final version of NPP, however, only recommended 30 per cent reservation in *Panchayats* and municipalities to be filled by election. During Rajiv Gandhi's regime, efforts were made to amend the Constitution so as to provide for 33 per cent reservation to women in local grassroots level *Panchayat* bodies. But the amendment (73rd) was made in 1992 under the next government providing for 1/3 reservation to women in the women *panchayats* with Schedule Castes and Tribes inbuilt quotas for women. The bill was released is April 1993.

The conferring of constitutional status on local self-government as an integral part of the Indian governance structure, and mandating 1/3rd reservation for women in all these bodies, with an in-built quota for Schedule Castes and Tribes women were quietly ratified in April 1993.

Between 1993 and 1996, women's organisations united for a joint demand for reservation in state assemblies and Parliament. The demand was accepted and featured in the manifestoes of the major parties:

Janata Dal (JD) : The reservation on 30 per cent elective post in local bodies for women has to be extended to union and state legislatures.

Congress	:	The Congress has already reserved seats for women in the *gram panchayats* and municipalities. It also proposes to provide reservation for women in state assembly and Parliament.
CPI	:	Having made a beginning with *panchayats*, the next step should be to reserve 1/3rd seats for women in state assembly and Parliament.
CPI (M)	:	1/3rd of the seats in legislature and Parliament be reserved for women.
BJP	:	In state assembly and Parliament and all elected position, 33 per cent reservation will ensure that at the dawn of the 21st century, Indian women will have true participation.
Samata Party	:	The party will initiate legislation for the reservation of constituencies for women candidates in rotation for one-third of the seats in both the Lok Sabha and state assemblies.

But against these theoretical assurances, the major political parties are taking vogue positions on the issue of caste-based and religion-based women's reservation regarding four sub-categories within the women quota — backward caste, Muslims, Christians and Sikhs. In September 1996, when the reservation bill was brought before the house, the first obstacle was about the fixed quota women from the Other backward castes (OBC). The main votaries were Sharad Yadav, Ram Vilas Paswan, Mulayam Singh Yadav and other OBC MPs. The main argument advanced by them was that with a blanket reservation, the upper caste women would corner all the party tickets and get supremacy in Parliament.

The pressure was mounting by the women activists. It gained momentum after the ratification in 1993. In 1996 general elections, only 34 (thatis, 6.3 out of 537 declared seats went to women.[7] Mainstream national level parties, which had a longer history of involving women such as Congress, the Janata Dal and the Communist Party, did not do much better. Only 103 women out of 388, who contested the election to the 11th Lok Sabha, were supported by the parties. Congress had 16 women in Parliament, BJP had 14 women and JD had only nine seats. Such induction reflects tokenism rather than powersharing. It could also be termed as the patriarchal frame of society, which has marginalised women in mainstream parliamentary politics.

1996: The Bill being Tossed Around

Amidst such a scenario of opposition, the double face of parties and MPs, the Constitution amendment (81st) Bill, 1996 was introduced by the United Front Government All hopes were dashed to the ground at the fag end of the discussion on an aggressive plea for proportional representation of seats for women belonging to OBC.[8] The bill was then referred to a joint select committee of 32 parliamentarians under gita Mukherji for amendments with a brief to see if the demand of having reservation for the OBCs from within the 33 per cent could be met. The committee in its final recommendation wanted the bill to be passed at the earliest and rejected the demand for an OBC quota. Both the houses witnessed clamorous scenes with members cutting across party lines.

1997

Once again the government failed to put the bill before Parliament due to strong objections to the bill in its present form. It was deliberately attempted to keep the bill in 'cold storage' by stating that the consensus needed to be evolved.

1998

Although, Prime Minister Atal Behari Vajpayee assured representatives of the women's organisation that he would not only introduce the bill in the Budget session, but also put it to vote and the Union Cabinet also approved the introduction of the bill, it was once again put under the lid on the issue that the quota should be slashed to 15 per cent for OBC women. The women's bill was stalled in the Lok Sabha and was finally deferred on July 17.

What does this show? Women's reservation bill is surrounded by sham and hyprocisy and more by male chauvinism. The shelving of the women's reservation bill calls for a serious debate on the text of the Bill.

Women's Reservation Bill

The proposed bill is debated upon from many angles. It requires analysis and discussion. The bill envisaged reservation by rotation of the constituencies through lottery system so any constituency could be selected for the reserved category. The debate and doubt is on the infirmity of rotational principle.

The Debate

Senior advocate of Supreme Court. Abhishek M Singhvi, has opined that though the rationale is unclear, it appears evidently to be actuated by a desire not to permanently shut men off. He reiterates that the constitutional mandate for rotation of constituencies reserved for women is impracticable and harmful.[9] Madhu Kishwar, womens activitists also contends that the bill has been drafted irresponsibly. She opines that the rotational principle means that neither male nor female aspirants will know which constituency they can stand from. The result: at least 1/3rd of male legislators will be routinely uprooted and denied seats from their chosen areas of work and influence, and an equal number of women will be told at the last minute where they can fight an election from.[10] This will further erode the incentive to serve a constituency because everyone will remain forever uncertain about whether or not they can actually get elected from their areas of influence.

To this problem, Madhu kishwar comes out with a suggestive measure. Instead of 33 per cent rotating lottery system of reservation, we provide for 50 per cent reservation by having double member constituencies.[11] This would give women a share of seats in proportion to their population. That is to say, each constituency should be represented by two members, one of which has to be a woman. The other constituency would remain open and general, which means there would be nothing to prevent even two women being elected from it on the basis of winning the highest common vote and the other on the basis of acquiring the highest vote among women candidates. This system will encourage team work among men and women in parties. It will also create a healthy competition between them to serve the constituency. Doubling the figure of MPs will also lighten the load of work and remove the possibility of '*biwi-beti* brigade'.

If the rotational principle is not to be eliminated, it may be provided that in case reservation for women in legislatures is to continue beyond the presently mandated duration of 15 years, the next round of reservation after 15 years may commence with new and rotated constituencies.

The delay and debate on the issue of absence of reservation for OBC women, impartially seen, has no actual link to the issue of women's reservation in general. It has already marred the process of the actual proposed bill. Reservation for backward classes generally never existed in Indian legislatures. Reservation for Schedule Castes and Scheduled Tribes on the contrary, was a subject of debate in the constituent assembly and found specific inclusion in a specific set of constitutional provisions. Ever since 1992, women reservation in Panchayati Raj institution operated without any linkage with the lack of reservation for OBC women in these institution. Even as CP Bhambhri rieterates that the logic that women should participate in the decision making process gets diluted if participation is on the basis of their religion or caste because they are reduced to the level of sectorial leaders and not women leaders.[12] Veena Nayyar, too on the issue contends that the talk of quota within quota is a blatant attempt to divide the women. That they forget about OBCs when it came to the 73rd Amendment because it concerned only governance at the village level and there was no need for considering a system of proportional representation whereby the legitimate political aspirations of each group can be satisfied without breaking down the whole system with competing quotas.[13]

Therefore, quota or no quota, only the most deserving should get the benefits. Why not pass the bill as it is first and later decide about the quota within a quota. Women have to begin somewhere. As Kannabiran and Kannabiran contend that women are fighting for the principle of representation. Women's representation in politics will some how improve the status of all women including the Dalits, OBCs, etc.[14]

Another argument put forth, disfavouring the bill in its present form, is the concern for creating a *zenana* dabba argument. The objection seeks to encapsulate the apprehension that men will limit women to only 33 per cent, which might become a maxima or an upper limit for women's presence in legislatures. But then assuming without conceding that in the first phase women's reservation will result in an upper ceiling of only 33 per cent it is for stronger presence than the present 6-7 per cent.[15] With the time pace, this would reflect a sufficiently strong voice to result in allotment of ever increasing number of seats.

The one more objection on proxy control and the '*biwi* brigade' deserves to be considered. The proposed reservation will be cornered by elite women, by wives, daughters, conflict of personal interest between them and the women at that level.

Basically, the OBC politicians used a clever tactic to stall women's reservation. Caste and commual card was used to confuse the whole issue. The OBC leaders too, were not sincere about either the backward caste women or the Muslim women's share. Supporting the quota for OBC, several women leaders too have come out with their expressions like Salija, Meera Kumar (CWC member) and Uma Bharti (BJP) Uma Bharti's comment "I'm for '*Mandal and Kamandal*" is indeed surprising.[16] Because what is essential today is the general involvement of women at all levels of power structure to ensure a true society, without any quota within quota for political leverage. Mamta Banerjee rightly affirms: "What percentage of OBC and Muslim women candidates Laloo Yadav and Mulayam Singh Yadav had put up in the last election ?" As Brinda Karat opines, there is no reservation for OBC in any state assembly or in Parliament, and nor has any such demand ever been raised by OBC. Therefore, to raise the demand, OBC women now is nothing but a pretext to shelve the bill, as it protects the interests of OBC men. The last Parliament had about 200 OBC male MPs. Why are OBC women not there if OBC women's representation is their real concern? Their talk of quotas within quota is a blatant attempt to divide the women. Madhu Kishwar maintains that mothers and mistresses of powerful men will be used by them as agents or nominees of proxy control. When party tickets are given to the wife of a Kamal Nath as a means of keeping him in power through her, or when wives of local politicians are given *panchayat* and *Zilla parishad* seats simply because a certain number of women have to be compulsorily fielded in the elections, it makes a mockery of women's participation of politics. Some of the women candidates may be representatives of the *parivar* syndrome, but it is not a permanent phenomenon. '*Biwi* brigede' would be easily overshadowed once women realise their power in a democracy; more and more women would come forward to participate in elections, and would be elected on their own merit. Evaluation reports have suggested that women leaders in *panchayats* have given a greater thrust to the developmental activities in their respective areas. Moreover, the *parivar* syndrome is not restricted to women alone, this malaise affects men too.[17] Could Laloo Prasad Yadav be stopped from bringing his wife? In any case would Prakash Singh Badal or Farooq Abdullah or Karunanidhi be stopped from fielding their sons? Just because they are men, no one points finger at them. So why question women? This very culture of male-female segregation prevalent in our society adds to the disabilities suffered by women in the political world.

Amongst the various objections to the proposed bill, the suggestion for constituencies may be clubbed into one and represented by one male and female member (as also suggested by Madhu Kishwar, discussed earlier in this paper) — is actuated by an apprehension that simple reservation for women would result in ghettoisation of women and pit women against women. But this does not have much innovation. This kind of suggestion does not operate in any legal system or legislatures in the world. Moreover, multi-member constituency would not fit in with our existing constitutional alteration of several provisions and chapters of our Constitution based on representational democracy. It would also raise several other issues regarding the total strength of our Parliament (whether it would remain 550 or become 1,100), the potential enhanced expenditure involved in maintaining double the member of MPs, the issue as to which of the two members would speak for the constituency.

Though probe and thought on all these issues still requires more open debate and discussion, one can impartially admit that through reservation the state intervenes to admit the imbalance in an effort to at least rectify it. Abraham Lincolnis (Lincolra's) concept of democracy is an ideal, unachieved in the world. Democracy falls short when women of whatever colour or ethnic group cannot vote or cast an effective vote, cannot expect success in electing representatives of their choice or being elected to the legislative bodies, and have little hope for enactment of laws they believe are critically needed.[18]

Arguments For and Against

The arguments pro and against the issue of reservation of women in Parliament, have been quite conflicting and mixed from various corners, even after the debate and discussion of the basic text. The politicians, women activists and thinkers are divided on the issue of women's reservation.

Against

Argument against the issue has come up from Shatkari Mahila Aghadi that experience of reservation in *panchayat* in Maharashtra has not been favourable. The relatives of established male leaders are fielded, with no impact on inefficiency and corruption. Yogendra Makwana calls the bill as an inflated one. What is needed is more women candidates in elections, rather that providing statutory reservation for them in Parliament. Nearly 50 per cent of the voters in our country are women. Should they not exercise their voting strength to get more tickets instead of begging for statutory reservation? He reiterates that in a country where a women ruled for 17 years as Prime Minister in BJP and Congress Vijaya Raje Sindhia and Sonia Gandhi have respectively reached the top position, Najma Haptullah is elected deputy chairperson of Rajya Sabha for the third term and earlier Violet Alwa was also elected to this position thrice — it seems paradoxical to talk of women's reservation in Parliament. Vishwa Hindu Parishad Lobby among BJP MPs does not want women reservation. Ram Vilas Vedanti — a VHP block Lok Sabha MP from Pratapgarh along with Uma Bharti and Ganga Charan Rajput agitates on women's quota business: "Women should not be given any reservation." The Congress Party was no better off than BJP on the women's bill. It forced even its women president Sonia Gandhi to buckle under party MPs' pressure. Rajesh Pilot and P Shiv Shankar led the revolt within the Congress. They demanded 27 per cent OBC quota within the overall 33 per cent women reservation. They questioned why shouldn't BC women get a share when the very concept of women reservation is based on the backwardness criteria. Madhu Kishwar counters the demand for reservation of seats in Parliament and the state assemblies for women with the contention that it would stultify the political process and prevent the emergence of outstanding women who practice better politics of renewal and change.

For : (On the other hand, Promila Dandavate, an avid crusader of women's rights, is in the forefront of the struggle for reservation and a chunk in the power structure for the women of the country. She opines that the quality of parliamentary debate will definitely improve with at least 180 women MPs.[19] Former Union Minister, Margaret too is playing a leading role in mobilising women MPs and other organisations, and is quite disgusted by the way the bill has been treated. Veena Nayyar also favours the bill, suggesting there can be no empowerment without power. With the amendment what women are seeking is not reservation but de-reservation that is, male representation be scaled down to 67 per cent from 95 per cent. It is only when women will acquire an 'effective voice' and become a legislative force will agendas for women in terms of education, health, shelter, access and control to set targets for their empowerment can be implemented. Margaret Alva has showed her concern for the 5 per cent of meagre representation of women of the total contestants. Of these who get elected constitute a still smaller percentage. Therefore the big task before us today is to ensure justice, to reduce the disparities in the opportunities and facilities available to women and make them equal partners in development.

However, it would be dangerous to conflate the two discrete spheres of political activity, namely that of Panchayati Raj institution and that of legislatures and Parliament. At the level of Panchayati Raj institution, what matters is the nature and strength of familial and social patriarchy, no matter what caste the women may belong to. On the other hand, the women who make it to the legislature and Parliament have usually attained a class status that enables their movement out of the household, and thus, it is the patriarchal power arrangement of the party that matters more. All parties have thus found it convenient to deploy women only strategically, resulting in the emergence of '*biwi* brigade'. But today reservation has become an imperative, not an option. The policy of 'tokenism' by having a few women in the legislature and executive wings of government offers serious obstacles to their acting as spokeperson for women's rights and opportunities. If this process continues, women would loose their faith in political process to change their condition. Reservation would provide an impetus to both the women and political parties to give a fairer deal to nearly half the population in the various units of government. The system would generate greater freedom to articulate their views, increase women legislators' sense of responsibility and concern for the problems affecting women, instill socioeconomic change and broadening the political elite structure.

Moreover, women reservation cannot lead to their becoming isolated pockets in the nation because women are not marginal to society as a minority group. It might be a transitional measure to break through the existing structure of inequalities. This will not be retrogression 'from the doctrine of equality of sexes and the principle of democratic representation' as felt by representatives of political parties and most women legislators, but it may serve a long-term objective of equality and democracy in a better manner. Women need to represent their own interests. Statistics and social indicators show that women's interest have not been served.

The argument that women should come into Parliament only on their merit, against the '*parivar* syndrome' is true, but then their representation is negligible in a merit based system. Reservation should result in less inequality and increased confidence of women. Women if encouraged to participate through reservation, will emerge even in non-reserved constituencies. Once women emerge, we can revert to a merit based system. Also, the argument that women's reservation is a play of the upper castes to bring their women into Parliament is not true. Schedule Castes and Scheduled Tribe and OBC men have come into Parliament either through constitutionally mandated reservations or by being given tickets by their parties, they have significant representation in Parliament within their party organisation. It is upto the 'same people' to ensure that party tickets are given for women from minorities and disadvantaged communities.

The possibility that 33 per cent reservation will ghettoise women, has its own reasoning. In the face of the fact that women today are already marginalised, this provision alone could arrest this trend. It will provide them an opportunity to escape from ghettosiation imposed upon them by patriarchal norms and practices.[20]

Reservation reflects the will of the people. It is the part of the common minimum programme of all parties, which make up the United Front (UF) government. The Thors Prime Minister had himself introduced the 81st Amendment Bill in Parliament. The leader of the opposition has fully endorsed the bill in his public address to the nation. The national Policy on women of the Ministry of Human Resource Development (HRD) has stressed the need for more women to be part of the political decision-making process. The national alliance of women's groups have strongly articulated the need for reservation for women in Parliament and the assemblies. Even after looking at over 100 submissions including the attorney general, the law ministry and the national commission for women, the select committee made up of representatives of all parties from both houses has strongly recommended that the bill as amended, be passed without delay and that necessary legislation to give effect to the provisions of the bill may be brought before Parliament at the earliest. So how can it be reiterated that reservation for women is the demand of only a few urban elite women and does not reflect the will of the people? It was indeed surprising, when a positive response in favour of bill, came from a male MP, Anand Mohan, on the fateful day of July 14, 1998. He seemed to be the only honest male politician in the house to have questioned amidst revolt, "speaker sir, what about the women's reservation bill?"

The bill would bring roughly 181 women in Parliament. The integration of women in the political process at all levels of political life is essential for the democratisation of politics. Although it is known that some sections of people in the country including the women should take more active interest in public life this cannot be ensured by a system of reverse preference to ensure a quota for women in legislature. This is the surest way of ensuring that women do not achieve equal status in life. The idea is to bring about a qualitative change with women's participation in these fora rather than bring the level of functioning down further with women simply joining as puppets in this enterprise.

In future electoral contests, parties that show themselves to be sensitive — voluntarily rather than under compulsion — to the need for greater female representation could well reap a proportional harvest. This would salvage the issue of gender justice from the detritus of caste prejudice that today surrounds it. Another strategy would be for a deligent study of the patterns of social representation that have emerged from the women's quota in local bodies. The large number of women who have recently assumed office as mayors of important cities is an index of the substantive impact of this measure. Objective observers are convinced that in their social origin, the women who have gained seats in local bodies are as representatives of the underlying caste sub-stratum as are the men. If the appropriate lessons are avidly disseminated before the extrapolation of the principle of reservations to legislative institution many of the political insecurities that have recently emerged well be placated.

References

1. 'Distribution of Seats between Men and Women in National Parliament (Geneva : Inter-Parliamentary Union, 1991) and the 'World's Women', 1970-1990, (New York, UN 1991).
2. Programme of Action for the Second Half of the United Nations Deeds for Women: Equality, Peace and Development. A/Conf. 94/34; 13 Aug. 1980: UN Publication, p. 3.
3. T.K. Rajalakshmi, 'Women in Politics' *Frontline*, March 21, 1997.
4. Asha Ramesh A Note to Support the Introduction of a Bill for Reservation at the Legislative and Parliamentary levels, National Alliance of Women; Fax 91-11-623139; 20/5/96; 12-23.
5. Basu, *Commentary on the Constitution of India* (3rd edition) p. 69.
6. Majumdar, Seminar, 457, Sept. 1997, 'Historical Surroundings', Vina p. 14-15.
7. Seminar, 457, Sept. 1997, 'Democracy and reservation', Malini Bhattacharya, p. 24.
8. The Hindustan Times, Sunday, July 19, 1998, 'Wanted a whole new pie,' Madhu Kishwar, p. 7.

9. Seminar, 757, Sept. 1997, 'The Women's reservation Bill' Abhishek, M. Singhvi p. 28.
10. The Hindustan Times, July 19, 1998, 'Wanted a whole new pie,' Madhu Kishwar, p. 7.
11. The Hindustan Times, July 19, 1998, 'Wanted a whole new pie,' Madhu Kishwar, p. 7.
12. The Hindustan Times, Aug. 4, 1998, 'Woes of Gender Politics', C.P. Bhambhri, p. 7.
13. The Hindustan Times, Mar. 11, 1998, 'Ending male monopoly' Veena Nayyar, p. 7.
14. Economic and Political Weekly, 1 Feb. 1997 Vasanth Kannabiran and Kalpana Kannabiran 'From Social Action to Political Action: Women and the 81st Amendment', p. 196-97.
15. Seminar 757, Sept. 1997 'The Women's reservation Bill' Abhishek M. Singhvi, p. 28.
16. The Hindustan Times, Sept. 15, 1996: 'Gender decide stallls quota', Kalyania Shankar, p. 6.
17. The Hindustan Times, Dec. 22, 1996, 'Men are scared of losing their seats', Promila Dandvate, p. 5.
18. Refer to democratic criteria in Arend Lijphart, 'Democracies' (New Haven : Yale University Press, 1984), pp. 2-3.
19. The Hindustan Times, Sept. 15, 1996, 'Gender decide stalls quota', Kalayani Shankar, p. 6.
20. Document sponsored by the National Commission for women, New Delhi, INDIA, 'Towards Justice'.

12

EQUALITY IN POLITICAL DECISION-MAKING [Some Implications of the Panchayati Raj System (Grass root Institutions) Amendment Act 1992 For Women in India]

Niroj Sinha

It is global a experience that in the formulation of polities and programmes for national and international goals, women barring a few, have seldom played an effective role. They have been marginals in politics and political decision-making process. In 1988, the average percentage of women represented in national parliaments worldwide stood at 14.6 per cent. What is more, it is decreasing considerably per cent. True, women in almost all the countries have de jure right to participate in political decision-making, but in fact they continue to be under represented and marginal in political decision-making bodies at all levels. How can there be, then, equality in political decision-making? The urgent need of the hour at this juncture is to find a way to increase the number of women in the politically representative bodies. In a democratic polity, it is expected that the processes and decisions reflect the will of the people and represent the interests of all the various groups and formations in the population of the country. It rarely happens. The decision, in fact, are made by the powerful in the society for furthering their self interests of various groups. Women form the largest minority group, almost 50 per cent of any country's population, but are hardly visible in the area of politics. They are so scarce, their voices can hardly be heard. They are the silent minority unheard and unseen. But democracy does not and cannot operate by proxy. Every citizen needs to take part in the political activities and perform the political duties. Women have to take processes to ensure the democratic nature of the polily and for this they have to be present in political bodies.

It is easier seen than done. Politics is an exercise of power and denotes the functioning of a whole array policies of public institutions and forms, which are involved in moulding the lives of people by way of decisions, which influence their interpersonal relationships.[1] Thus, politics throughout the ages has been constructed and moulded on the basis of those norms which have been identified, though loosely, as masculine. Rationality, self discipline, competition, aggression, orderliness, universality to mention a few, are the priced qualities in political parlance. On the contrary, irrationality, indiscipline, particularity, submissiveness, impulsiveness are some of the qualities associated with the feminine nature. The result is the distancing of women from every thing political.[2] Women are perceived as part of the social structure and not as part of power phenomenon. Simon de Behaviour calls as "being rather than doing".[3] The male-public and female private dichotomy in social perception has been found to be the greatest hindrance in the way of women's access to power and political decision-making, even in highly developed countries like the Nordic ones. "Democracy was still unfinished, since women constituted a minority in politics (as Drude Dahlerup remarks in *The Unfinished Democracy: Women in Nordic Politics*.[4] It is even more true in the countries where cultural norms and traditions still restrict women to the private sphere of action. Politics is not for them. It is strictly "public" and male dominated sphere of action.

It would be apt here to discuss and define politics in a slightly wider perspective. An important feature of the feminist efforts has been to proclaim the political nature of private life, and the relation between the sexes which has brought traditional politics into question and has forced the authorities to take account of problems hitherto regarded as belonging to private life.[5] It is now a well recognised proposition in women's studies/movement viz. that all spheres of lives involving any relationship is political; that millions of women are silently (and not always very successfully) waging a struggle against the patriarchal and feudal forces that seek to confine and contain them. It is not lack of consciousness of her human and political rights, but the vicious circle into which she is placed from the very beginning of her life. This struggle against patriarchy in its myriad forms is a prolonged and complex one, and it needs effective participation in politics in a visible and appreciable number at effective levels and in meaningful positions.[7]

This brings us to a theoretical discussion of what a sizeable number of women can do in the political bodies. Drude Dahlerup maintains that it makes a big difference whether women constitute a small minority or a large minority, although still a minority. She developed a theory of the 'critical mass' in which she maintains that if women's number rose to 25-30 or higher, these women reached a critical 'mass', which permitted them to intervene and benefit from the support of women colleagues in what was 'nevertheless' still a male-dominated body.[8] She considers support from outside by a strong feminest movement as a necessary requirement towards effectiveness of women's participation in the decision-making representative bodies. She quoted the developments in her own country where women now constituted approximately 25 per cent of all elected members of parliament and local councils. It is the same with other Nordic countries.[9]

Various strategies have been suggested for augmenting women's place in political bodies, such as changing the electoral laws (for instance proportional election systems tended to be more favourable to women than election systems with single member districts) women's political parties (the successful use of these in Iceland in 1983 was noted), and public campaigns' organisational structure of political life.[10]

Another important method is fixing a quota for women at all levels of political decision-making bodies. This question of quota, in order to increase women's presence in political life, was being discussed in Denmark and was applied in Norway in public commissions.[11]

With this theoretical backdrop, let us come to the Indian scene.

The Constitution of India guarantees gender equality in all spheres of life including political. Thus, Indian women (at least in law) have equal rights of political participation along with men. They can vote in elections, can fight elections and get elected to legislative bodies right from the federal to the grassroots level. They can hold executive and leadership positions at various levels. So it is that India can boast of a very strong leadership in the primeministership of Indira Gandhi for more than one-and-a-half decade, besides a number of powerful chief ministers and governor's. However, nothing much has happened for the masses of Indian women in the last four decades. There has been some mobilisation of women voters in the last two decades, especially during the Women's Decade (1975-85). The political parties to some extent have started to recognise the potential of women as a 'vote bank'. As regards their candidacy for elections, the number has risen constantly, but the percentage of women getting elected to Parliament has declined. A raincheck on the election data to Lok Sabha reveals that women's percentage in the lower house has never exceeded 8 per cent (see Appendix I).

Why is it so? There is the argument about a particular style of socialisation process for women, their generally weak economic position, lack of education especially in developing countries like India, and above all the danger of violence hanging over women in all spheres of life, and especiallys.

In the areas of politics. The political culture which is predominantly masculine, determines the attitude of political parties towards women tolerates a few weak women, but is very hostile towards the entry of women in a viable and strong position in politics.

Can we leave things as they are? The question of participation of women in politics and the political process has been debated in Parliament many times. There is the human rights argument that as 50 per cent of the population comprises women, it was unjust that women were underrepresented in Parliament. The existing conflict of interests between women and men was a determining reason for women's entry in politics. Men would simply be unwilling or less capable to represent women's interests in politics adequately.[12]

Despite the guarantee of constitutional equality, women have not been able to get equal treatment or opportunity because they are not present in the institutions and process relevant for it. Hence the need to get into these processes and institutions, again and entry into the functioning of the status and share control over the apparatus of state. This alone would lead to preserve and promote equality and justice, and bring about the necessary policy changes and social restructuring so as to usher in a humane and suitable social order.

So, this brings us back to the question of strategy, and one important strategy would be to fix a quota for women in all political decision-making bodies, atleast for sometime to come. This might mean, at least for a while, a certain compromise on the quality of participation. Fixing of 'quotas' or 'reservation' of seats for women would open up a possible entry point for them in politics, and this is necessary because it cannot be denied that a handful of women in legislative bodies cannot make their voice strong enough to be heard. How do they, then, equally share in the decision-making and policy formulations?

It is precisely at this point that the 73rd Amendment to the Constitution of India, known as Panchayati Raj Amendment Act 1992, could have very important implications for women's political participation. This act, although related to only the grassroots level institution 'nevertheless provides for 33 per cent reservation for women in local bodies, both at the deliberative and leadership positions.

It has not happened suddenly, India has witnessed a long-drawn debate on reservation for the various minorities and backward communities such as the Scheduled Castes and Scheduled Tribes and women. Although, reservation for the first two categories was provided by the Constitution, reservation for women has been rough weather from the very beginning. Reservation for women in all the elected bodies from the Centre to the local level has been a fiercely debated issue, and it began in the Constituent Assembly itself. One section of the women's movement had at that time suggested continued reservation of seats on the line of Government of India Act 1935.[14] Women members in the Constituent Assembly, however, rejected this as against the principle of social equality. Much later, the Committee on the State of Women in India (CSWI) decided to maintain the same position, through two members submitted a dissent note.[15] A group of the social scientists consulted by the committee strongly advocated reservation for women, especially at the *panchayat* (grassroots) level. The arguments given in favour of reservation for women in the legislative bodies at the state and central level are :

(i) That the declining trend in women's representation was the result of the reluctance of political parties to sponsor women candidates which, however, offers real obstacles in making the few legislators act as spokesperson for women's rights and opportunities.

(ii) That in a situation of political parties reflecting the established values of a male-dominated society, certain structural changes in the sociopolitical set up were necessary to make room for desirable social change; otherwise losing faith in the political process to change their condition of life', women might 'opt out' of the political system and become either passive partners or rebels.

(iii) That a system of reservation of a proportion of seats for women in elected bodies would pave the path for a 'fairer deal to nearly half the population in the various units of government; and,

(iv) That, a system of reservation could increase the women legislator's sense of responsibility and concern for women specific-problems, and this would lead to increasing mobilisation of women both in the electorates and within the political parties. Social scientists associated with the committee also hold the viewthat improvements in the political status of women constituted an integral aspect of the overall problem of socioeconomic change and 'broadening' the 'political elite structure'. It was pointed out very forcefully that a 30 per cent reservation of seats in the legislative bodies will alter the very character of our legislature and will compel the political parties to change them strategies and tactics and induce them to give women their due.[16]

There was opposition on this issue from the side of the representatives of the political parties and most women legislators. The 'Towards Equality' committee rejected the suggestion for a system of reservation for women to state assemblies and Parliament. However, it recommended "statutory women's *panchayats* at the village level to ensure greater participation by women in the political process as an integral part of the Panchayati Raj structures.[17] The recommendation was passed on to state governments, received mostly negative response and was, therefore, buried within the government. Some states, however, began a gradual process of induction of more women in the *panchayats*, as they began steps to entrust more powers and responsibilities to the *panchayats*. The most daring was the Karnatak *zilla parishads, taluk panchayats, mandal panchayats* and Nyaya panchayat Act of 1983, which provided for 25 per cent seats being reserved for women.

The National Perspective Plan (1988) proposed 30 per cent reservation to all elective bodies to be filled, at least in the initial years, by nomination or co-option. The debate organised by the national women's organisations refused the proposal for reservation in the state assemblies or Parliament, but recommended 30 per cent reservation for women in Panchayati Raj institutions "with due precautions to ensure representation of the weaker sections of women, especially Dalits and tribals.[18] The women's organisations were, however, emphatic on the need for elections to ensure the emergence of a new leadership from gramroots.[19]

The 64th Amendment Bill introduced by Rajiv Gandhi was a step further in this direction. The 22nd Amendment in 1990 proposed one-third reservation for women in the Panchayati bodies with an additional provision of one-third among the reserved categories of Scheduled Castes and Scheduled Tribes and among office-bearers. Ultimately, the 73rd Amendment was passed by the parliament on December 22, 1992 providing for 33 per cent reservation of seats for women in Panchayati bodies. It was ratified by half the states by April 1993. Undoubtedly, this act is most significant for the reservation provided to women along with the Scheduled Castes and Scheduled Tribes. If fully utilised as many as 7.95 lakh women, including those belonging to Schedule Castes and Tribes can become *panches* and *sarpanches* (member and chairperson) in the *Panchayat*. Following are the provisions of the Act :

1. Not less than one-third of the seats will be reserved for women (including the Schedule Castes and Tribes) and these may be allotted by rotation to different constituencies of the *panchayat*.

2. In the seats reserved for Schedule Castes and S. Tribes not less than one-third of total number of such seats to be reserved for women.

3. Not less than one-third of the total number of seats for the offices of the chairperson at each level would be reserved for women. This would be rotated among different *panchayats* at each level.

In addition, there are certain general features which could be taken advantage of by women, such as direct elections for membership and *sarpanch* (president) posts, at the local as well as the intermediary (block) level.

The duration in the case of such *panchayats* in operation would be five years from the date of its first meeting. Elections would be direct and held compulsarily every five years. For women it is significant in doing away with the old practice of cooption and replacing it with direct election, assuring that it would not become a stronghold and prerogative of women of rich and influential families.

The reaction of the states as expected have been varied. While states like Orissa and West Bengal did not even wait for the 73rd Amendment and amended their acts in 1991 and 1992, and held elections in 1992-93 electing about 25,000 women in each state of these bodies, the state of Tamil Nadu taking advantage of some loopholes may not genuinely implement the provisions because the ruling party is not is favour. Punjab held elections promptly after the amendment. Going by the old practice of coopting women and Schedule Castes, it has avoided a true election for another five years.

The Panchayati Raj system has operated differently in various states of India. In the particular context of women's representation, a good number of states showed adequate regeratation as in Maharashtra, Kerala, Himachal Pradesh, Andhra Pradesh, but the proportion varied. Only in the first two states mentioned above where was the reservation up to 30 per cent. In Orissa it was 33 per cent. In West Bengal, the government has not been too keen on reservation. Elections every five years have been held since 1978. The latest elections were held in May 1993. This election was held on the basis of 1992 Act, which gave one-third membership to women, to be filled up by election. In 1993 elections, the total number reserved seats for women was 25,460, and many more, about 41,000 women got elected. In some other states elections have been long over due. For example, Bihar had its last elections in 1978, Uttar Pradesh in 1988. Orissa and West Bengal amended their acts before the Panchayati Raj Act was passed by the Parliament in 1992. Elections in Orissa in 1992 brought 22,000 women to Panchayat Raj institutions.

The recent Panchayati Raj Institutions (PRIE) Act does have the potential to include women in a very good proportion to male at the grassroots level political institutions. Presence of 33 per cent women is likely to affect and influence the political processes of decision-making and policy formulations at this level. It will not only enable them to give a women's angle to the decision and policy formulation activity. It will also awaken them to the problems facing the community as whole. It will enable a journey from the private to the public sphere of activity. It will train cadre of women political activists for partaking in the affairs of state and federal politics. Total sharing and equality in decision-making may not happen for years to come, but it Panchayati Raj Institutions (PRIS) promise a path towards that goal. When women armed with physical presence of a sizeable proportion reach the position of a 'critical mass', their voices cannot be ignored. They have to be heard. No longer can they be ignored. It could be a road to women's political empowerment. However, for a wider representation effective sharing in power process, this needs to be extended to representative bodies right up to the federal level. Wider representation will not ensure instant quality. It will take time and practice, moreover many studies have already proved that democracy, even while being the best form of government, need not be the best government, that men as much as women are guilty of devaluating its quality all over the world. The experience of Orissa and West Bengal testify that women are guilty of devaluing its quality all over the world. The experience of Orissa and West Bengal testify that women are capable of efficient political performance given the chance.

However, a word of caution is necessary at this juncture. Women's effective participation at the grassroots through the *panchayat* system will not become a reality unless women are made aware of the realities and are properly trained for their new role. Reservation alone cannot deliver the goods. It will still be a weak need to rely on, in tackling attitudinal, social and structural barricades. Never-the-less, by getting this one gateopened, women's movement can (and must) flood the rural side with the potentialities and political contribution of women. This will need much intervention by way of action and other inputs.[21]

Political education is the first step. For political education there will have to be two types of target groups. Where-ever women have already entered the Panchayati Raj institutions through election or otherwise, these women need to be politically educated and informed. Such education should not be confined only to creating awareness among women of their powers, rights and functions but also about Indian polity, the nature of its democracy and constitution, policies and programmes for women and other weaker sections. For the general women it would mean mobilising them for voting in the elections, standing for elections, and even campaigning and questioning the candidates, both male and female.

Political information : For education, information on issues such as current political developments and trends, legislations, policies and plans is the basic step. Information should lead to mobilisation.

Support services are necessary inputs

1. For election - Possibility of creating a special fund or efforts for raising resources to help women for fighting elections. Election being fought on party lines, are becoming more and more expensive, corrupt and violent even at the grassroots level. Could women's organisations help the women candidates to raise funds for fighting election?

2. Need for the formulation of one a few models of curriculum development, and of designing a syllabi that would include the different areas in constitutional, political, socioeconomic, social rights and issues, as well as governmental policies, programmes and procedures.

3. Some type of political literacy manual which in brief, precise, easy/readable and commonly understandable style explains the various provisions for (general and women specific) rights, governmental policies, judicial judgements, non-governmental social actions, etc.

4. For sustained political education there is need for an organisation working at site, if not every village atleast

in a cluster of villages. Existisng women's organisations in the villages and NGOs working in a particular area can be trained to act as trainers provided they have the inclination, correct and strong approach to feminist issues and women's rights, and are somewhat natural towards political parties.

5. Formation of resource centres with full time social activists could help by emerging as forums for information, dissemination, discussions, reading materials and even counselling services. The social activists with the necessary skill in political understanding, raising resources and networking may organise various activities like group discussions, awareness camps, lectures by visiting scholars/social activities and politicians.

As elections are increasingly being fought on party lines, political parties need to be sensitised towards women's right of political action, by giving them some priority in fighting elections.

The strategy of reservation or quota for women at all levels of political deliberation has immense possibilities, but it alone cannot deliver the goods. It has to be backed by a strong women's movement from outside. Even more, the presence of women sensitised women's problems in deliberative and decision-making bodies, will give strength to their voice. With time and proper training, they will not only be concerned with women's issue, but in all issues and problems related to the whole society and polity. They will lend to women's angle to issues of war, militarisation, nuclear power, widespread violence and what not.

It is true that having been trapped by sociocultural norms, and traditions they have been out of the so-called 'public areas' of activities. But, this sad tale is not and should not continue any more, politics is as much a women's concern as a man's because it equally affects her life conditions. What is needed is proper mobilisation, awareness generation through political education and training. For this task, the government, NGOs, women's organisations, both academic and action oriented, need to join hands in their effort. For a healthy democracy, all need to participate in the shaping and sharing of power. If gender prevents half the population from participation in politics, it cannot be a democratic politics. For Indian women, the 73rd Amendment to the Constitution, the Panchayati Raj Act 1992 opens up the door to many possibilities. They have been given a chance, if one goes by the experience of some states. In India, the signals are very positive. The commonly held view that women have to be found for contesting elections has been somewhat disproved in practices so far. In the Orissa elections of 1992, 2,200 won at three levels. This was more than one-third reserved. In 1988 Karnataka elections out of 30,000 women 14,000 won the elections. A state like West Bengal saw 59.2 per cent seats going to women in 1993. Thus, besides the reserved seats, women secured seats also from the general quota. Maharashtra presently have nine all women *panchayats*.[22]

What is needed is awareness generation in women, their mobilisation and training for their new political roles. They have to know about themselves, their rights, the nature of their political system, the myriad problems facing the country, the political process through which decisions are made and policies formulated. A concerted effort is necessary by all institutions and individuals who care for women, and do not want them to remain political cripples forever, with proper training and guidance. Women could share effectively the political decision-making, at least at the grassroots level. Some day they might effectively hold power at the national level.

References

1. Sushila, Kaushik In Kamla Sanskaran (ed.) *Women in Politics : Forms and Process*, Published by Friedrich Ebert Stifting. New Delhi 1992. p. 35.
2. Coole M. Diana, *Women in Political Theory : From Ancient Misogyny to Contemporary Feminism* (Introduction) Wheat Sheaf, Sussex 1988. p. 9.
3. This has been the running theme of the work by Simon de Behaviour *The Second Sex* 1949 English translation by Parshley MM Fenguin 1987.

4. Dahlerup Drude, *The Unfinished Democracy Women in the Nordic Politics*, Press 1985. Oxford, Pergamon Press, 1985.
5. *Report of UNESCO* meeting of experts on the participation of women in political life and the means for increasing the participation, LISBON, Portugal December 13-16 1983.
6. Sushila. Kaushik, *Women in Panchayati Raj*. Haranand Publications. New Delhi 1993. p. 4.
7. *Ibid.*, p. 4.
8. *Drude Dahlerup* in final report of UNESCO 1984, on the international meeting of experts on *factors* influencing women's access to Decision-making roles in political, economic and scientific life. Dubrovnik, Yugoslavia. December 10-14, 1984, p. 9.
9. *Ibid.*, p. 9.
10. *Op. cit.*, Report of UNESCO meeting. 1983.
11. *Ibid.*
12. *Ibid.* P. 9.
13. *Op. cit.* Kaushik, *Women in Panchayati Raj.*
14. Ceraldin, Forbes, *Symbols of Power* (ed) Vina Majumdar. New Delhi, 1977.
15. Lolika Sarkar & Vina Majumdar Towards Equality, Report of Committee on the status of women in India, GOI, Ministry of Education and Social Welfare, 1975, pp. 355-357.
16. *Ibid.*, Towards Equality, pp. 302-303.
17. *Ibid.* p. 304.
18. National Perspective Plan for Women : A Perspective from the Women's Movement, Delhi. August 888 (mimeo).
19. *Ibid.*
20. *Op. cit.* Kaushik, *Women in Panchayati Raj.* pp. 25-29.
21. *Ibid.*, p. 4.
22. *Ibid.*, p. 41.

APPENDIX-I

Table - Pattern of Participation of Women (Lok Sabha Election)

Election year	*Voting perce-ntage of men*	*Voting perce-ntage of women*	*Total seats conte-sted*	*Seats won*	*Percen-tage of women candi-dates*	*Total seats*	*Perce-ntage of wo-men members*
1952	53.00	37.10	51	23	45.09	499	4.40
1957	56.00	38.77	70	27	38.57	500	5.40
1962	62.10	46.63	68	35	51.47	503	5.70
1967	66.10	55.48	66	31	48.43	523	5.90
1971	69.70	49.15	86	22	27.50	521	4.30
1977	65.62	54.96	70	19	25.70	544	3.40
1980	57.69	51.22	142	28	19.70	544	5.14
1984	63.61	68.17	421	159	28.30	544	7.90
1989	70.90	43.90	189	28	14.80	525	5.30
1991	52.56	47.42	307	33	10.75	503	6.60

APPENDIX-II

History of Panchayati Raj System in India

The Gandhian ideology ever since the 1930s believed in '*Ram rajya*' the rule of Rama, based on an economy of self-reliance and self-sufficiency of the villages, and village as the basic unit of administration. Gandhian line of thinking was based on the ancient village republics model of India. However, this idea did not find favour with the modernising sections of emerging political leadership. But the massive appeal of Gandhi's idea of self-governance or '*swaraj*' could not be totally resisted. Hence, the Directive Principles of State Policy (Art 40c) provides that the state should take steps to organise village *panchayats* and endow them with such power and authority as may be necessary to enable them to function as units of self-government..

The Community Development and Panchayat Raj system was launched in 1952 seeking to harness people's power and channelise their participation for social reconstruction. Following this, Panchayati Raj system was born in 1959 with the submission of Balwant Rai Mehta Committee Report in 1975. It provided for three-tier system of grassroots institutions from village to the district level. The block was the intermediary level — village *panchayat panchayat* at samiti and zila parishad. The process of establishing the three-tier system first started in Rajasthan in 1959. By 1962, this system was in force in the entire country except in few states by the end of March 1973, there were 2,22,050 village *panchayats* covering 5.65 lakh villages in the country.

13

WOMEN OF BIHAR: POLITICAL PARTICIPATION

Sarojini Sharan

(a) Importance of the Topic

It is assumed that active participatory involvement of Bihar's women, in the processes of decision-making will increase administrative and technical competence of officials add to the alternatives, from among which they will make their choice. Such options will be more responsive to the needs and aspirations of the people of Bihar, about half of which are women. These will provide greater legitimacy to Bihar's political system.

(b) Purpose and Objectives

The purpose of this study is to investigate women's participatory pattern in Bihar's politics and the visibility/ non-visibility of the impact of their political activities on decision-making or other actions of the government.

(c) Method

Material for this study were gathered from books, research works, interviews with women active in politics, talks with political women and my own observations.

(d) Definitions of Key Terms Used

Involvement of groups and individuals at various levels in political system is called political participation. Various kinds of political activities can be brought under this term. Orbit of political participation includes "those legal activities by private citizens which are more or less directly aimed at influencing the selection of government personnel/or the actions they take".[1]

Political participation can also be described "simply as activity by private citizens designed to influence governmental decision-making".[2] Hence people may be said to be participating in political life when, their activity relates in some way to the making and execution of policy for society.[3] Thus all kinds and all levels of activity may be brought under this rubric. It may consist of formal activities as voting, contesting elections, party activism pressure group membership, as well as extra institutional informal activity of any kind aimed at influencing the policy-makers.

The term visibility here may mean two things. In the first meaning, it is a question of the efficacy of women's political participation in Bihar's politics and governmental decision-making processes. In the second meaning, it is a question of how far the mass media, the opinion leaders and political and governmental agencies take note of women's political participation.

(e) Scope

In this study we are interested in learning about women's attempts to influence the authoritative allocation of values for Bihar's society. The scope of discussion will lie within the boundaries of governmental activities.

There are four sections in which the pattern of women's political participation in Bihar has been analysed. These are (i) participatory avenues; (ii) leadership; (iii) forms of participation; and, (iv) issues of political involvement visibility or less visibility of women's political participation and its causes have been discussed in the last part. Attempts have also been made to give some suggestions in order to improve the visibility of women's political participation and its causes have been discussed in the last past. Attempts have also been made to give some suggestions in order to improve the visibility of women's political participation in Bihar.

(f) The Study

(i) Participatory Avenues: The participatory avenues in Bihar's politics consist of all the modes and avenues of political participation like holding political or executive offices, seeking political or executive offices, active or passive membership in a political organisation, active or passive membership in an interest or pressure group, participation in public meetings, voting, demonstrations, rallies, *dharnas*, *gheraos*, strikes, fast unto death, and so on. Those who are involved in any one or more than one modes mentioned above, can be placed under two broad categories — professional political participate and non-professional political participants. To the former category belong the members of the Council of Ministers, legislatures and local self-government agencies, members of political parties and professional lobbyists. The primary calling of this category is government or politics. They are involved in political activities as a matter of routine job. The other category, that is, the non-professional/political participants are involved in politics, only intermittently and not as their primary calling. Politics is their secondary exercise.

Though many women of Bihar had entered legislatures and Council of Ministers in the early period of independent India, there were none who could acquire the stature of Sarojini Naidu, Kamala Devi Chattopadhya, Rajkumari Amrit Kaur and Aruna Asaf Ali. Yet, it was under the banner of the Indian National Congress that more women could find place in state or central legislatures, than under the banner of other political parties. The Congress women could attain name and fame also in state as well as central legislatures and Council of Ministers. Some of them did well in their new roles and were even appreciated by the erstwhile Prime Minister of India, Jawahar Lal Nehru. According to studies carried on by researchers on women and politics in Bihar,[4] during 1960s, greater number of women members of Parliament had belonged to south Bihar, fewer from central Bihar and still fewer from North Bihar in 1967. Elections of 1967 were important and a watershed in Bihar because political participation in general had increased. It was for the first time that Congress lost its monopolistic hold on the minds of the people. It started a period of non-congress governments in the state.

Still more vital than the year 1967 for women's participation in politics, were the turbulent years of 1970s, when Lok Nayak Jay Prakash Narain started his movement for eradication of corruption from politics. This movement activated and increased women's political participation in Bihar. It could be compared with women's participation in movements led by Gandhi. Jay Prakash Narain had jumped into the main current of the students' movement starting from the university and subsequently engulfing the whole of Bihar. The initial demand of the students was for the postponement of examinations. But it was channeled into demands for holding price-line and eradication of corruption specially from politics. Rising prices and corruption among politicians were issues in Gujarat agitations also. The male and female students of Bihar set up action committees, which demanded dissolution of the Bihar Assembly. But the Budget session of the assembly met complete with Governor's address. The protestors became violent and went on rampage. Agitation and police firings took toll of about 27 people.[5]

Jay Prakash Narain set up the organisation called Citizens for Democracy in New Delhi. He himself became its chairman.[6] He gave a clarion call to the youth to leave their studies in the universities for one whole year in order to go to rural areas for furthering the objectives of their agitations. His call was for "total revolution" (*sampurna kranti*). He asked, specially Bihar, along with whole of India to follow the path shown by the Gujarat students in 1974. Jay Prakash Narain cautioned the nation that a "1942 Quit India" type of revolution with bloodshed was imminent, if the corrupt political system continued. He believed in party-less democracy, for that he thought existing political system had to be dismantled. It could be done through the path of *sarvodaya*, according to which groups of villages could be taken up when *panchayats* could be organised and youth power could be channeled for revitalising the rural society.

The young women participated in all the modes of the J P movement. In July 1975, Jay Prakash Narain called forth the youth, for throwing the Bihar administration out of gear, by crippling the economy. He asked them to mobilise a "no tax campaign" and *gherao* the officers in the Bihar government. Jay Prakash Narain announced four point programme on October 14, 1975.

First the people were asked to establish parallel governments at the village, *panchayat* and block levels. Secondly, it was decrided that if the Council of Ministers along with the Bihar Assembly were not dismissed by November 4, 1975, a people's assembly was to be convened at Patna. Thirdly, it had utilise all the means available, in order to paralyse the state government, and fourthly, a "no tax campaign" had to be started immediately. Bihar was in the grip of agitations, arsons and rioting. The women in very large number also participated in the programme.

Bihar's women legislators of the early Independence period were well educated and some had brilliant academic careers. They belonged to 'well to do' upper and middle class families. Almost all of them were inspired by Mahatma Gandhi, Binova Bhave and Jay Prakash Narain. Most of them had been involved in social movements since their childhood. They were engaged in welfare works among the *adivasis* and Harijans. These political workers formed several organisations for women and children under their leadership. Two women MPs of Bihar had held ministerial posts in the Union cabinet, in earlier years. They were Jahanara Jaipal Singh and Tarkeshwari Sinha. They held important posts in the cabinet. The former held the portfolio of transport and civil aviation and was nominated for the Rajya Sabha in 1966. Tarkeshwari Sinha was the first woman deputy finance minister in the Nehru ministry. She had also led a delegation to the U.N. and Tokyo. For last few years it was Ram Dulari Sinha – an important Congress worker of Bihar, who held the post of Governor in Kerala. There had been some other prominent women of Bihar, who occupied ministerial positions in the Centre as well as in the state.

As regards the non-Congress parties, it was in 1957, that some women of Bihar started contesting elections from few constituencies. These parties were Swatanatra, Samyukta Socialist Party and Praja Socialist Party. Two women from the old Janata Party could be returned with success from the south Bihar constituencies.[7] After a gap of fourteen years when again the old Janata Party set up its women candidates for contest, they were defeated in elections. The Swatantra set up three woman candidates in 1962, and that was the only occasion when it took the risk. They lost the elections. Several independent women took their chance of contesting in 1971 elections and then in 1977, but were routed.

Since 1967, the Congress Party went on losing its popularity with an exception in 1985. Congress tickets spelt bleak future for women in elections. On the other hand, the roots of some parties like the Swatantra and Janata (old) had not gone deep in Bihar till then and so they avoided involving women in contests. The left parties like Praja Socialist Party RRP, JKD and the CPI in Bihar did not consider women's candidature in elections seriously.

In 1977 parliamentary elections, the new Janata party also did not give any thought to offer a ticket to any woman for parliamentary seat. As regards Bihar Assembly elections, it distributed 10 tickets to women, all of whom performed well in the elections by winning seats from their constituencies. As against Janata women the Congress women, could retain only two seats.[8] The new Janata Dal came to power in Bihar in 1989, after ousting the Congress. Though the Janata claimed to stand for the oppressed including the women, it could not accommodate more than one woman in its record-breaking large ministry.

Membership in political parties and organisation has been an important factor in professional political participation. Since it was the influence of Gandhi in pre-Independence and early post-Independence period, which involved masses of women in political participation, it was again as members of the Indian National Congress that most women participated in protest demonstrations. They courted arrests, carried out picketing of wine shops and shops selling foreign goods. Political activities shifted to governmental sphere after Independence. It is important to note that in its organisational structure, women have not been placed in important positions by the Congress Party.

Active membership of women in non-Congress parties in Bihar had remained low for a very long period. Even when they began their political activities as party members, they were less perceptible. Information regarding women membership in the newly created Leftist parties like the Indian People's Front, Maoist Unity Centre and the like are scarce. Their field of activities lies in deep rural areas. It is presumed that these must have been enrolling a large election of women, belonging to the agricultural sector. Whenever there is a call for a rally, the village women seemingly impoverished are visible on the streets of Patna in very large numbers.

The political activities of the educated sections of women has shifted to the educational institutions mainly in their professional associations. Some of the prominent among these women members have belonged to the Leftist parties like CPI.

Till date there are very few women members in trade unions in industrial towns. Though Bihar may boast of being one of the initiators of peasant movements and organisations in the country under Sahjananda Saraswati, women are no where to be seen and their activities no where perceptible in this field.

In Bihar, there are several women's organisations and action groups with women membership, with political ideologies. Some of them had been in existence since long. But it was J P movement which gave a fillip to mobilisational activities and militancy in youth organisations including that of women. Prominent among the organisations with Marxist leanings are today Samajwadi Mahila Samiti, Pragatisheel Mahila Manch and Bihar Mahila Samaj.

Several organisations were founded in Bihar under the leadership of Jay Prakash Narain, or under the influence of his ideology. Two youth organisations were born under the direct inspiration of Jay Prakash Narain viz. Chhatra Yuva Sangharsh Vahini and Sampurna Kranti Manch. The former came into existence in 1975 and the latter in 1984. When Janata Party formed government at the Centre, Chhatra Yuva Sangharsh Vahini allied with it. These two had considerable number of women activists participating in their programmes. Another organisation with women membership was the Vidyarthi Parishad also under the influence of Jay Prakash Narain. This group associated with BJP. Young women came to join still another voluntary action group known as Nav Bharat Jagritikendra, again owing its inception to Jay Praksh Narain from whom it drew its inspirations. Besides the above mentioned voluntary action groups in Bihar, other important groups had also come into existence for mobilising women besides other programmes. They were the Peoples' Union For Civil Liberties, Rashtriya Lok Samiti (head quarters at Varanasi), Nav Bharat Jagirit Kendra and Jan Jagran Kendra (Hazaribag), Prayaas (Patna and Gaya), Catholic Centre (Khagaul) and Xavier's Institute of Social Service (Ranchi)[9]. Except Prayas all the above groups including Chhatra Yuva Sangharsh Vahini (Patna and Gaya) were part of wider national movements. But their operational style and focus were specially Bihari. Some of these organisations and their activities have been discussed later on in this paper.

(ii) Women Leadership in Bihar: Bihar is proud of dedicated social workers of very high stature like Prabhawatijee, wife of Sri Jay Prakash Narain. But as mentioned earlier, Bihar has not thrown up women leaders of very high stature in politics. In neighbouring Bengal, such women leaders had arisen who had courage to confront the British colonial power with violent activities. If one examines the recruitment processes in Bihar, one finds that more often it was the family's political background, which helped the women in coming into leadership positions. This happened more during the hay-days of the the Indian National Congress. These prominent women had been working in the political field with the male members of their families, who themselves belonged to the leadership

clan. Like other states of India, Bihar also had displayed liking for dynastic prominence in politics. There are several instances when the male leader had died, his party itself provided tickets to the wife or other female members of the family, for contesting elections. This proved successful for a while. Such constituencies had been a sort of "raj" for the hereditary candidate, who belonged to the landlord's family of that place. Leadership was conferred upon this group of women, they had not acquired their positions solely by their personal toil.

More than often, leadership was provided by non-Bihari women. For instance, in BJP, the initial women leadership was provided by a woman fondly called 'Taljee' from Maharashtra. It was she who made efforts to mobilise women to attend meetings addressed by BJP leaders and participate in other political activities of the party.

Some of the political activities point out that leadership of women in political field has been intermittent, halting and temporary. Those who possessed leadership capacity could not make themselves free from their household chores. Therefore, they could not remain in the lead from beginning till the end in all the phases of political activity. Leadership has been carried on in breaks, as and when the women leaders feel free. There have been instances when budding leaders left their original parties to join another party, in search of better political opportunities.

The youth organisations founded under the influence of Jay Prakash Narain threw up some women leaders and activists. They played their new roles with zeal. But when internal divisions occurred, there was a decline in the leadership role of the women. This point has been discussed later on under another subheading.

(iii) Forms of Political Participation by women in Bihar: In rallies sponsored by IPF, CPI and CPI (M), rural women participate in large numbers. They are brought from rural areas on some payments and conveyance facilities. Participation in these rallies is partly mobilised and partly voluntary. The rural male cadres organise them because on their own these women cannot organise themselves.

Their participation is also voluntary because they perceive their leaders to be rooted in villages like themselves and sensitive to their sufferings. There seems to be an understanding between the leaders and the led. Most of these women are Dalits, Harijans and come from other oppressed castes and class. They have no inhibitions against coming on streets. They see hope for their future in these activities.

The upper middle class of women do not like to participate in field politics. The lower middle class women are too much occupied with their household chores. These sections need more mobilisation.

Other forms of protest and political participation of elite group of women have been strikes, dharnas, gheraos, collective fasts, cease work, rallies and formation of human chain against price-rise (on one occasion in Ranchi). In most of these, it is the working women from educational institutions, who have been involving themselves along with their male colleagues, in order to pressurise the government to release funds for their institutions, to improve their service conditions and status of their universities/colleges/technical institutes and for 'take over' by government of sick but important institutions. In all such forms of political participation, the women have played less prominent roles.

In recent years, some aggressiveness had been shown by women in Bihar under the guidance of BJP. In October 1990, women group from Bihar had also gone to Ayodhya to participate in the *kar seva* (voluntary service) for the construction of Ram Mandir (temple). Under the same guidance, women had geared the Doordarshan (TV station) for blacking out of Ayodhya incidents in their news telecasts. In their other aggressive activities, they pulled down vulgar posters of women and carried agitation on the streets. They forced the authorities to take action against those involved in the display of indecent posters. For launching gherao of the Parliament, a group of women had also gone to Delhi from Bihar and participated in it.

The Chhatra Yuva Sangharsh Vahini, in which there are enthusiastic young women members, showed more militancy than any other organisation with women membership. Vahini's militant agitation against dowry deaths forced the authorities to take cognizance of such cases and activated police action against the culprits.

In Bihar, Chhatra Yuva Sangharsh Vahini was established in 1975, but Jay Prakash Narain proclaimed it a national organisation on September 30, 1978. During and after Emergency (1975), the membership rose to the high point of 10,000. In addition, there were several others who supported it informally.[10] But the core of its support always remained in Bihar.

The Chhatra Vyva Sangharsha Vahini carried out struggles against issues connected with the impact of dam projects in Bhagalpur and Singhbhum. Other issues in which the Vahini involved itself concerned fishing and forest rights of the local and forest people. Most important of its activities had been concentrated in the struggle against the *math* (temple) landowners of Bodh Gaya. The success of this struggle was acknowledged by the social researchers. The Vahini assisted landless *musahars* (low caste) to put up their struggle against Bodh Gaya Math, for almost 10 years. Many *Vuhini* members decided to live full time in those villages and stood with the exploited. They confronted violent retaliation from vested interest and the police[11].

Fundamental dissensions had developed in the Chhatra Yuva Sangharsh Vahini in June 1984 in Alwar (Rajasthan) on the issue of the use of violence along with other radical methods in their struggle against injustice in society. The radical group of Vahini brought out a booklet in 1985, propagating its strategies. The other group was moderate. It declared its position on Gandhian lines for employing peaceful strategies in their struggle. Radicals expelled the moderates from the organisation. But it seems that moderates have come to control the Bihar level. These divisions within the Vahini mellowed the impact of their struggle against the Bodh Gaya Math landowners.[12]

The establishment of Sampurna Kranti Manch in 1986, widened the split in Chhatra Yuva Sangharash Vahini. The Manch was launched as a national movement in Bodh

Gaya in October 1986. It was to be a movement for '*total revolution*' of Jay Prakash Narain's dream. V.M. Tarkunde — a former Supreme Court justice was appointed its convener. Tarkunde had already become secretary of Citizens' for Democracy founded by Jay Prakash Narain during the 1970s. Tarkunde also was installed as president of the People's Union for Civil Liberties. Initially, the Sampurna Karnti Manch decided that members of the voluntary Organisation, which had accepted funds from foreign sources, would not be eligible for its membership. However, this was not strictly observed. Hence, the more militant in the Chhatra Yuva Sangharsh Vahini called for its boycott.

There were other causes for Vahini's decline. The members largely belonged to middle class and could not analyse the rural situation in Bihar properly.

Women had been in active role in all forms of political participation adopted by the Chhatra Yuva Sangharsh Vahini. But they had to struggle hard, to be felt in the organisation and also to focus upon issues especially related to women. Chhatra Yuva Sangharsh Vahini did not give importance to women's issues in its programme. An activist Manimala in the forefront of Vahini's struggles remarked, "we thought that we could begin the fight with the struggle for land and then the fight against the many other inequalities in social, cultural, political and educational realms, would ultimately get linked with the struggle for land rights, leading to a movement for total change. However, there was no clarity about how the different forms of inequality involving exploitation were related to one another. Therefore, without any analysis, by unifying and organising the issues more systematically, the struggle for land became not just the focal point of our efforts, but our total struggle. The other issues usually got taken up or left behind according to the conditions laid down by the struggle for land."[13]

The Vahini women campaigned and carried on limited struggle on two fronts. On the one hand, they agitated against liquor and domestic violence on female members of the family, on the other, they struggled for getting land allocated to women. These activities were successful to a limited extent. These women members of the Chhatra Yuva Sangharsh Vahini also won prestige and recognition for their activities within the organisation which remained male dominated.

Another action group, the Nav Bharat Jagriti Kendra, based upon Jay Prakash Narain's goal of 'total revolution was registered in 1974-75. It was located in Hazaribag district in Chouparan block, known as Bahera Ashram. It enlisted the cooperation and support of specially the oppressed castes and classes like Harijans and women. Harijans were placed as secretaries at different levels of the organisational structure. Women also participated in its activities, but it was not very encouraging.[14]

Besides action groups influenced by Jay Prakash Narain, another group was established in May 1982 and registered under the name of Prayas Gramin Vikas Samiti. It combined traditional development programmes along with strong emphasis on education and mobilisation of women. It put special emphasis on legal education. In its initial period it established its centering six villages in Phulwari Sharif block in Patna districı. It established a few years ago a sub-centre in Amas block in Gaya district. Prayas concentrated its activities mainly upon the issues related to *musahars* (untouchables) and landless labourers. It also included other disadvantaged groups notably the Muslim women. Women are playing prominent role within this organisation in aggregating, articulating, campaigning and struggling for the disadvantage groups. They have formed even a parallel women's organisation known as Mahila Jagaran.[15]

One of the forms of political participation of groups of women's organisations was visiting scenes of violence against women. The Samajwadi Mahila Samiti, Pragatisheel Mahila Manch, Chhatra Yuva Sangharsh Vahini, Bihar Mahila Samaj and such others visit and make "on the spot" inquiry in Padaria village, where media had reported mass rape of women by men in uniform. These action groups activised the authorities to the extent of establishing special agencies or the enquiry and hearing of rape cases, though ultimately, the women organisations had to face failure in getting the culprits punished.

In recent elections, some women members of BJP and the Janata Dal played active roles as campaign managers and canvassers also. BJP women collected large groups of women at BJP meetings, they themselves addressed large gatherings, collected and contributed money for transporting women to meetings and back home. They also distributed party pamphlets in many areas.

Voting is the most important form of political participation in which the masses of women participate periodically. The size of women electorate is congruently increasing. The election statistics indicate a general trend of increasing turnout of women voters. The amendment in People's Representation Act during Rajiv Gandhi's regime lowered the age of voters from 21 to 18. That has considerably increased the size of the women electorate. But the irony of this situation in Bihar has been that with the widening of women electorate, their representation among the political elite is dwindling. It is very important to note that since 1967, women have been increasingly involved in voting participation, but at the same time their number is almost nil in power positions of politics. There are almost no women 'power brokers' in this state. In the role of 'contact persons' their performance is poor in influencing governmental decisions for the benefit of their clients. Based on the TV reports, latest trend in women's voting seems to be unhappy. Since 1989, Bihar has been witnessing largescale violence, murders, intimidation of voters, resulting in terrorising of women voters.

(iv) Issues of Involvement: The issue which has attracted women's involvement in politics has been of general nature, concerning all sections of the populace. Among issues related to women, specially important have been those of sex exploitation (i) through vulgar display of female body in advertisements and posters; (ii) dowry deaths not taken cognizance by the police; and, (iii) mass rapes by policemen

not proved and not punished. Other important issues were of economic nature viz. distribution of land to women. Some issues were of social and educational nature, which could mobilise women for asserting their legal rights within family and in society.

Among the general political issues which agitated women's minds like their male counterparts are: (i) caste privileges based on governmental policy of reservation; (ii) the *mandir-masjid* issue at Ayodhya; (iii) the biased news telecast of the Doordarshan; (iv) multiplying corruption in public life; (v) expansion of communalism; and, (vi) rising prices.

Among the economic issues women have shown concern with regard to equitable land distribution, among social issues, their efforts had been to uplift the status of oppressed and disadvantaged groups, and on educational front, their aim has been to train the disadvantaged groups for holding organisational positions.

G. Invisibility/Visibility of Women's Political Participation and its Causes in Bihar

The impact of political participation of women in Bihar does not seem to be much. The vulgar advertisements still appear on walls displaying female body. Prices are spiralling high, making household management more and more difficult. Women are finding it difficult to enter legislatures or executive political positions in government or recognised political parties and action groups. Even in voting participation they are often unable to register their choice because of rampant intimidation and violence during elections.

We can now identify those causes which make political participation of Bihar's women less visible or invisible. These could be placed under the following categories — political environment, social structure, traditions and cultural norms, availability of alternate avenues for women's activities and attitude of the media.

(1) Political system in Bihar shows lack of stability. It is highly fluid, loosely structured, opportunistic, non-ideological

and personalised. It is infested with rival factions extending horizontally and vertically. Violence in the temper of Bihar,[16] placed great limitations upon voluntary political participation of women.

The impact of women's political participation has been nil in the electoral process of Bihar. Politics has become criminalised, violent and dominated by muscle and money. The techniques for winning elections have been booth capturing, bogus voting, ballot box looting, printing fake ballot papers, intimidation of officers in polling booths, kidnapping and murders of candidates, etc.[17] Every political party is learning the art of these and chiselling and polishing these instruments to win elections by hook or by crook. Women have not even made efforts to make a dent in this process. In fact, they do not have that capacity. The general body of women are increasingly alienated from politics, which is stained with blood and violence.

The number of women in state and central legislatures shows a decline in Bihar. The reasons are that elections are becoming costlier for every political party. Hence, the contestants themselves have to meet a major portion of the election expenses. For that they have to depend upon their own sources. Women do not have sources which can give them money in abundance. The second reason is that these days every political party employs musclemen and arranges for its 'private army', for competing with other political parties in booth capturing, looting of ballot papers and boxes, bringing bogus voters to booths and such other corrupt practices. Women cannot arrange for their 'private armies', unless the party leaders do it for them. Moreover women in Bihar have not become adept in the art of such manipulations.

Absence of political information is another great handicap for women political participants. Some of the women's organisations had led agitations for demanding the benefits of reservations for women under the Karpoori formula. But the agitationists could not get the total picture of vacancies in Bihar and hence could not verify whether the number of jobs to be given to women would really tally with the above formula. The modern age demands from women technical and managerial skills, without which they will remain on the periphery of the communication structure. Women in Bihar have made very little effort acquire the above skills. An information service specially for women could provide accurate information in various fields of society. This may help women in bettering the visibility of their political participation. Women should be given incentives to acquire science and technical training.

(ii) The social structure of Bihar makes political participation of women more difficult. The reasons are: the patriarchal structure of the family; the hierarchical basis of the community; the stratification of the society with upper, middle and lower caste clusters; the lingering feudalistic attitude in every walk of life; failure of Bihar's leadership to effectively mobilise women after Jay Prakash Narain's death; government's insensitivity to women's issues, creating a feeling of apathy in them and lack of any awareness about the efficacy of women's political participation.

The above factors do not permit the women of Bihar to become an homogeneous group. These work against any aggregation of interests common to all women. This heterogeneous section of Bihar's population is constantly clamouring for male guardianship and protection for every political activity. On the reservation policy of the government of Bihar, the women are bitterly divided on ground of forward and other backward castes (OBC) or most backward castes (MBC) like the male members of their group.

(iii) Women generally shun political activities because they perceive politics as dirty and immoral. Going for active politics would mean for them character assassination and a fallen social image. They do not wish to prove themselves deviants by accepting roles violating the expectations of Bihar's feudalistic and fatalistic society. Moreover, those few who have taken to active politics seemed to have entered a ready-made male political culture, wherein they seem to lose their feminine qualities.

(iv) With the growth of liberal and technical education, it seems that middle class and upper middle class young women are finding more avenues to perform socially useful functions. They are competing successfully for all-India and state services. They are also going for untraditional jobs like that of police, engineering and others. With these avenues, they seem less interested in the unstable vocation of politics. Hence, the decline in the number of women in active politics of Bihar or of India.

(v) Attitude of the media does not seem to be much sympathetic towards the activities and achievements of women. In the second meaning of 'visibility' as mentioned earlier, society, the opinion leaders and the mass media do not give importance to women's political participation in forms other than voting. The media is interested only in events like dowry deaths and rape cases, which they consider as having news value. Women activists do not get due attention.

The role of mass media, governmental or non-governmental, is to a large extent responsible for image building or image bursting. Media has created and conferred personality on less competent men. But it remains silent about women and rarely takes to image-building of women elites. It rarely reports what the women have been doing in Bihar, specially in the social and educational field of rural Bihar. Though every daily, weekly or monthly newspapers and journals have their 'woman columns', the focus is only upon the problems beleaguering them and not how they are struggling to solve them. If the media could highlight the achievements of women in Bihar and could also give the news items a better placing, perhaps the insensitivity of the bureaucrats could be broken. Perhaps then women's efficiency in politics may improve.

H. Some suggestions to Improve Efficacy of Women's Political Participation

To make the political participation of women more visible and effective the following suggestions are made:

(1) We should make an intense drive for illiteracy eradication among women in rural as well as urban areas.

(2) We should encourage the girls in schools to study

science subjects. The college/university women should be given incentives for acquiring technical and managerial skills.

(3) We should make an intense drive for legal and political education for women.

(4) More and more women should join different political organisations and action groups.

(5) Women should strive to enter into important organisational positions in political parties, action groups, trade unions and such other organisations.

(6) Similarly, oriented women's organisations should be unified or coordinated in order to attain strength.

(7) The educated women should enter the profession of journalism, in order to focus upon the activities of women in all walks of life.

(8) Agencies for better political communication should be established from where accurate political, economic and educational informations can be given.

(9) Men interested in women's political participation should be invited and welcomed to involve themselves in women's action groups and the like.

References

1. Political Participation in Greenstein, F I and Polsby N.W. (eds.), *Handbook of Political Science*; Vol. 4, p.1. Massachusettes, Addison- Wesley Publishing Company 1975.

2. Huntington, Sammuel, P and Nelson Joan H, *No Easy Choice*, p. 4, Cambridge, Harvard University Press, 1976.

3. Easton, D, *'A Framework for Political Analysis'* p. 32. Englewood Cliffs, N.J. 1965.

4. See Verma Madhubala, *Women of Bihar and Politics Since 1917*, A thesis accepted for Ph.D degree by the Patna University, p. 55 (Unpublished).

5. Butta Vishnu, *Indira Gandhi, Promised to Keep*, p. 72. National Publishing House, 23 Daryaganj, New Delhi-110002. India First Published 1980.

6. *Ibid.* p. 72.

   Also see

   Charan Sarojini and Vivekananda Franklin, A socio-Economic Study of Bihar During the Regime of Two Gandhis; (under publication) Bethany Books, Stockholm, Seden.
7. Verma, Madhubala, *op. cit.*, p. 58.
8. *Ibid.*
9. Eldridge, Dr Philip, and Ratan Nil, *Voluntary Groups and popular Movements in Bihar.* 1983. Report in A.N. Sinha Institute of Social Studies, Patna Bihar (India) (Unpublished).
10. *Ibid.*, p. 12.
11. *Ibid.*, p. 15.
12. *Ibid.*, pp. 16-17.
13. Mani Mala, Zameen Kenkar, Jote Onkar, *The Story of Women's Participation in Bodh Gaya Struggle.* ANUSHI, Jan. Feb. 1983, Vol. 3, No. 2, pp. 2-16.
14. Eldridge, Dr. Philip and Ratan Nil, *op. cit*, pp. 19-22.
15. *Ibid.*, p. 39.
16. See Sharan Sarojini, Anatomy of the Temper of Violence in Bihar Politics; Proceedings of the Ninth International Symposium on Asian Studies, 1987, pp. 433-440. Asian Research Service, G.P.O. Box 2232 Hongkong.
17. See Tyagi Bhuwendra , *Vote booth ki Loot* (Hindi) (Journal) *Dharmayu* of 1st June - 15th June 1991, pp. 8-13, The Times of India Building, Bombay 400 001.

14

GENDER AND POLITICS: JOURNEY FROM INVISIBLE TO VISIBLE

Chandrakala Padia

In contemporary feminist literature, the word 'women' has been replaced with the term 'gender' as a new category of analysis to assert that much of sexual differentiation is a social and political construct, related to but not determined by biological sex difference. It (Gender) "is seen as the process by which individuals who are born into biological categories of male or female become the social categories of men and women through the acquisition of locally defined attributes of masculinity and femininity".[1] Therefore, the feminists argue that this replacement (from women to gender) provides deeper analysis of present inequalities, and thus challenges the structure of current social, economic and cultural processes.

In fact the invention of this new word 'gender' is the result of two decades of intensive thought and research. In its most recent usage, gender seems to have first appeared among American feminists who wanted to reject biological determinism implicit in the use of such terms as 'sex' or 'sexual difference'.[2] Two major theories of gender are prevalent today: the psychologically focused theory of gender; and the historically and anthropologically focused explanation of gender.

The former is represented in the writings of Simone de Behaviour, who says that "one is not born but rather becomes a woman."[3] She claims that it is a whole process by which femininity is manufactured in society. To quote her, "she is defined and differentiated with reference to men and not he with reference to her; she is the incidental, the inessential as opposed to the essential. He is the subject, he is the absolute — She is the Other."[4]

Simone Behaviour argues that it is the child-bearing role of women which excluded them from the productive process, and prevented her from seeing themselves as subjects in their own right. Thus, an artificial idea of womanhood was created by the society. She exhorts: "No biological, psychological or economic fate determines the figure that the human female presents in society, it is civilization as a whole that produces this creation, intermediate between male and eunuch who is described female."[5]

Nancy Chodorow also subscribes to the above viewpoint and substantiates her argument from a psychoanalytical point of view. She argues that since women have always been assigned the responsibility of primary parenting and nurturing, she develops a psychology of being more suited to the task of nurturing and caring and thus herself chooses the role of a care given and confinement to the private. On the other hand, man from the very beginning is encouraged for more and more individualisation and attaining status resulting into such personality traits impelling him to associate himself with the public.[6]

The second theory of gender, based on historical and anthropological explanation, proclaims that in most of the societies so far, gender has been a socially constructed category rather than biologically determined. However, the proponents of this theory have also stressed that the nature of this social construction differs from one society to the other. So, there cannot be any uncausal, unavailable and ahistorical explanations of it. Anthropologist Michelle A Rosaldo supports this theory on the basis of her cross cultural research which reveals that women are subjected to the authority due to the existing dichotomy between the public and the private.[7]

Historian Linda J Nicholson also rejects the unicausal explorations of inequality of sexes. She also emphasises that it has been affected by various causal factors in different social contexts. She stresses the need to fight against the powerful tendency present in political theory to reify the public-private distinction and to perceive it as rigid.[8] She believes that one can comprehend this distinction only through the study of history for the gender structure irregular time and place is less affected by other contemporary stressors, such as political, economic, than by the previous history of gender. Joan W Scott also stresses the centrality of history in analysing different aspects of the construction of gender. She explains (a) how cultural myths and symbols reify the suppression of woman; (b) how these symbols create the 'binary opposition of masculine and feminine, male and female; (c) how social institutions family, labour markets, educational instructions, and polity reinforce this dichotomy; and (d) how the subjective identity formation of individuals is psychologically determined.[9] She, therefore, emphasizes the need to expose the social construction of gender by deconstructing it. This calls for:

> "....a refusal of the fixed and permanent quality of binary opposition, a genuine historicization and deconstruction terminism cannot be monolithic in its issues, goals and strategies, since it constitutes the political expression of the concerns of women from different regions, classes, nationalities and ethnic backgrounds. There is and must be a diversity of feminisms, responsive to the different needs and concerns of different women and defined by them for themselves.[10]

The most positive part of the whole discourse is that these concerns are reflected in practice also. Women involved in different social movements are fighting against injustices on their own cultural terms. Environmental activists, such as Vandana Shiva are speaking of the need to decolonize northern assumptions such as the concept of sustainable development, and appeal to save environment through knowledge based on poor women's experience.

Thus, feminist scholarship has brought sweeping changes to social and political theory. It has cautioned us against constituting gender as a super-ordinate category of analysis. It should neither be an automatic starting point of analysis of adjustment, nor should it be ignored as a potential starting point. We must avoid approaches that are gender-blinded or gender-blind. Then only we can have true meaning of democracy and participation.

This has eventually led to the dichotomy between morality and power. Women in the name of being more moral have been excluded from the public realm. Even the suffragists argued in favour of women's franchise by claiming women's superior morality as it would usher the state in a reign of peace. This is why Elshtain alleges that suffragist instead of challenging the separation of the public and private, merely "perpetuated the very mystifications and unexamines presumptions which served to rig the system against them.[11]

Against this background, one can understand the significance of the feminist slogan; 'The personal is the political.

The feminist argue that public realm of politics can be rational, noble and universal as the messy content of the body, meeting its needs providing for production, caretaking and attending to birth and death, are taken care of elsewhere.

So a modern reflective political theory should recognize that the glory of the public is dialectically, entwined with the exploitation and repression of the private and the people restricted to that sphere so that they can take care of people's needs. In view of this, feminists conclude that 21st century politics requires a basic rethinking of this distinction and its meaning for politics.

Feminists are trying to develop a theory of social practice on the following premises: First, there should be no sexual division of labour in workplace and in political organizations of all ideological persuasions; second, it believes in a differentiated social order within which various dimensions are distinct but not separate or opposed, and which rests on social conception of individuality, which includes both women and men as biologically differentiated but not unequal creatures.

We must expand conception of politics, based on the understanding that power relations between men and women are not confined to the 'public' world of law, the state and economics, but that they pervade all areas of life. This means that, contrary to the assumptions of traditional political theory, the family, reproduction and sexuality must be included in political analysis.

The question arises how far this public/private dichotomy and its deconstruction is relevant to the women of the Third World? Can this empowerment epistemology rooted in White women's experiences, subjectivity and identity fulfil the interest of Third World women?

However, in the post colonial discourse, women of North have themselves understood the significance of Third World women's realities and they have themselves rejected the monolithic nature of earlier feminist discourse on the grounds that it ignores difference, indigenous knowledge, and local expertise. For example, modernity is equated with Westernization, industrialization, and superiority, whereas non-modernity is equated with non-Western countries, tradition and inferiority.[12] In the 1970s, Ester Boserup's pioneering work *Women's Role in Economic Development* asserted that modernization had marginalized women and their contributions in the Third World. Chandra Mohanty also questions the Western approach. How, she asks:

> "...is it possible to refer to 'the' sexual division of labour when the content of this division changes radically from one environment to the next, and from one historical juncture to another? At its most abstract level... concepts such as the sexual division of labour can be useful only if they are generated through local, contextual analysis. If such concepts are assumed to be universally applicable, the resultant

homogenisation of class, race, religious, and daily material practices of women in the Third World can create a false sense of the commonality of oppressions, interests, and struggles between and among women globally.[13]

Sen and crown too cautions against adopting a concept of gender that ignores difference and diversities. They believe this diversity is built on gender oppression and hierarchy. He exclaims:

"The most fundamental and general of these opposition associates women with nature and men with culture. Nature is always seen as of a lower order than culture. The feminists like Ortner argue that the opposition between women/nature and men/culture is itself a cultural construct and not given in nature.[14] Firestone in her work *Dialectic of Sex* argues against this separation of private and public. Women necessarily suffer from a fundamentally oppressive biological conditions. It is their role as reproducers that has handicapped women over the centuries and made possible men's patriarchal power.[15]

The consequences of the public-private dichotomy are disastrous. Due to this, only women have been deprived of political power and effective participation. Citizenship for women is always seen as "an elaboration of their private domestic task." Thinkers like-Ruskin could argue that "man's duty as a member of the commonwealth, is to assist the maintenance, in the advance, in the defence of the state. The women's duty as a member of the commonwealth is to assist in the ordering, in the comforting, and in the beautiful adornment of the state."[16]

References

1. N Kabeer, 'Rethinking Development from a Gender Perspective: Some Insights from the decade', Paper presented at the Conference on Women and Genders in Southern Africa, University of Natal, Durban, 1991.
2. See, Joan W. Scott, '*Gender*: a Useful Category of *Historical Analysis,' American Historical Review*, 91, 1986, p. 1054.
3. Simone de Beauvoir, *The Second Sex*, trans, HM Parshley, New York, Vintage Books, 1974, p. 301.

4. Simone de Behaviour, *The Second Sex*, Harmondsworth, Penguin, 1972, p. 16.
5. *Ibid*, 295.
6. Nancy Chodorow, 'Family, Structure and Feminine Personality', in MZ Rosaldo and L Lamphere (eds), *Women, Culture and Society*, Stanford, Stanford University Press, 1974, pp. 43-66.
7. See, Mechelle Z Rosaldo, 'The Use and Abuse of Anthropology', *Signs*, 5, 1980, 3, pp. 389-417.
8. See, Linda, J Nicholson, *Gender and History*, New York, Columbia University Press, 1986, p. 83.
9. Joan W Scott, 'Gender: a Useful Category of Historical Analysis, *American Historical Raview* 91, 1986, 5, p. 1067-69.
10. G Sen C Grown, *Development, Crises, and Alternative Visions: Third World Womens' Perspectives*, New York: Monthly, Review Press, 1987, pp. 18-19.
11. JB Elshtain, 'Moral Woman and immoral Man: A Consideration of the Public-Private Split and its Political Ramifications', *Politics and Society*, 4, *1974*, pp. 453-61.
12. See, Hagen 1962; Huntington 1971; Lerner 1964; Sutton 1963.
13. Chandra Mohanty, 'Cartographies of Struggle, Third World Woman and the Politics of Feminism,' In Mohanty *et. al. Third World Women and the Politics of Feminism*, Bloomington, IN; L Indiana University Press., 1991, pp. 67-68.
14. See, SB Ortner, 'Is Female to Male as Nature is to Culture?, in *Women, Culture and Society*, (ed.) MZ Rosaldo and L-Lamphere, Stanfard, Stanford University Press, 174, pp. 72-87.
15. S Firestone, *the Dialectic of Sex*, New York, W Morrow, 1970, p. 255.
16. J Ruskin, 'Of Queens' Gardens,' in *Free and Enobled*, (ed.) C Bauer and I Pitt, Oxford, Pergamon Press, 1979, p. 17.

Index